O9-BUB-868

Chicken Soup for the Soul

The Magic of Mothers & Daughters

Chicken Soup for the Soul: The Magic of Mothers & Daughters
101 Inspirational and Entertaining Stories about That Special Bond
Jack Canfield, Mark Victor Hansen, Amy Newmark.

Published by Chicken Soup for the Soul Publishing, LLC   www.chickensoup.com
Copyright © 2012 by Chicken Soup for the Soul Publishing, LLC. All Rights Reserved.
No part of this publication may be reproduced, stored in a retrieval system or transmitted in any form or by any means, electronic, mechanical, photocopying, recording or otherwise, without the written permission of the publisher.

CSS, Chicken Soup for the Soul, and its Logo and Marks are trademarks of
Chicken Soup for the Soul Publishing LLC.

The publisher gratefully acknowledges the many publishers and individuals who granted Chicken Soup for the Soul permission to reprint the cited material.

Front cover photo courtesy of iStockphoto.com/digitalskillet (© digitalskillet). Back cover photo courtesy of iStockphoto.com/gradyreese (© Grady Reese). Back cover and interior photo courtesy of Photos.com.

Cover and Interior Design & Layout by Pneuma Books, LLC
For more info on Pneuma Books, visit www.pneumabooks.com

Distributed to the booktrade by Simon & Schuster. SAN: 200-2442

Publisher's Cataloging-in-Publication Data
(Prepared by The Donohue Group)

Chicken soup for the soul : the magic of mothers & daughters : 101 inspirational
  and entertaining stories about that special bond / [compiled by] Jack
  Canfield, Mark Victor Hansen, [and] Amy Newmark.

     p. : ill. ; cm.

  Summary: A collection of 101 true personal stories by mothers and daughters of
all ages about the magical relationship between mothers and daughters, with stories
ranging from funny to inspirational to heartwarming.
  ISBN: 978-1-935096-81-8

  1. Mothers and daughters--Conduct of life --Literary collections. 2. Mothers--
Conduct of life--Literary collections. 3. Daughters--Conduct of life--Literary collections. 4. Mothers and daughters--Conduct of life--Anecdotes. 5. Mothers--Conduct of
life--Anecdotes. 6. Daughters--Conduct of life--Anecdotes. I. Canfield, Jack, 1944- II.
Hansen, Mark Victor. III. Newmark, Amy. IV. Title: Magic of mothers & daughters V.
Title: Magic of mothers and daughters

PN6071.M7 C483 2012
810.8/02/092052   2011942714

PRINTED IN THE UNITED STATES OF AMERICA
on acid∞free paper
21 20 19 18 17 16 15 14 13 12   02 03 04 05 06 07 08 09 10

Chicken Soup for the Soul®
The Magic of Mothers & Daughters

101 Inspirational and Entertaining
Stories about That Special Bond

Jack Canfield
Mark Victor Hansen
Amy Newmark

CSS

Chicken Soup for the Soul Publishing, LLC
Cos Cob, CT

www.chickensoup.com

Contents

Introduction xi

❶

~A Daughter's Love~

1. Face Time, *Lisa Tiffin* 1
2. The Secret, *Barbara LoMonaco* 4
3. Nailing It, *Nancy Hegan* 7
4. Quarters of Hope, *Malinda Dunlap Fillingim* 9
5. Gracefully Grateful, *Rachel Gilmore* 11
6. The Bird Incident, *Mary Beth Case* 13
7. The Gift of the Penguins, *Kathy Melia Levine* 16
8. The Ice Bucket, *Drema Sizemore Drudge* 19
9. Thankful, *Michele Arduengo* 22
10. Burgers and Butterflies, *Carmen Goldthwaite* 26

❷

~Rites of Passage~

11. Nobody Ever Told Me, *Sally Schwartz Friedman* 33
12. Separation Anxiety, *Sue Sanders* 36
13. Reconnecting, *Anita Mellott* 40
14. Mom Jeans, *Carol Band* 44
15. Beautiful Girls, *Christy Chafe* 47
16. Invisible Mom, *Deanna Ingalls* 50
17. A Training Opportunity, *Stacey Gustafson* 53
18. Taking a Back Seat, *Victoria Koch* 55
19. A Carton Tied with String, *Sally Schwartz Friedman* 58
20. My Feng Shui Nightmare, *Nancy Lowell George* 61
21. The Wedding Dress, *Carol Harrison* 64

❸
~A Mother's Love~

22. Mom to the Rescue, *Mimi Greenwood Knight* 71
23. The Sound of Music, *Jan Cline* 74
24. A Labor of Love, *Mary Elizabeth Laufer* 76
25. Love, Mom, *Amber Chandler* 80
26. Roots, *Kathryn Roberts* 82
27. A Promise Is a Promise, *Tessa Graham* 85
28. My Mother, My Father, My Everything, *Natalie Scott* 88
29. Standing Out, *Patricia Gordon* 91
30. Whatever You Want To Be, *Caitlin Q. Bailey O'Neill* 94
31. Mother or Daughter? *Jacqueline Rivkin* 97
32. A Mother's Last Lecture, *J.D. Chaney* 100
33. Unconditional Love, *Angel Therese Dionne* 104

❹
~The Face in the Mirror~

34. Generation Gap, *Therese Guy* 109
35. The Lady in the Mirror, *Terri Lacher* 112
36. Full Circle, *Stephanie Wolff Mirmina* 114
37. Self Defense, *Alice Muschany* 118
38. The Pied Piper, *Cathi LaMarche* 122
39. Here Come the Brides, *Annmarie B. Tait* 127
40. Crashing into Grace, *Janeen Lewis* 131
41. When I Wasn't Looking, *Davalynn Spencer* 135
42. Family Fusion, *Alyson Gerber* 137
43. When I Laugh, *Nina Guilbeau* 142

❺
~Family by Choice~

44. The Jacket, *Carol Sharpe* 149
45. Mother by Proxy, *Kathryn A. Rothschadl* 153

46. That's What Moms Are For, *Joan Oen* 156
47. Hope for the Future, *Tricia Downing* 160
48. Loving Her Through the Fear, *Chantel Friesen* 163
49. Learning to Trust, *Samantha Ducloux Waltz* 165
50. A Little Bite of Love, *Mary Ulrich Jackson* 169
51. A Second Chance, *Cynthia Lynn Blatchford* 171
52. Redemption, *Danika Cooley and*
    Amber Nocole Vanderzanden 173
53. Towel Folding, *Karen Robbins* 177
54. To My Other Mother, *Penny Smith* 179

❻

~Away We Go!~

55. The Great Navigators, *Crescent LoMonaco* 185
56. A Changing of the Guard, *Marcia Rudoff* 188
57. High Five, *Sallie A. Rodman* 192
58. Tent Lessons, *Ann Barnett* 196
59. Broadway Follies, *Amanda Koehler* 199
60. A Better View, *Kim Cooper Findling* 202
61. My Travel Companion, *Patricia M. Rompca* 205
62. The Stormy Cape Cod Day, *Dianne Bourgeois* 207
63. To Russia, With Mom, *Amanda Kendle* 210

❼

~Learning from Each Other~

64. Fearless, *Sharon M. Stanford* 217
65. The Strong One, *Jackie Allison* 220
66. Thunderstorms, *Tiana Lawson* 223
67. Magic Baggies, *Carol S. Rothchild* 226
68. Be Careful What You Tell Your Children,
    Judith Morton Fraser 230
69. Her Own Person, *Lil Blosfield* 233
70. Hair, *Kelly Reidenbaugh* 235

71. The Second Promise, *Linda J. Hinds* 238
72. Mom's Sage Advice, *Natalie June Reilly* 242
73. Ripped Pants, *Bobbi Dawn Rightmyer* 244
74. Choices, *Samantha Ducloux Waltz* 246

❽
~Healing and Second Chances~

75. Hope and Acceptance, *Laura Wisniewski* 253
76. I'm the Mom, *Cindy Gore* 257
77. She Never Stopped Loving Me, *Leigh Ann Bryant* 260
78. Card Shop Quandary, *Shauna Hambrick Jones* 264
79. Childhood's End, *Lynn Sunday* 266
80. Understanding Lori, *Pam Bostwick* 270
81. To the Owner of the Great Gray Dollhouse,
    Michelle Sedas 274
82. A Mother Is Born, *Ann Blakely* 277
83. No More Ditches, *Sioux Roslawski* 279

❾
~What Goes Around Comes Around~

84. The Lessons We Teach, *Marcia Byalick* 287
85. Refrigerator Magnets, *Hope Sunderland* 290
86. Cheer Leader, *Victoria LaFave* 293
87. Some Things Never Change,
    Sally Schwartz Friedman 297
88. Just a Good Mother, *Courtney Conover* 300
89. I'm a Barbie Girl, *Debbie Acklin* 304
90. A Mother Who Read to Me, *Jennie Ivey* 307
91. Monster in the House, *Jeri McBryde* 310
92. My Three Mirrors, *Kristine Byron* 314

10
~Dreams Fulfilled~

93. The Rest Is Unwritten, *Shannon Kaiser*...............................319
94. A True Daughter, *Barbara LoMonaco*.................................322
95. A True Success, *Dallas Woodburn*.......................................324
96. Girl Scout, *Tara Henson-Cameron*......................................328
97. What I Gained When I Lost My Daughter, *Jo Eager*...........330
98. Reading with Rosie, *Susan H. Young*...................................334
99. Following in Our Footsteps, *Priscilla Dann-Courtney*.........336
100. A Sign of Love, *Elizabeth Veldboom*...................................338
101. First Wonder, *Talia Carner*..341

Meet Our Contributors..347
Meet Our Authors...364
Thank You...366
About Chicken Soup for the Soul....................................367

Introduction

"**S**TEP AWAY FROM THE RACK!" the voice boomed through a megaphone. The police helicopter whirred loudly overhead and I was caught in the beam of a spotlight. I quickly put the item back and stepped away, my hands in the air.

Okay, it wasn't exactly a police helicopter and there weren't paratroopers sliding down ropes to apprehend me, but it sure felt that way when my sixteen-year-old daughter caught me examining a jacket that she deemed too "matronly" at Bloomingdale's. It was not the only time I heard "Step away from the rack," or "You can *not* be seen in that," or "Just because it still fits doesn't mean you're allowed to wear it."

Thanks to my daughter, I have donated half the contents of my closet to the church thrift shop over the past few years. One time, I was very excited when she rescued a couple of items, one-piece "jumpsuits" that had been all the rage in the late 1980's and had gotten me past the bouncers' ropes at trendy Manhattan discos with admirable speed. She said that she "had to have them" and I felt vindicated that she liked my cool clothes, until she added... "in case I go to a costume party."

The flip side, of course, is that the clothing... and shoes... that she deems acceptable seem to disappear with some regularity. I remember picking her up from college one May, and discovering half a dozen pairs of my missing shoes and sandals in one of her boxes. I was secretly pleased. What mother doesn't love sharing with her daughter, enjoying when we wear the same size and like the same things?

As they get older, our daughters become more and more like us too. The little girl who wanted to be just like her mommy, wearing matching nightgowns, turned into the somewhat disdainful teenager who wanted to create her own identity, and then turned into the young adult who smiles when she is told "you are just like your mother." Our husbands and sons shake their heads in amazement when our daughters make the same gestures, use the same wording, or even walk just like us.

Over time, we mothers find ourselves emulating our daughters too. I always tell mine, employing a technology-world term, that she is "Version 2.0" — me, but much improved. I learn so much from her — not only about how to dress, but about fitness and nutrition, current events, human relationships, and all the other areas where she has a fresh perspective, one that was "seeded" by me but has grown in different soil, in a new generation with updated ideas and knowledge. And I find my own mother, who I see every time I look at myself in the mirror, asking me for advice too, at the same time that I still listen and learn from her.

There truly is magic between mothers and daughters, and that is why our editors D'ette Corona, Barbara LoMonaco, and I had so much fun putting together this volume of stories that celebrate that special bond. We hope you will enjoy reading it as much as we enjoyed creating it for you.

~Amy Newmark

The Magic of Mothers & Daughters

Chapter 1

A Daughter's Love

A daughter is a mother's gender partner, her closest ally in the family confederacy, an extension of her self.

~Author Unknown

Face Time

Kids spell love T-I-M-E.
~John Crudele

I am not Mrs. Wilson. But I have opened cards addressed to her. And I know that each and every one of those cards will have a teacup or teapot gracing the front. I know this because each and every one of those cards is from my mother who taught me, with tea, what real love is.

"Hello, Mrs. Gastin? It's Mrs. Wilson. And I'm here for tea."

Every few days, my five-year-old voice would ring out this greeting, hoping my mom, Mrs. Gastin, would be ready to have a tea party with me.

I was always Mrs. Wilson—a name I conjured from my imagination. After my mother answered the make-believe door and poured the tea, the two of us would sit at the kitchen table, drink tea and nibble cookies together.

In essence, we'd have a tea party. I know the words "tea party" evoke images of frilly clothing, fancy dishes and stuffed animals, but that's not how it was for us. I could always come as I was, and during our tea parties my mom and I would chat about anything and everything. It was the highlight of my day.

In fact, this childhood ritual is among my favorite memories. Maybe it's because whenever we had a tea party my mom treated me with the same attention that she gave her own friends when they visited. Just like them, I got to sit at the table and share what was on my mind, and I had my mother's undivided attention.

Our tea parties laid the foundation of our relationship. As a teen I never had the stereotypical mother/daughter angst many of my friends experienced. Instead, I enjoyed seeing my mother after school. I even wrote a poem about what it meant to me to see her car in the driveway each day as my bus rounded the corner, knowing she was ready to greet my siblings and me and hear how our day went.

When I got older, my mom would stay up late — well past her bedtime I later learned — talking to my older brother and me while my younger siblings slept. No topic was off limits: religion, politics or life in general. To know I had a listening ear and a guiding hand throughout the toughest years of my life was priceless and no doubt helped form who I am today.

Even in my adult life, I live not too far from my mom and still chat with her by phone every day. Now, I talk to her about my own children, discuss my career and even provide a listening ear. No matter how old I get, I still enjoy her conversation, advice and opinions.

In other ways those tea parties set the stage as well. There's nothing I love better than hosting my own friends for a cup of tea and some homemade banana bread. As our children play, we chat, offer advice, or become sounding boards for career choices, childrearing discussions, and day-to-day happenings.

A missionary friend once explained the Chinese concept of "giving face" as a way of showing respect. Mary and her husband had come from halfway across the U.S. to visit my mother, and I dropped in after dinner to say hello. To me, I was simply being polite and doing what I had been trained to do. When people visit, you make the effort to spend time with them. It's what my mother did for me, and what I always try to do for others.

But to Mary and Len, I was honoring them by my presence. I suppose that is what is at the heart of what I loved so much about my childhood tea parties. From my mother, I learned that the simple act of sitting and sharing with another person could mean so much more than a glitzy gift or a quick e-mail. That face time is the gift of telling the other person that they are valuable; they are worth my time and attention and they matter to me.

From my mother, I learned to give that to my friends as well as to my own children. Plenty of people joke they are afraid of becoming like their mothers, but for me I can only hope that I might be like her—kind, caring and in tune with what other people need. I hope that like her, I remember to honor others with my time and my attention.

Every time I see a pretty teacup or anything with a tea theme, I think of my mother. In fact, we often give each other gifts involving tea because it represents so much more than a girlhood game. Instead of playing at being a grown-up, I truly learned how to be one.

I have boys, so I don't expect they'd ever be interested in having tea parties with me. That's okay. I've still found ways to pass along my mother's lessons. Through conversations over board games or during long car rides I hope I've taught them lessons like the importance of spending time, giving face and being present in the lives of those we love. It's an important gift I hope they pass along someday.

For this gift—the gift not only of her time, but the gift of the lesson, the gift of learning how to love—is truly one of a kind. And for that, I say, "Thanks, Mom." And yes, the teacup thank-you card signed by Mrs. Wilson is in the mail!

~Lisa Tiffin

2

The Secret

What a teacher writes on the blackboard of life can never be erased.
~Author Unknown

It was the start of another summer session at the university. I was enrolled in a psychology class—the lecture part and the laboratory. I was majoring in both education and psychology and since this particular class involved techniques for teaching children with learning disorders it would help me greatly. The class was very popular and the lab was one-of-a-kind. Therefore the class was extremely difficult to get into. Lots of students were put on a waiting list but I was lucky. I got my spot in the class—both lecture and lab—on my first try.

I had enrolled in this class not only because of the subject matter but also because of the professor. I had heard wonderful things about her. Learning disorders were her specialty and her techniques and teaching methods were known across the United States. She traveled around the country lecturing; she had published many articles and books, including an entire series of classroom books used by children with learning disorders. Those books had been translated into many languages and were used around the world. She ran a full-time school on the university campus that enrolled elementary age children who had trouble learning. It would be an honor to learn from her. And I had a secret.

Today was the first day of class. I was excited. The professor entered the crowded lecture hall and made her way to the front of the room. I had taken a seat about halfway back and a little over to one side. Because of the stadium-style seating in the lecture hall, I had a perfect view of her. The professor faced us, looked around, and the room quieted. It was time to start. Could she see me? I didn't know. She smiled. She was my mother.

When I was growing up, my mother and I had a great relationship—most of the time. I felt that I could talk to her about anything. She didn't judge me and didn't get angry. I don't mean to imply that she let me do anything I wanted. Far from it! I was an only child and she was very overprotective but she was also fair and she listened. If I disagreed with her I'd let her know how I felt—that is, after I got over being mad! Sometimes she would change her mind based on what I had to say. And sometimes she wouldn't. But she did listen. And we could talk. I felt she was my friend, but first and foremost, she was my mother and I knew she was in charge.

It was strange seeing my mother at the front of that lecture hall. I didn't know how I was going to feel about that. After all, we had just had breakfast together that morning and talked about the usual mother/daughter things we always talked about. Could I get past the fact that the professor was my mother and really learn something? Would she have information to teach me? What if someone in the class said something unkind about her? Could I let it go?

My mother welcomed everyone to the class and gave a brief overview of what we could expect during the eight weeks the class would be in session. And then my mother started the lecture. She didn't use any notes. She never did. She knew her topic so well that the information just flowed from her in her easy style. And the information was very interesting and informative. I listened and took copious notes and somewhere along the way my mother turned into a professor. She was so good and had so much information to share that I got completely lost in the subject matter and forgot that my mother was the person lecturing. But occasionally I'd blink and, once again, my mother would be the one standing up there in front of the class.

At the end of the lecture, the professor disappeared and my

mother was, once again, the person standing at the front of the class, answering question from the students who approached her. I looked around at some of the students. Did they know my secret? Did they know that the professor was my mother?

That summer school session passed quickly. My mother and the professor morphed back and forth from one person to another during the whole time, like those toys that transform from one thing to another with the twist of a wrist. Sometime she was the professor. And then, sometimes, she'd become my mother again.

The lectures were very informative and the experience in the lab, actually assisting the students with their lessons, was incredible. The facts and techniques I learned would prove to be very valuable when I became a teacher.

Did the other students in the class ever learn my secret? Well, yes they did. Did I tell? No. But someone else did. It happened on the last day of the session at the very end of class. The professor was summarizing what we had learned and wishing us all well in our various careers. When she was finished, she asked me to stand. She introduced me. She told the class that she was very proud of me and just wanted to let them know that I was her daughter.

My mother, who had accomplished so many important and noteworthy things in her life, was telling her students that the thing she was proudest of was me! Over the years I heard her lecture many times but I have never been more proud to be her daughter than I was that day when she introduced me to the class.

~Barbara LoMonaco

Nailing It

It's important to have a twinkle in your wrinkle.
~Author Unknown

What could I give my mother that Hanukah that I had not given her before? I didn't want to repeat anything. I had given her clothes, jewelry, and flowers. She abhorred my taste in perfume. She loved parties, but I had done that twice, both times as a surprise that pleased her. She was eighty-five years old; I wanted to do something different, something out of the ordinary.

I racked my brain, and suddenly I saw her fingers appear, small as a child's, with ragged, chewed fingernails. How they embarrassed her. How often she wore gloves, even in summer, to hide them. In fact, they hurt, and sometimes bled. I knew what I could do for my mother.

We kept it a surprise. No one provided her the slightest clue. She was mystified. On the day before Hanukah, I picked her up for lunch.

"Do I get the surprise today?" she asked.

I nodded my head yes.

"Is it at your house?"

Again, yes.

I threw open the front door. I led Mom into the kitchen where Rachel sat at the table, the tools of her trade arrayed before her. My mother recognized neither Rachel nor the implements.

"Is she my present?" She was puzzled.

"Mom," I said, "Rachel is going to do acrylic nails for you. You are about to have nails for the first time in your life! You won't be able to bite them anymore! You won't need to hide them because they'll be beautiful!"

My prediction was correct. Mom was thrilled with her glorious nails. She took to waving her hands about when she spoke, displaying her nails prominently.

We decided she needed a mother's ring to complete the effect. That was her birthday gift the following year. She loved the ring and the special cake we made. After the celebration I went home to rest, congratulating myself on another great choice. Then Mom called, agitated.

"Something's wrong with my new ring." she told me. "There are stones missing."

I drove three miles in eight minutes. Mom held her hand up to my face, waggling her tiny fingers with the blatant red tips. Horror of horrors! Where the topaz and emerald should have been, representing my daughter and son, the ring was white. She wrenched it off and thrust it into my hand.

Some lunatic impulse caused me to lick the ring. It tasted extremely sweet, and I continued, despite the alarm on my mother's face.

When all the congealed white frosting was gone, there were all the stones—intact. They had just been covered with frosting!

"Well," she said, laughing. "I'm old. I'm allowed to make a mistake. I guess you'll never let me live it down."

As usual, she was right. But it was Mom who referred to the birthday cake fiasco frequently and enjoyed the story and her nails every time.

~Nancy Hegan

Quarters of Hope

A wise lover values not so much the gift of the lover as the love of the giver.
~Thomas á Kempis

My daughters, Hope and Hannah, have been blessed with many things: loving parents, keen intellect, great humor, athletic abilities, and beauty… inwardly and outwardly. My home is full of ribbons, medals, certificates, and various other awards they have accumulated over the years.

But the one thing they have never had in abundance is money.

In fact, with parents who work as ministers, they will never get a lot of money from home. They have worn hand-me-downs, thrift store clothing and have done without many things because of our low income. They never complained, never cried out for something we could not afford. In fact, I think they are more appreciative and well rounded because their feelings of worth do not come from external things.

When my older daughter Hope was five years old she was looking for a gift to give me for Christmas. Not having any money of her own, Hope went to different neighbors and asked if she could do odd jobs to make some money. I don't know how she did it, but that Christmas she gave me a gift I will never forget.

Because money was so tight, I had not been able to subscribe to the newspaper. Reading a newspaper is one of my pleasures, and I would gather one at doctors' offices or anywhere else a free one might be found.

Hope knew this as we often read these freebies together. Thus, her gift.

It was wrapped tightly in bright festive paper and taped together with several layers of clear tape.

Small enough to be held in the palm of my hand, I questioned the contents of this precious gift.

Hope laughed, "You'll love it!"

Inside were two quarters.

"It's for a newspaper," she said. "We can go get one fresh out of the machine!" I held those precious quarters in my hand and knew then that I was a vey rich woman.

That was many years ago. Hope is in college now. When she left for college, I gave her a jar of quarters, a reminder that her love was priceless to me. It was a reminder that love costs nothing, but means everything to a mother and her daughter.

~Malinda Dunlap Fillingim

Gracefully Grateful

What the daughter does, the mother did.
~Jewish Proverb

"Y ou can go home now. We'll get her settled in," the ER nurse said to me while starting to help my mom out of her street clothes and into a hospital gown.

I caught my mom's eye over the nurse's shoulder, winked at her and said, "My mommy wouldn't leave me alone in the hospital. I'll stay."

The nurse turned and gave me a funny look, shrugged her shoulders and went back to the task at hand. I then settled in for what became a very long wait to get my sixty-eight-year-old mother admitted and into a room. And what became apparent to me over the next two weeks during her hospital stay was that most people there did not have family around to visit with them, advocate for them, comfort them, or look out for them. My mom was definitely in the minority.

However, according to Carol Abaya, a nationally syndicated columnist and recognized expert on aging issues, twenty-five percent of Americans are caring for both their own children and their own parents. Welcome to the Sandwich Generation. That's me. I just earned a new badge of honor, kind of like that first gray hair. I don't particularly want it, but I've got it.

Which brings me back to the ER nurse. I find it interesting that she really seemed to think I was just going to pick up and leave my mom alone in the emergency room, scared and in pain. I didn't think I was being heroic or the model daughter. I actually didn't think twice about staying.

And what I told the nurse was true. My mommy wouldn't leave me alone in the hospital, at any age. If the roles had been reversed, my mom would have told the nurse the same thing and sat herself down in that visitor's chair just like I did. For better or for worse, we are linked genetically and generationally. Now, I know that physically I resemble my mom and my gram, and every day my daughter looks more and more like me. But the DNA didn't quit there, because mentally, emotionally and spiritually, we are a line of strong, independent, determined, stubborn women… with mothers and daughters often butting heads when our similarities challenge our differences.

But while my gram's stubbornness and need for independence had a negative effect on her personality in later years when her health declined, I've seen a whole new side to my mom through this medical adventure. Gracefully grateful is what I'd call it.

Her broken hip and hand radically interrupted a very full and busy semi-retired lifestyle. Yet the determination is clearly there to get back to her old schedule, with the stubbornness and independence hovering just below the surface. Still, a new quality has emerged… a softer, gentler side from which appreciation flows. I must say I like what I see.

So if the Sandwich Generation is my new identity, my new reality, then I hope I continue to resemble my mom in later years, and I hope my daughter is able to say, without missing a beat, "My mommy wouldn't leave me alone in the hospital. I'll stay." I'd thankfully accept that badge of honor.

~Rachel Gilmore

The Bird Incident

At the height of laughter, the universe is flung into a kaleidoscope of new possibilities.
~Jean Houston

As a vibrant, hard-working teenager, I recognize the intrinsic value of sleep. As a vibrant, hard-working woman in her twenties, my sister does as well. My mother, however, doesn't seem to subscribe to the same notion. That can be the only explanation for the strident cry of "Mary Beth! Bonnie!" at 8:00 on that particular Saturday morning.

Grumbling, I rolled over and shoved my face into the pillow, assuming that this was just the usual thing: clothes left in the dryer, dishwasher gone un-emptied five days in a row, etc. You know, the usual mom nag-type things.

However, I couldn't escape a tiny bit of doubt. I lifted my head and eyed my mother from my cocoon in the blankets, unwilling to completely surrender my strategically advantageous position. Then I saw her stricken face and immediately sat up.

"Girls… it's an emergency." The yelling was gone, replaced by a trembling voice. My mom walked back down the hall, and after a hasty attempt to snatch glasses off bedside tables, my sister and I followed.

It was not at all what we expected.

From Mom's sober pronouncement, I anticipated that at the very least we would find one of the beloved cats struggling for breath or suffering an early-onset heart attack. Luckily, that wasn't the case. Instead, we found both cats, Tazz and Ferdinand, throwing themselves against the bathroom door, clawing and meowing desperately in a way that I hadn't heard since the last time I took them their breakfast twenty minutes late.

With my right eyebrow raised, I turned to my mother and questioned, "Um… what's the emergency?"

Grimly, and with a great sense of ceremony, my mother announced, "There's a bird in the bathroom."

Jaws dropped and eyes popped as my sister and I both thought, "We were dragged out of bed for this? A bird!"

Noticing our incredulous expressions, my mom pleaded, "Come on, guys, I can't do this alone." That, combined with a wide-eyed, pouting face that shouldn't be effective on a mature woman, caused my sister and me to crumble. And it wasn't even Mother's Day.

After luring the crazed cats into my bedroom with the promise of catnip, all three of us entered the battlefield, armed with nothing but our wits which, admittedly, are not that strong so early in the morning. The bird had perched on the towel shelves. At least, it was perched there until my sister and I went anywhere near it. In a whirl of plumage, the bird launched itself into the open air of the bathroom and towards its only chance at freedom. Sickening crunches filled the room as the bird smacked its small head against the skylight over and over again. As the gruesome noises escalated, my sister attempted to take control.

"Mom, open the window. Mary, climb up on the toilet and block the skylight with a dark towel." Opening the window seemed like a great idea. The bird needed a way to get out, right? Climbing onto the toilet closer to the bird's sharp, yellow beak? Not so much.

"Um… maybe, if we just open the window, the bird will figure it out?" I pointed out hopefully, but, knowing my sister, already resigned to my fate.

"Mary, just get up there." For such a nice girl, my sister sure can be bossy. Of course, my mom, after wrenching us brutally from the

Sandman's domain, merely stayed back near the sink and let us do the work.

Resentfully, I slowly put one foot on the toilet and then the other, and, finally, leaning as far from the skylight as I could and with my eyes screwed up to prevent puncture wounds, I hung the towel up. And with that, the bird came careening straight towards my face and I dived off the toilet. Anyone would have reacted the same way. It wasn't really my fault that I jumped straight into my sister. As we landed on the hard tiles, both destined for serious bruising, the bird—that God-forsaken bird—flew sedately out the wide-open window. The worst part, however, was the gleeful laughter of our mother.

"You guys... you guys look so funny! It's just a little bird!"

With my entire body throbbing, I stood up and opened my mouth to deliver a scathing retort about "emergencies," but stopped when I heard my sister laughing uproariously. Well, even if bruises seemed imminent, it was still the most fun I'd had with my mom and my sister in a long time. The Bird Incident can still, to this day, make us break into uproarious laughter.

~Mary Beth Case

The Gift of the Penguins

Other things may change us, but we start and end with the family.
~Anthony Brandt

How do you say goodbye to your mother after she's given you a lifetime of love? I had well over a year to come up with an answer to that question after she was diagnosed with a terminal illness. Would my goodbye take the form of a letter? A party to celebrate her life? A simple but profound conversation? Or something more lighthearted, like a scrapbook filled with eighty-three years of stories and photos? Turns out I didn't need to plan a thing. When the heat in her building broke down one cold winter day, I found an opportunity for a mother/daughter event that brought us closer in an unexpected way.

She was frail during that last winter and I knew that even a few hours in an ice-cold apartment wouldn't do her any good. So although she'd been housebound for many months—and preferred sleeping in her own bed—she reluctantly agreed to come to my house and spend the night.

For some families, this might be routine. But in the thirty-five years since I'd left home, my mother had never once slept at my house. Our family was big—and the last time I had a chunk of time alone with her was when I stayed home sick from school. Much as I loved her, I couldn't help but wonder what in the world I would do with her. Would we play cards? Sit around and chat about old times? I decided to rent a movie to keep her entertained. As I walked through the aisles of the rental store, I rejected the off-color comedies, erotic romances, and bloody thrillers. When I came upon the wildlife documentary, *March of the Penguins*, I had a hunch I'd found the right diversion.

Mom didn't seem particularly delighted with my choice at first. But once I set her up on the couch with pillows and a blanket—in the same way she'd cared for me years earlier—she immersed herself in the story. And what a tale it was! The documentary followed a colony of Emperor penguins during their perilous rites of starting a family. Each year, hundreds of them march in single file through the brutal terrain of Antarctica to the breeding grounds where they conduct their mating rituals. The pairing off is instant, instinctive and destined to last for a lifetime. Soon after the choice is made, the female penguin lays a single egg and passes it on to her partner for safekeeping while she takes on more pressing tasks.

My mother and I watched in awe as one male penguin began the challenge of protecting his precious bundle, balancing the huge egg between his feet and stomach for months, enduring icy winds and frigid temperatures over 100 degrees below zero. Did I mention that the father-to-be couldn't eat throughout this entire period? Hundreds of other male penguins were in the same situation, huddling together and defying the odds to keep each other warm. My mom laughed as she recalled how my dad—though he loved his five daughters—couldn't even change a diaper! As the drama continued, we saw the mother penguin begin her arduous journey to the sea in treacherous conditions to stock up on fish for herself and her family. When she finally returned months later, she instantly spotted her partner from among the hundreds of penguins waiting—and recognized the call of her newly hatched chick.

Once the movie was over, the beauty of the story moved us to talk about the joys, the struggles and the occasional heartbreaks that come with raising a family. Though my parents never faced the menacing conditions of Antarctica, they too had their challenges. Finding the perfect partner, making a lasting commitment to each other, taking on the sometimes harsh responsibilities of raising children weren't always easy. But with family, there were always rewards.

On the first—and last—night my mother slept in my home, we settled in the comfort of those lasting rewards. For a unique tale set in ice-cold Antarctica had reminded us of the soothing warmth of family, as it melted the chilling fears that ruffled our hearts.

~Kathy Melia Levine

The Ice Bucket

Don't ever save anything for a special occasion.
Being alive is the special occasion.
~Author Unknown

After leaving home for college, I never felt like I quite fit in with my family again. A layer of ice seemed to form between my mother and me as I began spouting opinions radically different from those with which I had been raised. I felt the chill of disapproval. Mom and Dad came from blue-collar families and remained so themselves. Though I saw nothing wrong with that, I preferred the artistic life, one that they didn't seem to understand.

"What kind of a job can you get if you're an English major?" my mother asked. I knew her concern was only because she wanted a better life for me, but it infuriated me.

"I never tell you how to live your life. Don't tell me how to live mine," I would say. "I want to be a writer." It's funny that when you're in the middle of a situation you never realize what a cliché your "problem" is. You think you are the only one to ever disappoint your parents. Eventually we learned not to talk about certain topics, but it hurt to feel like I hadn't won my parents' approval.

My parents came from more conservative times, and one of the symbols of that to me was Mom's ice bucket, which sat atop the refrigerator. My parents didn't usually have parties, but during my childhood my mother did have a Tupperware party. She planned it for days and we children helped her prepare the house for it. Mom and her friends had a great time, and Mom obtained enough hostess points for the one item in the catalog that she coveted—the ice bucket with tongs.

When it came, it was unwrapped carefully and reverently put in that place where all household treasures resided—the top of the refrigerator. Though we moved several times after that, that ice bucket was carted from house to house and a new house wasn't home until the ice bucket was placed on top of the refrigerator.

The bucket was never used. I think Mom was saving it for a "special occasion." The only occasions we ever had were the usual milestones—someone's twenty-first birthday, a baby or a bridal shower. I suspect that Mom was hoping for a slightly more glamorous occasion—perhaps a cocktail party, or a New Year's Eve celebration where everyone wore something besides jeans. I think in her heart she thought that life (and their income) would get better.

A few months ago, Mom called to say she was bringing over some things for me to sort through. She and my father had moved into a smaller place for their retirement, and they just didn't have room for all the stuff they'd accumulated. I rooted through the box and gladly rescued a few ceramic roosters from the thrift shop pile before I saw a bag with a familiar shape peeping out from the top.

"Do you want this?" Mom asked as she sadly handed me the ice bucket. "Wait," she said, not letting me respond. "I know the tongs are in here somewhere." Daintily she handed me the items, pinkie outstretched, the same daintiness that would not have been out of place in a queen's court had her life circumstances placed her there.

"Of course I want them," I said.

I knew then that she was still hopeful about my future, still believed my life would be better than hers had been, and that the ice between us had started to thaw. That ice bucket told me there were unexpressed desires in my mother's heart for me and that she wasn't as different from me as she might appear.

Some time later, I threw a surprise birthday party for Mom. I stipulated that the dress code was to be "Sunday Best." Not since that Tupperware party had my sisters and I spent so much time fussing over a party. Once I told them about it, the whole family was on board; my dad even bought Mom a new dress "from the mall," he told me proudly.

The star of the party was, however, the ice bucket. We elevated it in the center of the table, swathing it in pink tulle, filling it to overflowing with ice.

The surprise party flabbergasted my mom. After the initial greetings, I put Mom to work. "Would you get us all some ice?" I asked, as I handed her the tongs. Standing there in the teal silk dress that made her blue eyes sparkle, pinkie extended, she complied, dipping into that bucket as if she were handing out gold coins.

Afterwards she introduced me to her new friend from church I hadn't met.

"Lisa," she said, "have you met my daughter... the writer?"

~Drema Sizemore Drudge

Thankful

Fill your paper with the breathings of your heart.
~William Wordsworth

I felt honor-bound to eat every one of those oranges—to savor each one as long as possible. Every day for the last fifteen days, I had stared at that cardboard crate of premium oranges. Occasionally I had picked up an orange and peeled the loose skin with my thumb to reveal the juicy flesh, and I had eaten several of them. I would inhale deeply, the citrusy aroma gently nudging me from my grief. The oranges were beginning to show signs of their trip from some distant tropical clime to Wisconsin, where they had sat on my kitchen table for a week. Several of them were already inedible and had to be discarded.

Juice dribbled down my chin when I took my first bite of the one remaining orange. I wiped the sticky sweetness from my chin with a damp cloth and sat alone for a few moments while my daughter was at her first day of daycare, my husband was at work and I floundered through my last morning of maternity leave.

A pile of birthday cards lay scattered on the kitchen table beside me. I needed to write thank-you notes to several people. Writing thank-you notes at the kitchen table was a childhood habit. When I was a little girl, my mom would make me sit at the table after every birthday or Christmas, or anytime I received a gift, and write thank-you notes. To pass Mom's inspection the notes had to be high-quality, neatly written, grammatically correct and specific: where I was going to wear the clothes or what I was going to do with the money.

Early on, I protested writing those notes as a chore, and then later I embraced writing them as a challenge. In the exercise of writing those notes, I developed a genuine love of language and a fascination for how words work. I got my start as a writer at my mother's knee. She taught me how to consider my target audience, to stick to a purpose, to revise and edit, and never to be satisfied with a first draft. I use all of those skills on a daily basis in my work as a science writer.

I sighed, biting into another wedge of orange. I couldn't help smiling as I remembered the one thank-you note that escaped my mom's quality control and created quite a family kerfuffle. My cousin had sent me a craft project he made in a school class. The item was constructed of a discarded frozen juice can that had been covered in gold felt. To one end of the juice can, my cousin had attached the flat side of half of a Styrofoam ball, which he had also meticulously covered in gold felt. The result was a gold mushroom, the top decorated with colorful sequins, each held in place with a straight pin.

I crafted a glowing thank-you note describing how beautifully the colors and the design worked, what a nice job he had done constructing it and how I really appreciated the time he put into making the gift. The problem was that I wasn't sure what it was. I thought it might be a pincushion, but I hesitated to be specific because I was I afraid I might offend him if the gift wasn't a pincushion. So I concluded my glowing comments about the gift's construction with the words: "By the way, what is it?"

My cousin was crushed. My aunt was furious, and she called my mother. My mother ended up furious with my aunt, and I was upset because I really had intended no harm and had been completely misunderstood.

I shook my head and smiled to myself as I picked up the final wedge of the orange. Writing those mandatory thank-you notes had turned me into a writer. I was always writing in journals and notebooks when I was a teenager, entering essay contests, and attending writing camps and summer writing programs.

I remember one time I was in my room, sitting on the floor writing in one of my diaries about the day's events. Mom and I had some sort of mother/daughter spat, and I had stormed into my room, slamming the door behind me. My escapes after Mom had "ruined my life" in some fashion or other usually involved writing. I hadn't been writing long when Mom opened the door to my room.

"I guess you're writing all sorts of horrible things about me in there." She glanced at my journal.

"No." I grunted, turning my back on her. A moment of silence, then I heard the door shut.

I remember thinking that I should have said more. But I didn't know what to say.

That was a long time ago.

I remember thinking a few weeks ago how I should have said more when she commented over the phone from her hospital bed, "You know, you'll miss me when I'm gone."

But I didn't know what to say. She died that night.

The last wedge of the orange was dry and bitter. I spit it out.

A generic computer-printed card lay in the now empty orange box in front of me, a white card with the words "A Gift for You" printed on the top, and inside simply: "Love, Mom." The oranges had been a gift from my mother, pre-ordered for my forty-first birthday well before she died. They would be the last gift that I ever received from her.

I reached for a pen and a note card.

Dear Mom,

Thanks for the premium oranges that you sent for my birthday. The aroma transports me from February in Wisconsin, and I think of you and all of the adventures we had together. I miss you. I've decided that I will start a tradition of ordering a box of premium oranges for my birthday every year, and I will eat one a day until they are gone. It will be a won-

derful way for me to remember you and remind myself to go through life
grateful for all of its blessings, large and small.

    Love,
    Michele

~Michele Arduengo

Burgers and Butterflies

I think that if ever a mortal heard the voice of God
it would be in a garden at the cool of the day.
~F. Frankfort Moore

The doctors had recommended "a facility" but Mom and I had other plans for her last few months. With her doctors' concurrence, she rejected aggressive cancer treatments with, "I've lived a long and full life and I want to live while I'm here. I'd rather go home to my flowers, birds and butterflies." I joined her in that wish, tough decision though it was, and moved in to stay with her, to read poetry and drink tea in her garden, rejecting hospice for a while.

For decades, Mom's "garden of love" had been a place that nourished her soul as she nurtured it, a place where she turned in times of loss, anger, fear, joy, and gratitude. There she would bury her frustration or feed her exultation, pulling weeds and planting seeds… sculpting her yard.

A delightful young woman stayed with Mom while I finished teaching my university classes. During the late spring, I cooked on the grill and we dined at her old picnic table amid the flowers and shrubs. About once a week, though, I'd call on the way home from class. "How about I stop by Dutch's and pick up some hamburgers?"

"And French fries," Mom said, relishing foods with salt that she'd long ago foresworn.

When I arrived, our helper would leave and Mom and I would picnic at the red cedar table in the backyard, with her dog by her feet.

At first, the roses were flush. Then the sweet honey fragrance from the arbor of Carolina jasmine shouted over the burgers and fries. In that quiet spot, we ate and laughed as we remembered our years together in many flowerbeds and lawns across Texas.

When butterflies would light on our shoulders or hair, she'd say, "Remember... a butterfly's kiss is a kiss from God." She'd said that as long as I could remember. That saying lingers in my heart.

The heat, mid-summer, sent us inside to air conditioning. I'd read aloud to her from a book of poetry, taking comfort from the wisdom of old souls. Her young friends and neighbors would drop by with hugs and cookies and a chat about business and politics. Mom enjoyed staying abreast of the world.

Early and late in the day, we'd walk, and try to ease each other's fears, and grieve the coming goodbye. When her disease advanced, she'd ride in her wheelchair over her lawn, checking out what had bloomed, what needed tending to, and most often just pausing to admire. She had planted flowers, trees and shrubs so that there would be "something blooming every month that I can cut and take in the house." And we would cut and take color into the house for this woman who had been reared in the Texas Panhandle, where the sky's blue dome might be the only hue contrasting with the tan earth.

My classes started again in August, and we took up our routine of "want a burger... and fries?'"

As the summer heat waned, we moved back outside, to a patio those young neighbors, whom she called, "my angels," had built. It included a wheelchair ramp. By now, Mom napped more than wandered. On one late, cool September afternoon, I strolled around her backyard. When she awakened I said, "Mom, looks like your fall flowers are up... they're a copper red... in among your roses."

"The asters," she said, her eyes bright as the first star at night. A childlike glee swept her face.

"Let me take you." I helped her into her "chariot" and rolled her to her favorite flowerbed. She strained. Her vision had deteriorated even more, from macular degeneration and perhaps "the disease process." She followed my hand as I pointed out the flowers. "I see them.

I see them. Yes. It's them," she said. And then, a small yellow butterfly landed on her hand, "a kiss from God," she said, as usual.

We did not know that would be our last outing. Late that night she succumbed to the pain and the weakness and stopped going outside. Only a few more nights and days remained when she could call my name. A few days of ragged silence followed, her breathing labored, and then stilled. Within moments, as if in salute, a pair of mockingbirds flew figure eights through her front porch and patio. "She can see them now... and hear them," a friend who had stayed with us said.

In that time between the dying and the burying, that time between so much to do and so little, I stopped for a burger and of course added the fries. When I returned home, the young woman who continued to help, departed. Mom's rascally dog and I kept company at the red cedar picnic table.

And then a winged visitor joined us. A rust and copper butterfly, about the size of a silver dollar and unlike any I'd ever seen in Mom's yard, fluttered around. It lit on strands of my hair, kissed my eyelids, my cheeks, my nose. It flew from ear to ear with stops on my shoulders, circling and circling, then down my arms to my hands, resting for a bit on my knuckles, then hopped to the burger. Its forefeet rubbed together like a child's hands in anticipation. While I ate, the winged visitor nibbled my burger, then hopped to the French fries, then back to the burger, then up my hand and back to my face, then back to the burger. And the fries.

"Thanks, Mom. You're present in a way that only you and I would know. Enjoy the burger and fries; you've lifted my heart." I sat beneath her bush of bridal wreath and ate. And smiled... perhaps for the first time in days. The butterfly stayed, nibbling, and dancing between the burger, the fries, and me... a "kiss from God" she would have said. But for me, in this time between passage and memorial service, the butterfly and burger combination signaled a kiss from Mom.

Today, another year later, her house now my home, I sit beside her bridal wreath and gaze upon her roses and asters when in season, and enjoy my mother's passion, her garden of flowers, butterflies and birds. When the cloud of grief drifts by, not as severe as those early days, I still go to her "garden of love and hope." And while I've never again seen that particular species of butterfly, Mom's spirit blossoms and my memories of her bloom in this, her place of solitude and treasure.

~Carmen Goldthwaite

The Magic of

Chapter
2

Mothers &
Daughters

Rites of Passage

Do not squander time. For that's the stuff life is made of.

~Benjamin Franklin

Nobody Ever Told Me

A daughter may outgrow your lap, but she will never outgrow your heart.
~Author Unknown

Nobody ever told me, when I became the mother of a newborn, that I would tremble with terror as I carried her home from the hospital, wondering how in the world I'd know what to do with her. She seemed like a tiny, helpless victim of my ineptitude.

When I diapered Jill, back in the days of cloth diapers and diaper pins, and I once clumsily stuck a pin into her velvety-soft body, I wept with shame.

When I bathed her, I was positive she would drown.

And when she cried, I felt pangs of guilt that I couldn't figure out what was wrong.

Nobody ever told me that despite all the sleepless nights, the high anxiety, the fear that I would drop her or starve her or overfeed her, I would fall madly, hopelessly in love with this perfect miniature who somehow survived all my first-baby fumbles.

Nobody ever told me when our second daughter was born that I would feel slightly more confident, but just as overwhelmed. Bringing Amy home from the hospital was a bit less traumatic and more routine — but it also taught one young and still-novice mother that two babies somehow added up to more than twice as much work and exhaustion and worry. Nobody can explain the math.

Nobody ever told me that somehow, a mother's love multiplies easily, and that there's more than enough to go around.

Then along came another daughter.

Nobody ever told me that as much as I'd yearned for a son, a little boy to play baseball with my husband and be named Jonathan, I'd cradle a six-pound wonder named Nancy and lose my heart to her the moment her tiny hand curled itself around my finger.

I had only two hands, and needed six.

I had only twenty-four hours, and needed at least ten more.

I finally knew exactly how to bathe and diaper and burp a baby—but I didn't know how to push down the feelings of desperation when Nancy, cursed by colic, screamed in pain.

Nobody told me that colic passes, and that I was actually developing that elusive, amazing, powerful thing called maternal instinct, even though I was the last to know it.

Infant girls turn into babies, babies turn into toddlers, and toddlers pick themselves up one day and walk away, right out into the world.

Nobody told me how it would feel to walk three little girls in turn to "big school," and turn them over to a smiling usurper with the official title "kindergarten teacher."

I managed that feat three times, blinking back tears on each momentous walk to the kindergarten door.

I somehow sweated out those first days of school praying, "Let her be okay. Let her love school!" And three times, I was lucky. Kindergarten was an unqualified success.

Nobody told me that those school years would tumble onto one another leaving this mother wondering how those little girls in their plaid dresses had grown into teenagers who thought I was stupid, mean and a general embarrassment.

But those years passed, too, and suddenly, I was walking Jill, then Amy, then Nancy into dormitories on college campuses. Those walks might have been on a tightrope, so dangerous and traumatic did they feel—and not for my daughters.

I was the one who sobbed as I hugged them goodbye. I was the one wondering, "Will they be okay? Do they know all they need to? Will life ever be the same again?"

Nobody ever told me that yes, everything changes when daughters leave home. That it gets better in some ways, and ineffably sad in others.

Then each of our daughters took a different walk, this one down a path in our garden to meet their grooms in three memorable home weddings.

Nobody ever told me that there would be room in my heart for sons-in-law, young men who would forever change our family constellation—and make it better.

And then my daughters—women now—had children of their own. Nobody ever told me what it would feel like to look down at the child of my child and glimpse eternity.

I'm supposed to be the expert now—the wise, all-knowing grandmother. The elder of the tribe.

I'm supposed to know all the secrets of life and pass them on.

Nobody ever told me that the longer I live, the more humbled I feel by how little I know, but how much I love.

Nobody ever told me that mothers and grandmothers grow second hearts just to store up all that love.

And now, at last, nobody has to tell me that motherhood/grandmotherhood is my most profound, most monumental gift.

That I know every single day of my life.

~Sally Schwartz Friedman

Separation Anxiety

My thoughts are free to go anywhere,
but it's surprising how often they head in your direction.
~Author Unknown

The green backpack Elizabeth was stuffing with clothes for summer camp was almost bigger than she was. At ten, my daughter would soon be off to sleep-away camp for the first time. As she placed Stripey, her stuffed tiger, on top and snapped the bag shut, there were plenty of emotions swirling around the room: nervousness, agitation, the effects of insomnia.

And that was just me.

It was her first time away from home and I worried that she wouldn't make friends or that she'd be homesick and cry herself to sleep each night. But two days later, driving through Vermont's lush green hills on the way to camp, Elizabeth was her usual chattering self. She was apprehensive about the upcoming swimming test, but excited to get there, unpack and meet new friends. After my husband Jeff and I helped lug her backpack and duffle bag up the hill to her cabin we strung mosquito netting, in an intricate cat's cradle of cord, over her top pine bunk. As we sweated and grimaced, Elizabeth introduced herself to a new friend, dug her bathing suit out of her duffle bag, and trotted off to the bathroom to change. The girls skipped together to the lake for their swimming tests, leaving two sets of nervous parents struggling with their children's bunks. When the girls returned, jabbering to each other nonstop, it was almost as if we'd become invisible. Jeff and I kissed Elizabeth goodbye and left. I was relieved she seemed so happy.

For the first time, we began to think about life without a kid, and what we would do for the next two weeks. It was our first extended time alone (we met when Elizabeth was four) and the possibilities seemed endless. Jeff started the car and as we bumped along the gravel road away from camp, I was elated—sending her to camp was the right thing to do. Jeff reached over, rubbed my back and smiled. But something still felt slightly off-kilter.

The first night, when I walked by Elizabeth's room, I got an uncomfortable feeling that some part of our lives was missing—like a phantom limb, something that should be there but isn't. I peered in, almost expecting to see her sprawled under her comforter, the dog curled into a crescent at her feet. But her bed was empty. Even the dog avoided the room, as if staying in Elizabeth's room without her was as wrong as jumping onto the sofa.

The next evening, Elizabeth haunted our first dinner date, too. Instead of gazing dreamily into each other's eyes, we took turns guessing what she might be doing at that very moment. And our conjecture transformed into my worry. Had she made any friends? Was she homesick? Were any girls bullying her? I had flashbacks to my preadolescence and my mind swarmed with the faces of girls who'd taunted me. Jeff assured me that I was fretting for nothing—my childhood was my issue, better left to a discussion with my therapist than making myself nuts over my daughter's imaginary tormentors. He reminded me of how she was when we'd left her at camp—ecstatic with a new friend. Surely, not that much had changed in twenty-four hours.

After a few days, we settled into our new, child-free routine and started to enjoy ourselves—until we received our first postcard. In careful squiggles on a pre-stamped, pre-addressed postcard Elizabeth wrote, "I'm having fun. I'm doing distance swimming. I've had no mail. Please send letters." A picture of a sad face was etched next to the map she'd drawn of the lake and her distance-swimming route. A week before she left, I'd posted two letters so she'd have a couple of notes from home waiting for her. They probably just hadn't arrived yet.

A few days later we stopped at the mailbox late at night, returning from a date in the city. Flipping through the catalogs and bills, there was another card: "I like camp. Please send mail. I'm the only person who didn't get any mail." Next to the note was a picture of a blank piece of paper, a pencil, and a stamp. Underneath was a caption: "0 mail."

I started to panic. Where was her mail? Was something insidious going on? Was it a plot to keep mail from her? A mean girl in charge of mail duty, purposefully hiding letters from our daughter? Had a bomb obliterated the quaint Vermont post office? I was obviously losing my mind. But she should have received at least a few letters by now. Her dad and I had mailed four or five. Her grandparents had sent mail and a friend had mailed her a postcard. Why had she received "0 mail?" It was too late to call the camp, so I shot off a quick e-mail to the camp administrator, crawled into bed and slept fitfully.

Early the next morning the camp director called. It was Saturday and the office was closed, but she said she'd checked with Elizabeth's counselor who said our daughter was happy. The director said she would contact the office Monday morning when it opened to see what had happened to Elizabeth's mail.

Despite the director's reassurances, I couldn't stop worrying that Elizabeth was really miserable at camp. It's not that I'm usually a neurotic, overprotective parent. Sure, when Elizabeth was a newborn I made my parents scrub their hands before they held her, but by the time she was thirteen months old I was picking up the goldfish crackers she'd dropped in the sandbox, dusting them off, and handing them back to her. At three, she skipped happily off to preschool—and I spied on her through the classroom's window for only the first few days. She was pretty well adjusted and I liked to think that I was, too. But somehow the missing letters had turned me into Crazy Mom, envisioning anything—and everything—that might possibly go wrong.

Finally Monday arrived. The post office was open. The village director called and said she'd talked to Elizabeth. She had finally received the mail, and, most importantly, had been having a blast all along. Somehow her cards to us had crossed paths with ours to her. When I heard this, I realized that even though we had sent Elizabeth to camp to learn about herself, I was the one who needed to learn... about letting go. Subconsciously, I was still longing for the tiny baby who depended on me for all her needs, but my daughter was growing up. And sooner, rather than later, she's going to have a life without me.

Jeff and I enjoyed our last week alone.

When the final day of camp arrived, we drove up, parked the car and hiked up the hill to Elizabeth's village. She actually looked taller, more poised and more sure of herself. "May I show you around my camp?" she asked, and without waiting for our answer, took our hands to show us around and then begged, "Can I come back next year — please?"

~Sue Sanders

Reconnecting

The art of mothering is to teach the art of living to children.
~Elain Heffner

We bought our older daughter a twin bed when she turned two. As my husband assembled the bed, she reached up now and then to run her tiny fingers along the golden-grained oak headboard. When Jim put the mattress on the box spring, she scrambled up and stretched out, a huge smile lighting up her face.

"She'll be fine." My husband pulled me away as I fussed with the guardrails later that night.

The next morning, I awoke to an unfamiliar touch. As I sat upright, my daughter's little fingers pushed down on my side of the mattress. Her upturned face stared back at me. Standing on her tiptoes, her curly head barely came over the top of the bed. She grinned, her eyes sparkling.

She came to our bedroom every morning. On Sundays our bed became a playground, where draped in sheets, she and Jim chased each other. Sometimes, at the soft patter of her footsteps in the hallway, he'd pull the covers over himself. She'd throw herself on top of his blanketed, growling form, squealing as she tried to capture the "lion."

As she grew older, we'd meet in the kitchen where I'd get my morning coffee. Together, we'd walk to my bedroom. She'd set her sippy cup of milk on the nightstand, climb into bed and prop herself up on the pillows. Taking her toddler Bible out from the nightstand drawer, she'd "read" it, sometimes upside down, while I had my quiet time. Sometimes we'd lie in bed, and snuggle and chat. Peals of laughter filled the room when I pretended to fall asleep and snore.

Our morning ritual continued as the years passed. It connected us somehow. The camaraderie we shared lingered through the day.

When she entered her preteen years, she became quieter. Sometimes shoulder shrugs and rolled eyes met my questions.

Our morning ritual began to wane.

"I miss you coming to bed in the morning," I'd say. She'd look away.

As her adolescence progressed, the easy conversations we once shared gave way to occasional awkward silences. Quite often, I hurt her feelings with what I said or didn't say. Her friends' opinions counted more than mine.

"It's just a phase," my husband said as he tried to comfort me. But I hated the disconnect I felt. I struggled to find a way to relate to her… to communicate with her. Though I tried to choose my battles, I felt I had morphed into a mean ogre, demanding she do her chores, pay attention to instructions and be more responsible.

Things climaxed sooner than I anticipated.

One afternoon, I pushed the vacuum cleaner into her room, trying to ignore the clutter of lip gloss, nail polish and lotion bottles that obscured the surface of her dresser. Was it unreasonable to expect a fairly neat room?

She lay on her bed, listening to her iPod. She looked over her magazine as I began to vacuum.

I rounded the corner of her bed. A few Kleenexes and candy wrappers lying between her bed and the nightstand ignited my temper.

"This is unacceptable."

"Huh?" A blank look greeted me.

"How can you leave trash lying around in your room like that?"

"What's wrong with my room?" I turned the vacuum cleaner off and stared at her.

"What's wrong with your room? You have to keep your room clean. Do you want to live in a messy house when you grow up?" I gestured to the books askew on the bookshelf, shoes and socks scattered under her bed, the pink butterfly chair piled with magazines, and the overflowing trash can.

"I like my room the way it is." I couldn't believe my ears.

"We didn't raise you to be messy!"

"But it's my room."

"Which happens to be in my house. If you can't obey my rules and keep your room clean, I'll... I'll take it away...." I swallowed hard. What a stupid thing to say.

Another time, we would have dissolved into giggles at the incongruity of my threat. But she shrugged and turned away.

"If that's your attitude," my voice began to rise a few decibels, "you're in charge of cleaning your room from now on." I threw the vacuum cleaner handle on the floor.

"Fine by me."

"Fine." I glared at her. She stared at the floor.

I stalked out of the room convinced I'd lost my daughter.

The next day, Jim and I set out our minimum expectations for a clean room.

Each week as I cleaned the house, I'd pause outside her room.

Would the easy relationship we once shared ever return?

Her room wasn't perfect, but she was trying. That was enough for me.

Several months later, I had an unexpected epiphany. Twelve tweens took over our home for a few hours to celebrate her birthday.

She greeted each of them at the door, and made sure she introduced everyone. She sat next to the quietest girl in the group and tried to include her in the rapid conversation. As they dared each other during Hot Potato, she was careful that no one would be embarrassed. She ate pepperoni pizza instead of her favorite, cheese, so that her vegetarian friend and others who liked cheese pizza would have enough. She remained at the table long after the others left, keeping a friend company who ate slowly.

"Ssshhh, my little sister is sleeping upstairs," she cautioned when the giggles and squeals threatened to raise the roof. Warmth seeped through me as I saw her through new eyes.

As the strains of the last song in *High School Musical 3* faded, they noticed the cake and ice cream on the counter. "Oooh, vanilla and chocolate ice cream!"

"Mrs. Mellott, can I have both?"

"Yes."

"Really?"

"Wow!"

My heart softened. Though fairies had given way to Hannah Montana and the Jonas Brothers, though lip gloss and shopping at Claire's were cool, and playing with dolls wasn't, they were still little girls at heart.

When the last goodbye was said and the last crumb vacuumed up, my daughter kissed me. "Thank you, Mama. That was fun."

A few days after the party, our toddler came down with a cold and fever. Exhausted from tending to her through the night, I eased myself against the pillows on my bed and picked up a book. A knock sounded and my daughter peered in.

"May I lie on the bed with you?"

"Of course." I put my book aside. Sliding down the pillows, I stretched out beside her.

We stared at each other in awkward silence for a few seconds.

I closed my eyes, pretended to fall asleep and snored. She giggled.

Suddenly she began to chat. We talked about everything and nothing. We looked into each other's eyes, we laughed and squealed.

I was content—for a brief moment in time I had reconnected with my daughter in the way I needed.

~Anita Mellott

Mom Jeans

If I were a cat, what would make me purr?
A pair of really comfortable blue jeans, and massages.
~Cinnamon Stomberger

I f you're like me, and still think that thongs are footwear, you probably don't wear low-rise jeans. You probably wear Mom Jeans. And, if you're like me, they make you look fat. That's what my teenage daughter says. She says that my faded jeans, those that button at the waist and taper at the ankle, are really unflattering. She says that hip-hugging, dark-rinsed, flared jeans are more slimming. Like anyone who weighs 103 pounds would know.

But the 103-pound youth market is what the fashion industry is courting. And who can blame them? My skinny kid is flush with babysitting money and has the stamina to beg me to drive her to the mall whenever a new issue of *Teen Vogue* or *Elle Girl* hits the stands. I, on the other hand, haven't bought a new pair of jeans in years.

That's because, for me, shopping for jeans is a traumatic experience. It's not just the three-way mirrors that reflect my doughy self three painful times in baggy underwear, it's finding jeans that fit. If they glide over my hips, the waist is huge. If the waist size is correct, I can't pull them up past my knees. They are always too long or the legs are too tight or they make me look fat. That's why I've been wearing the same jeans since the Clinton administration. I think of them as timeless classics.

"They're Mom Jeans," my daughter says. "They make your butt look big."

My daughter is nothing if not honest, so with her withering fashion commentary ringing in my ears, I don a sweater long enough to cover the aforementioned region and we head to the mall.

Going shopping with my teenage daughter is like hiking a small hill with a Nepalese Sherpa. You are in expert hands, but you don't necessarily speak the same language.

"Do you want flares, tapered or straight leg? Acid washed, sand-blasted or dark wash? Low-rise, super low-rise, mid-rise or curvy?" she asks, as we rummage through shelves of obsessively folded jeans in The Gap. I checked for a womanly size twelve lurking amid the twos, fours and zeroes. (What kind of size is zero?)

I looked for a price tag and remembered that a friend of mine once advised, "Never worry about cost when you are buying jeans." Or was it when you're buying a bathing suit? Maybe it was life insur-ance. Anyway, I figured that if I found a pair of jeans that actually made my matronly posterior look smaller, it would be worth a little extra money… heck, it would be priceless.

"Try the boot cut," my daughter shouts over the store's pulsating sound track. "They make your legs look longer."

"Then I'll have to buy boots," I hollered back.

I finally found a pair that were my size and took them into the dressing room.

They were perfect. They weren't cut too low and the hems didn't drag on the ground. I thought they made my butt look okay, and, best of all, they were comfortable. In these jeans, I'd be able to kneel down to pick up Legos off the living room floor and not worry about my underwear sticking out. I'd be able to reach up to the highest shelf in my kitchen without the rest of the family losing their appetite. I could even bend over to kiss my children as they sleep.

My daughter says I did it again—I got another pair of Mom Jeans, but I don't care. I have a Mom Body and Mom Jeans fit me just fine.

~Carol Band

Reprinted by permission of
Carolyn Hiler ©2011

Beautiful Girls

Beauty comes as much from the mind as from the eye.
~Grey Livingston

I promised my daughter that she could do my make-up on Saturday night. My husband and I were going to a party, a casual affair, outdoors, and I thought, why not? My girl would love this chance to play with all the goodies in my make-up drawer, and I could always re-do any collateral damage in the car.

I was ill-prepared for the grandness of the event at hand. Not the party... the makeover. When I came upstairs to dress, she had arranged all of her tools and color choices on the counter. Brushes, shadows, blushes, liners, concealers and powders, all artfully displayed in my bathroom.

"Ready, Mom?"

"I'm dressing first, and then I'll be ready for make-up, Abigail."

"I'm not so sure about that black shirt," she says, eying me.

I take a deep breath.

"I think it's good with the rest of the outfit, Abby."

She gives me a look filled with doubt. She is ten.

"Mom, I'm just saying... long sleeves?"

"Yes," I answer, realizing suddenly that I have stepped into an episode of "What Not to Wear, The Tween Years."

The make-up portion of the evening is sounding better and better, so I finish dressing and approach the bathroom.

I begin to moisturize, and she watches.

"What kind do you use?" she asks. I tell her, and take the moment to talk about sunscreen.

"Good point," she says.

She reaches for the blush, and I stop her, needing to first blend in a mineral foundation. She watches, entranced.

"Oh, shoot!" I exclaim. "I forgot my eye cream."

"What's eye cream for?" Abby asks.

"Dark circles."

"Yeah, you're gonna want that."

I feel my lips twitch with unspoken words, but she is right.

I blend in the under-eye cream, and then it is her turn. She begins with my eyes, showing me her color choices, seeming shocked that I don't question her decisions. There is no need; she is right about everything. The browns, the golds, the colors to highlight my best features and conceal the imperfections. There is even a little extra sparkle for nighttime. She holds my face in her hands and uses a light touch. It takes a while, and I am in no hurry. I let her apply my eyeliner, my mascara, and then powder, lipstick, and blush.

"I want to use a darker blush, Mom. I think it will be pretty."

I okay the decision, and when I look in the mirror, it is her face I see first, next to mine, waiting for a reaction. For a moment, I am stunned by the job she has done. My make-up is soft, it is lumi-nous—it is exactly the way I would want to look for this particular night.

"Abby, you did such a good job. A really, really good job. I'm beautiful."

"Do you think so?"

Do I think so? That's a huge question. How often do I feel it? Like many women, perhaps rarely. And say it out loud? Perhaps never. But she had created on me (and in me) such a difference, that it was easy to give in to the moment. I was beautiful, by her hand, and she had given me this unexpected gift. This beauty. This beautiful moment.

I add the cardigan to the black T-shirt. I'm not sure if she is impressed and I find myself actually wanting her opinion, but it is late, and I need to leave.

"You need more gloss," she says.

I stop in the doorway of the bedroom and allow her to touch up my lips.

"There," she says, satisfied.

"Thank you," I say, meaning it.

"You're welcome." She is beaming.

How is it that I feel like a movie star but it is Abby's face that is shining, with no make-up at all?

Hers is true beauty glowing from within… no compacts, no glosses, no tubes. And if I could bottle up that beautiful feeling, that beautiful moment, that beautiful girl, I would. And on a day that is bound to come, a day when she questions her own beauty, I would open that bottle and give back to her this beautiful gift that she has so freely given to me.

~Christy Chafe

Invisible Mom

See everything; overlook a great deal; correct a little.
~Pope John XXIII

t had the potential to be a happy day. My thirteen-year-old daughter had been selected to join the National Junior Honor Society at her middle school and parents were invited to the induction ceremony. But at the supper table the night before, my daughter's words squelched my excitement.

"You know I won't be able to talk to you tomorrow," she informed me in her matter-of-fact tone.

"That's fine," I remarked casually, wishing inside my little girl still wanted me by her side. "After the ceremony, I'll leave quietly. You'll never know I was there." My words seemed to reassure her.

"Well, I just wanted you to know, that's all."

"Don't worry, Jelly." Her eyes widened at the mention of her family nickname. "I won't do anything to embarrass you."

The morning of the ceremony, I stood in my closet, hands on hips, surveying my wardrobe. I decided on a beige shirt, black pants and black shoes. Plain and simple. That way I could blend into the background. Never be noticed. My hand instinctively grabbed my denim jacket, the one my daughter calls my "mother coat." I sighed, leaving it on the hanger.

I arrived at the school fifteen minutes early hoping to get a good seat. I figured if I couldn't talk to my daughter, at least maybe I could get a good look at her when she got her certificate. I chose the second table from the front so as not to appear overly anxious, yet still be close enough to snap a quick picture as her name was called.

I glanced down, noticing a small strip of my lower calf was revealed. My daughter's voice whispered inside my head: "Not cool, Mother." I quickly pulled my sock up, then tugged my pant leg down. Now there was no skin. My daughter would be proud.

I scanned the rows of students already seated in alphabetical order by the stage. Several were peering around the audience for a familiar face. They waved, then smiled, obviously spotting their parents in the crowd. I wished I could be so lucky.

Finally, I recognized a delicate pink ribbon in the back of my daughter's hair, her body straight like a statue, feet on the floor facing the stage.

Several brave moms ventured down to where the students were seated minutes before the ceremony started. With cameras in hand, they called their children by name. Did they not receive the same instructions I did last night? Or maybe they chose to ignore them. My camera sat quietly in my lap. Not long ago, I was one of those moms. But not anymore. I had promised I wouldn't embarrass her.

The ceremony began. One by one, each student's name was called. Each received a certificate. A few parents snuck down close to the stage, crouched to the floor and snapped close-up pictures of their children. Instead, I pressed the zoom button on my camera and hoped I would get a good shot. I clapped quietly as her name was called. No whistling. No yelling. No standing up to cheer.

After the ceremony there was a reception in the cafeteria. I stood alone, scanning the crowded room for my daughter. Finally, I spotted her across the room in a circle of friends. She was laughing and talking, obviously enjoying the day's festivities. I wanted to run up to her, throw my arms around her and tell her how proud I was. How much I loved her. I took a deep breath and remembered my promise.

Parents were starting to leave. I couldn't see my daughter any longer. She must have gone back to class. I would have to wait until she got home to tell her how proud I was.

Suddenly, I felt a tap on my shoulder. It surprised me since I didn't know that many parents at her new school.

"What are you doing standing over here all by yourself?" my daughter jokingly asked. Had she forgotten her instructions from the night before? Before I could fully appreciate her gesture, she excitedly jumped in with another question.

"Would you take a picture of me with my friends?"

Would I? I couldn't unzip my camera case fast enough. She even introduced me to her friends.

By now, the crowd was dwindling as parents filed outside and students headed back to class.

"Well, I guess I better be going," I announced reluctantly, not wanting this rare closeness to end.

"Well, you have a good day, Mother." My daughter beamed like a ray of sunshine. My heart swelled with pride once more. And suddenly, it was a happy day after all.

~Deanna Ingalls

A Training Opportunity

Don't worry that children never listen to you;
worry that they are always watching you.
~Robert Fulghum

"Let's go. Are you ready? Why are we still standing here? Do you think I have all day?" my daughter nags. Burning rubber like a NASCAR contender, we zoom to the nearest department store.

At the mall, we shop for the many back-to-school needs of a nine-year-old girl: school supplies, school shirts, jazzy headbands, cool jeans and… bras. In keeping with my promise, my daughter and I search for bras. Underwire, padded, strapless, backless, the styles of bras are endless. But today, we shop simply to satisfy my daughter's desire to be a mature young lady. We seek a training bra.

She enters the lingerie department in a trance. Different colors and varieties of bras hang across the junior department, like a sea of flags at the United Nations. My daughter looks around in wonder, preparing to enter preadolescence one bra at a time.

After much contemplation, we complete our selections. White and simple, these are bras a mother dreams about for her daughter. With purchases in hand, we march to the only checkout lane open and drop the items on the counter.

Dark-haired and attractive, our teenage clerk, Kyle, turns to face us. With a flash of pearly whites he asks, "Did you find everything you need?"

My daughter and I smile knowingly at each other, our purchases forming a bond between us as only a mother and daughter can experience. She is growing up.

Kyle scans our purchases and I hear only one soft beep. But, how can that be? We selected two bras. My mind wrestles with the pros and cons of the next step. Two choices exist. We slip out of the store quietly, stealing the bra that didn't scan, or I humiliate my daughter and possibly the store clerk by pointing out his error. I decide to be honest. After all, I am a parent—a role model.

"Wait! You only rang up one bra. You missed the other one."

By my side, my daughter melts like butter on a hot plate. Kyle attempts to pull apart the AAA training bras tangled together. I reach over to help, and the tug of war begins. As he yanks upward, I jerk to the left and right.

"Thanks a lot. This is the most humiliating day of my life," snarls my daughter.

Kyle avoids eye contact and my daughter tries to hide behind my purse. I quickly glide my Visa card across the scanner to pay. Then we charge through the automated doors and out of the store. Ashley stays close by my side, still grumbling and embarrassed.

"Mom, he was the cutest boy! And did you notice how embarrassed he was?"

Bra shopping is not for the meek. Maybe my husband was right to stay home, avoiding the whole thing. Despite the checkout debacle, my daughter lights up in anticipation of trying on each training bra. Once home, she puts on the bras over her tank top and prances around the room, modeling her updated figure for her dad and brother. My son yells at her to quit blocking the TV but Dad offers her the attention she craves.

"Yes, Ashley, you look all grown up."

Smiling and glowing, she confidently strolls out of the room.

~Stacey Gustafson

Taking a Back Seat

Two wrongs don't make a right, but three lefts do.
~Jason Love

I vowed I would not be a back seat driver. My husband sat up front next to our daughter. I told myself he was better suited to teach her. Our fifteen-and-a-half-year-old daughter was now behind the wheel of our car and driving us to Eugene's Sweet Life bakery for the first time.

"Do you think she's ready to back out of the driveway?" I muttered. Dan was instructing her to stop at the sidewalk first and then again before the street. She pulled back slightly too fast and didn't stop until after the sidewalk.

"Don't you think she should slow down?"

I was making comments from the back seat and we hadn't even made it to the street yet. I tried to stop my words, but they just kept coming.

"I know you see Nina's truck."

She confidently straightened the wheel as she narrowly slid beside the small blue pickup.

There was a car coming behind us now and our daughter deliberately put the car into drive and slowly proceeded down the road. Before we started, I had told her to never worry about what the other drivers might think about her slow and careful driving. I also shared what my father had told me as a teenager: "Always drive like the other driver is going to do something stupid or wrong." I took a deep breath and reminded myself to sit quietly and let her father handle it.

We drove down our quiet street. She was doing fine. She had to turn left and then right, driving for a few blocks on one of our busier streets. I held the car door.

We were back on a quiet street and she was driving too fast. I mentioned how I seldom rode in the back seat and it seemed faster than in the front seat. My daughter countered with how it seemed faster when you were in the driver's seat. But she didn't slow down.

Dan had her move down to a crawl when we saw a pedestrian and a bicyclist. A yield sign was on the corner and Dan didn't have her stop. I couldn't hold my tongue. I had to mention that while learning to drive I thought our daughter should stop at the yield signs. You never knew what might be up ahead. I continued to hold the door armrest… a bit tighter.

Dan had our daughter park near our neighborhood playground. Neither of us was ready for her to maneuver the car into one of the restaurant's tight parking spots. She stopped as she scraped the tire against the curb's edge. But she straightened, set the brake, pulled out the keys and smiled broadly.

She and I, and she and her dad, had been practicing at our local fairgrounds' parking lot but this was her first real on-the-road driving experience. We praised her as I walked on wobbly legs to the bakery.

Inside, I looked across the table and saw my daughter, this young woman, staring back at me. She was already two inches taller and far more mature than I ever was at her age. Full of sugar now, we strolled back to the car and our daughter used the fob to open the doors. I took my dutiful place in the back seat. We were going to the fairgrounds and, of course, I couldn't help commenting on how we were going to get there without traversing those "busy" streets. Dan had it under control. I sat with my hand on the door handle as if I thought I could make a quick exit if necessary.

But then, as our daughter drove us further down the street, it hit me. Was I not only holding onto the handle but holding too tightly onto my daughter as well? When I told her to slow down her driving, was I really telling her to slow down her growing-up process?

She drove on and made it safely to the fairgrounds. I sighed and let go of the armrest. Was I being overprotective? Did I fear relinquishing her to those busy streets?

She was driving with confidence in this confined space and made her way to a small bridge that crosses over to the outer parking lot. We were heading to the smaller neighborhood streets just beyond the fairgrounds. I took some more deep breaths.

Being a parent, watching one's child grow from her first cherished steps to her first time behind the wheel, is nothing short of a whirlwind miracle. I sat up straighter. I let go of the door handle. Then I leaned forward and quietly told my daughter, "You're doing an amazing job."

~Victoria Koch

A Carton Tied with String

If nothing ever changed, there'd be no butterflies.
~Author Unknown

I came upon it on a recent search for an old serving tray in the basement where cartons from our last move—eight years ago—stood like sentries of guilt. We never did get to that final unpacking, surrendering too soon.

And there among the leftovers, in our daughter Nancy's unmistakable handwriting, was a carton marked "Nancy's Stuff—Keep!"

And we had. Not just for years, but for decades.

While I can barely remember the name of the movie we saw last week, I can still remember with astonishing clarity the history of this cardboard box and its impact on me.

Upstairs in her bedroom, door tightly shut, Nancy, who had just turned thirteen, had spent half a day on a "project." I smiled when she called it that. "Projects" usually involved dioramas for science or history that, in turn, meant multiple trips to various shops for obscure craft supplies. But this, Nancy told me, was a "personal project."

The next announcement, some hours later, was that Nancy had finished. I rushed up to her room to see it stripped bare of every object that could possibly be linked to her childhood.

The stuffed animals—gone. The frilly curtains—removed, so that only shades remained on her bedroom windows. Even the canopy of her bed was relegated to a corner of the room, ready to be carted off.

Nancy had done the task neatly and well. In those first several hours as a teenager she had swept away her past.

What I felt, standing in her bedroom that day, was awe and sorrow. I felt the kind of crazy mother-panic that heralds endings of the ready-or-not variety.

Nancy, the baby of the family, the last of our three daughters, was walking to the beat of the calendar while I was crying out, silently of course, for just one more month, one more year. With this daughter, every first had brought its own peculiar ache, every last a resounding finality.

Nancy was always the ruthless teacher of lessons I didn't want to learn. She was the one who reminded me that there is nothing shorter than a last daughter's childhood.

Ironically, it was she who was the clear-eyed, sane and rational pathfinder. I was the crybaby.

For Nancy, packing away Raggedy Ann and Winnie the Pooh and even the panda with the button eyes and the red felt tongue was sensible. For me, it was wrenching to see that little paw sticking out through one of the flaps of the carton.

Our youngest daughter needed that space now for lip gloss, jeans of a particular cut, and posters of rock stars. She joyously welcomed the gains and I mourned the losses in this emotional tug-of-war with time.

Guess who lost?

I had traveled those treacherous seas of change twice before, and now a last adolescence was nipping at my heels. I was not a good sailor. And that fat little panda bear, not quite settled into the carton, was an instant metaphor for it all.

I remember being grateful, that day, that at least the rocking chair I loved, the one that had traveled with Nancy from her nursery to this room, had survived the purge.

I'm sure I told Nancy that her bedroom definitely looked bigger now. I do recall that soon afterwards, Nancy requested — and received—new wallpaper, as we stripped away the whimsical pattern she had loved just a few years before.

There would be other transitions, but none quite as stark as this one, represented by a carton tied up with string in the basement of our empty nest.

"Nancy's Stuff—Keep!" was what she had ordered on that long-ago day. Who knows why?

But I will surely obey.

~Sally Schwartz Friedman

My Feng Shui Nightmare

What we see depends mainly on what we look for.
~John Lubbock

I picked a bad time to become a minimalist. My daughter had just moved home from college with armloads of clothing and boxes of electronic gadgets. She planned to live at home for a few months before her wedding.

On move-back day, she struggled to carry the box we had purchased four years earlier for under-bed storage.

"Don't you want to leave that in the garage?" I asked.

"No, these are my shoes," she answered.

My recent vow to clear my house of unnecessary stuff was quickly buried in piles of college T-shirts, mismatched kitchenware and boxes labeled "Italian flashcards."

I was living in a feng shui nightmare!

I decided to declutter after spending a summer week living in a Vermont college dormitory room while I attended a conference. A college dormitory without students is a blank canvas—no posters, no carpet, empty shelves and gaping closets. In my small white room with no television, no computer, no telephone and no distractions, I slept better than I had in months.

Inspired, I returned home and cleared bookcases, boxed photographs and cleaned closets. And then Emily returned home to plan her wedding.

The capable, organized daughter who had navigated college

with skill now left a trail of destruction in her wake—soggy tea bags, empty snack packages, straws, lists, junk mail.

Had I forgotten? Was she always like this, or had I become one of those cranky women who would rather dust than rock her babies? In high school Emily had left a trail of burning lights. I could follow her path around the house by snapping off lamp switches. But I didn't remember being bothered by her trails of clutter.

Before Emily moved home, I had imagined that the three months before the wedding would be girl time when we could watch movies, shop and talk. I didn't anticipate turning into Clutter Cop—constantly chiding her about her housekeeping and depositing her bits of trash in the doorway of her room, where they stayed… unnoticed.

I had once considered myself to be quite flexible and easygoing about messes. When my three kids were younger a neighbor asked, "Just how many kids do you have?" There were so many children in the yard, he could not figure out which belonged to me.

I never minded when my kids finger-painted, shook thousands of sprinkles on homemade cookies, or dyed Easter eggs. A few splatters of paint on the wall or colored sugar in the kitchen corners was a small price to pay for creativity and family traditions. But that was before my children left for college and I became enamored with simplicity and order.

When Emily moved home, I realized that the problem with being a minimalist was that it didn't leave room for the clutter of family life. Where does a minimalist put a four-foot-tall stack of bridal magazines with color-coded tabs? Rolls of ribbon to tie on tiny vials of bubbles? Or a note that says, "Mom, sorry about the mess, I'll pick it up when I get home. I love you."

A minimalist can get quite grumpy when her children move home. That's why I decided to postpone becoming a minimalist. Because if I didn't, I was afraid I would find myself in that small, white room again, but this time there would be padding on the walls.

~Nancy Lowell George

Just think darling... one day, all of this will be yours!

Reprinted by permission of
Carolyn Hiler ©2011

21

The Wedding Dress

A garden of Love grows in a Grandmother's heart.
~Author Unknown

I listened to my daughter describe the perfect satin and lace wedding gown. I visualized how beautiful she would look when she walked down the aisle with the heavy satin train flowing behind her. We arranged to go dress shopping in the near future. My excitement about this special shopping trip was offset by my worries about how we would pay for the wedding dress of her dreams.

My daughter Marles had been planning every detail of her wedding since she was a little girl. Satin and lace played a huge part in those plans. I hoped we could find a bridal shop offering huge discounts, even one with a "going out of business sale" like we had found two years earlier for my oldest daughter's wedding. Ideas popped into my head but I dismissed most of them as unrealistic.

But there was one idea that I couldn't dismiss as I thought about my mother's wedding photos and her model-like build, so similar to Marles'.

Forty-five years earlier my mother had eagerly planned her own wedding. Each month she saved whatever she could from her $100 pay cheque. Finally her savings grew large enough and she boarded a bus for the city, where the dress of her dreams awaited her. The ivory satin dress, with a flowing train, had lace panels inserted around the skirt. Tiny satin covered buttons covered the back of the dress. Matching buttons fastened delicate lace sleeves at the wrist. This elegant dress fit her tall, slim body beautifully. She saved enough to pay the sale price of $125.

As a little girl I had always admired the photos of my mother as a beautiful bride. By the time I reached my teens and began dreaming of my own Prince Charming and our wedding I had the story of the dress memorized. Sometimes Mom would open the cedar chest, lift out the dress and let me touch the soft, shiny fabric. Yet no matter how much I loved her dress, I knew I would never be able to wear it. The inches I lacked in height and shoulder width compared to my mother had settled around my waist making the dress an impossible fit for me in more ways than one. Warmed by the wonderful memories, I now dared to hope the dress would fit Marles.

I called my mom. "Mom, is your wedding dress still packed away in the cedar chest?"

"Yes. Why?" she replied.

"Marles wants an ivory satin and lace dress. I don't think we can afford that and I hate to disappoint her. I've been trying to figure out a way to give her what she really wants. Then I thought of your gorgeous dress."

Mom replied delightedly, "Well it's just been sitting there for years. I didn't think anyone cared about it. She'd be the only one it might fit."

Before I could say another word she added, "But the lace is starting to disintegrate. I think the satin's okay but we'd have to find lace. It's worth a try."

"Thanks Mom. I always loved your dress but it never fit me. Marles has seen wedding pictures so she has some idea of what it looks like. Can we get it sent to her?"

A few days later I watched Marles lift the folds of satin from the shipping box. Her fingers caressed the softness as we examined the lace, noticing small tears in the fragile fabric. We knew we could replace the lace... as long as the dress fit. And it fit well enough, as there were generous seams on each side of the bodice that could be let out. Marles twirled and waited for the train to settle around her ankles. The look on her face was priceless.

The next morning we found an ivory lace with an almost identical pattern to the old one. For the $95 cost of the lace and with free labour provided by a talented friend of mine, we had Marles' dream dress. Months later, Marles walked down the aisle with her satin train flowing behind her. Tears pooled in my eyes as I noticed the loving look that passed between my mother and my daughter. The fulfillment of two beautiful young women's wedding dreams, forty-five years apart, was wrapped up in one gorgeous, ivory-coloured satin and lace dress.

~Carol Harrison

The Magic of Mothers & Daughters

Chapter 3

A Mother's Love

A mother is a person who seeing there are only four pieces of pie for five people, promptly announces she never did care for pie.

~Tenneva Jordan

22

Mom to the Rescue

A mother's heart is a patchwork of love.
~Author Unknown

I think my friends and I started planning our senior prom when we were freshmen. Seriously. We talked for hours about what we'd wear, how we'd do our hair, how we'd pose for our pictures—as couples, then in a group, just the girls, then just the guys—where we'd eat, even rehearsed what we might talk about at the restaurant. I know. Get a life. But it was that huge to us. We painstakingly choreographed every minute and, with all that planning, we expected nothing short of an idyllic prom experience.

The big day arrived and we started getting ready before lunch. Between phone calls to each other, we worked on our hair, nails, make-up, shoes, dresses and purses. The restaurant where we'd made our reservations—three months ahead of time—was forty miles away. Ten of us were to meet there, three hours before the prom, eat together, then convoy to the dance.

The time came for my boyfriend, Rusty, to pick me up. No Rusty. Ten minutes passed. Still no sign of him. Twenty minutes. This was before cell phones so all I could do was wait—wait and experience a major meltdown. Thirty minutes. Forty. How could he do this to me? This was my only senior prom. He'd better be dead, I thought, or seriously injured. As my friends gathered in the restaurant, I paced the family room, burning a hole through the clock with my eyes. How could this happen? I'd planned everything so perfectly.

When Rusty finally peeled into our drive—an hour late—his tuxedo was rumpled and mottled with grease. The ruffled shirt was plastered to his chest with sweat. His face was flushed and his hair was tussled. He'd had a blowout on the interstate and had his first-ever tire changing experience only inches from rushing traffic. I tried to muster some sympathy for him but all I could see was my perfect prom night going down the toilet.

Little did I know that, while I was pacing the front room, my mom had been hard at work. She'd defrosted two steaks and roused my father to light the backyard grill. She'd gathered my grandmother's best china, crystal and lace tablecloth, thrown together an elegant dinner and then sent my little sister and nephew upstairs to don their Sunday best and serve as waiter and waitress.

By the time Rusty arrived, she'd transformed our living room into a private dining hall complete with candlelight and music. As our friends were returning from their formal dining experience, we were just sitting down to ours. I never saw Mama that night. She sent my sister and nephew through the door with dish after dish, from salad all the way to dessert. And while we ate, she washed, dried and ironed Rusty's tuxedo shirt.

We made it to prom with time to spare and a story to tell. Looking back now, I can't remember if I ever thanked my mom. I was probably more concerned with not spilling anything on my dress and making sure we got to the dance on time. She was content to remain in the shadows remedying yet another mini trauma in my life. By the way, thanks Mom.

~Mimi Greenwood Knight

Reprinted by permission of
Carolyn Hiler ©2011

23

The Sound of Music

Mothers and daughters are closest, when daughters become mothers.
~Author Unknown

The words every mother dreads rang in my ears. "Mom, it might be cancer." How could this be? It's funny how life changes in an instant. One minute I was enjoying a newfound relationship with my grown daughter, and the next I was gripped with fear that it might all come to a tragic end.

Now that my daughter was grown, with children of her own, we had a bond that never existed before. Even though she and her husband moved all over the world, we stayed in touch by phone. For the most part, the phone had been our lifeline to each other. Just being able to hear each other's voices bridged the time and distance between us.

I took that privilege for granted until a few years ago. After her first pregnancy my daughter developed an enlarged thyroid, and it was feared by the physicians that it might be cancerous. Surgery was scheduled, and her dad and I traveled clear across the United States to be with her. We didn't know what the surgeon would find inside our child's neck. When we met with him following the operation, he explained that the diseased thyroid had been wrapped around her vocal chords. He warned us that, although he was confident he had been careful, there was always the chance that her voice would be permanently damaged.

After strict orders not to talk, she embarked upon the process of healing. We flew home and waited for her voice to return. Little did I know how difficult the next few months would be. I had come to depend on our frequent phone conversations. Now, I wondered if I would ever hear my daughter's voice again. We e-mailed back and forth, but it just wasn't the same. The biopsy results were negative for cancer, and we rejoiced. But still, we waited for the healing to be complete. I longed to hear her speak again.

At last I received a call from her—or was it her? Hearing the voice on the phone that day broke my heart. She could barely squeak out audible words, and I had a hard time believing it was my daughter. I could hear the thickness in her throat, and the high-pitched sounds were foreign. I cried as soon as we hung up. Was this how she would sound from now on? Did it hurt her to talk? I was afraid for her, and even scolded her about straining her voice by calling. But I didn't stop to think that she might have missed my voice as much as I did hers.

Over the next several months her voice gradually improved, until finally it was back to normal. I will always be grateful that it was not cancer, and that once again, we can share our lives though our phone conversations. We talk more often than ever now. Sometimes she rambles on and on. But I don't mind. The sound of her voice is music to my ears.

~Jan Cline

A Labor of Love

Happiness is not a goal; it is a by-product.
~Eleanor Roosevelt

My mother carefully guided a piece of red fabric under the sewing machine needle. When she came to the end of the seam, she glanced at the clock and exclaimed, "It's four o'clock already? I have to start supper!" She jumped up from her chair and rushed to the kitchen.

The red cloth Mom set aside was going to be a dress for me. I needed something special to wear to my cousin's wedding, so every afternoon Mom sat at her Singer, the cabinet wedged halfway between the dining room and living room, right in the middle of all the commotion that came with having seven children. As soon as the needle started clicking, Mom went into a trance-like state, her face becoming more and more relaxed.

She hung the unfinished dress on a hanger in the dining room, and in the evening when my father came home he stopped to admire the work-in-progress as if it were a painting on an easel. First it was just a shell. The following day, dotted-Swiss sleeves appeared. A ruffled collar showed up next. "That's coming along nicely," Dad said, and Mom beamed.

By the end of the week, the dress was ready to be hemmed. As I slipped it over my head, goose bumps broke out on my arms, for this was the most beautiful dress my mother had ever made. I stood still on a chair while she held a yardstick to the lower edge and pulled straight pins from between her lips. She pinned up a few inches at a time, gradually moving around me until the pins in her mouth were gone and the hem was above my knee.

Mom hemmed the dress by hand, ironed out every wrinkle, and hung her masterpiece in the dining room one last time. "It's done," she announced with a sparkle in her eye, something that was missing when she mended torn crotches, darned my father's socks or stitched merit badges on my brothers' Boy Scout uniforms.

I couldn't remember a time my mother didn't sew. In the toy box were little dresses and bonnets she'd made for our baby dolls years ago. Clothing she'd crafted hung in every closet. She was always working on something: a bathrobe for Dad, a shirt for my brother, an angel costume for the youngest to wear on Halloween.

When the Home Economics teacher gave my tenth grade class an assignment to make a dress, I thought of my mother's handiwork and assumed it would be easy. I flipped through pattern books in the store and picked out a complicated design with a collar, cuffs and a twenty-two-inch zipper.

"Isn't this a cool dress?" I asked my mother.

"Maybe you ought to start with something simpler," she said.

I insisted and bought the pattern, along with a knit fabric, although my teacher had recommended cotton. When I got to school, I unfolded the directions and stared at the long list of steps. I didn't need directions. I'd seen my mother go through the process a thousand times.

I cut out the onionskin pattern pieces, pinned them to the fabric and snipped around them. After sewing my first seam, I gasped, "Oh, no! I sewed the wrong sides together!" The teacher handed me a seam ripper, and I grumbled as I tore out the stitches.

For weeks I struggled with the sleeves, collar and zipper. The knit fabric kept bunching up, and I daydreamed about sneaking my monstrosity home to Mom. She would have whipped it together in a few hours.

Finally I finished the dress, but unlike my mother's projects, you could tell mine was homemade. The collar didn't lie flat, and the zipper was bumpy. My teacher gave me a D plus, and she was probably being kind.

"Sewing is too much work!" I complained when I showed my mother the dress.

"My sewing is a labor of love," she said.

I rolled my eyes. I was sure she sewed because it would have cost a fortune to buy clothes in the store for seven kids.

My mother's sewing continued to be part of every stage of my life. She made a dress for my graduation from college, the bridesmaids' dresses for my wedding, and a maternity smock when I was pregnant with my first child. Inside every garment, Mom sewed a tag that said "Handmade by Betty." I still couldn't figure out why anyone would sew unless they had to.

One day, my husband told me that his mother had bought a new sewing machine and offered us her old one. He wanted to accept it so I could sew insignia on his Navy uniforms. Reluctantly, I agreed. The pine cabinet sat unused in the corner of our bedroom for a long time.

Right after our second child was born, my husband went to sea and I was overwhelmed with taking care of the kids and house alone. My mother came for a visit, and although she didn't say anything about the idle sewing machine, after she left a package arrived in the mail from her. Inside were a new sewing basket and a pincushion that looked like a tomato.

Where would I find the energy to sew? I didn't need any more work!

A few days later, the kids were driving me crazy, and I wondered how my mother kept her sanity with seven children. I gazed at the sewing basket and remembered the peaceful look she always had on her face when she sewed. It was close to meditation, as if she were blocking out the world and gathering strength. "Let's go to the fabric store," I said to my son. I grabbed my purse and strapped the baby in her car seat.

At the store, I chose two patterns: one a simple sundress for my daughter, the other easy pajamas in my son's size. I found cotton printed with yellow roses for the sundress, and my son picked out some flannel with airplanes for his pajamas.

During the baby's nap, I ironed the cotton fabric, pinned the sundress pattern on it and cut out the pieces. Later, when my daughter was happy in her playpen, I dusted off the sewing cabinet, set up the machine and began to sew. The motor hummed and time flew. I felt focused and free.

The next day I finished the sundress and eagerly started on my son's pajamas. Creating clothing was so different from housework! It wasn't like a washed floor that my kids spilled juice on before I even put the bucket away. It wasn't like a big dinner that was quickly eaten, leaving a stack of dirty plates. I felt a sense of accomplishment when I made clothes for my kids. The final products were nowhere near the quality of my mother's work, yet somehow it didn't matter.

Years before, when my mother called her sewing "a labor of love," I thought she was saying it was a tedious job, but she did it anyway, out of love. But now I saw her sewing in another light. Not only did she do it with love, but she loved doing it!

~Mary Elizabeth Laufer

Love, Mom

A hundred hearts would be too few
To carry all my love for you.
~Author Unknown

I can't say I was sad to see my daughter Zoey go to kindergarten. I love school so much that I have been continuously in school for three decades as either a student or a teacher. I'd say I was more excited for her than anything else. Zoey is like me—a rule follower, a bookworm, and a social butterfly. She entered kindergarten knowing how to read, and I was confident she'd enjoy every minute of school.

As I packed her lunch on the first morning, I decided I'd write a little note. I went to our dining room table, and I dug through the craft supplies. I found a piece of construction paper and some stickers. I created a very silly little card. I wrote, "Happy 1st Day of School Lovey Dovey! Have fun. Be good. Remember manners matter! Love, Mom." I did feel a small twinge as I thought of my little girl in a loud and chaotic cafeteria. I felt better knowing she'd open her lunchbox and see my note.

In the midst of telling us the details of her first day, we didn't think to ask about lunch or the note. However, as the days turned to weeks, I continued to make little cards—frequently related to the seasons or a holiday. Some days I cut out a heart. Other days, I wrote a poem. Occasionally, in the rush of the morning, my notes were mediocre, but I felt strongly that I should always include one. The notes became inside jokes with us — or so I thought.

One day, on the drive home from school, I asked Zoey, "Do you like the notes I write you?"

Perhaps I was having some parental insecurity or it was just a random thought. To my surprise, she replied, "We love them!"

What did she mean by "we?" What she said next inspires me to go the extra mile, even if it seems to be a small matter.

"We all read your notes. We take turns. Sophia, Courtney, Piper, and Emilee. One day the lunch lady who walks around had to tell us a word. She couldn't believe I could read!"

"What do all your friends think of your notes?" I asked, immediately worried they were yanking them from her tiny little hands and mocking her. Perhaps in her naïveté, she wouldn't know if they were making fun of her.

"They L-O-V-E my notes!"

"Oh, good," I said, relieved. I was now very thankful that I had always provided a note, albeit a lame one sometimes.

"Want to know something?" she added.

"What?" I asked, contemplating my new wider audience.

"No matter who reads the note, we always know how it ends. When we get to the end part, we always say 'Love, Mom' together, really loud!"

"That is a very good thing to remember," I told her.

"We know! It is our favorite part," she replied, tugging her backpack out of the car and smiling at me over her shoulder.

~Amber Chandler

Roots

Be grateful for the home you have, knowing that at this moment,
all you have is all you need.
~Sarah Ban Breathnach

am the daughter of a master gardener. My mother kneels, dirty, digging, knowing not only where to plant and what, but why. Each spring and summer she nurtures the relationship of soil and seed and sun. Some years I watch, wondering at the work — the weeds and water and endless cultivation of earth. I marvel at the transformation she culls from the depths of half-dead potted plants salvaged from the clearance rack at the nursery. I don't understand this garden, this patient plucking and pruning for fleeting beauty. I don't understand her.

Growing up, I avoided the invitation to sit beside my mother as she planned her plots, as she leafed through catalogs of seeds and stems months before breaking ground. As a late spring frost caressed the stems of the upcoming grass, and I bemoaned the prolonging of winter, my mother prayed the bulbs she planted last year would withstand the weather and the ground would thaw to release life and allow her hands to help it along.

My mother tried to include me despite my disinterest. She bought me an orchid to grow inside. I photographed it and soon forgot it. Each February and March she left the catalogs out where I could browse them, knowing I loved the roses and iris best. When I wanted to arrange flowers she indulged me, allowing me to cut the stems despite my inattention as she tried to explain the flowers and their features. Still, I was indifferent. Gardening was her passion: her dirt, her insects, and her identity… not mine.

As I aged I lost interest in our family's traditional Mother's Day tour of nurseries. I begged my father to let me stay home, to hide in my room with my music. He refused, reminding me of the respect I owed my mother, imploring me not to ruin the moment, the day. I trudged along, unable to understand the allure of the seven varieties of the same plant and how different they could possibly be. Pick one, I thought, and we can go home. What does it matter what you choose?

This year I turned twenty-four, the age my mother was when she married my father. I envision her then as a young woman, free-spirited, with her soft brown eyes concealing a spark. Now I see her in her early eighties, wearing polyester and big-rim glasses that she puts away when she sings, her voice carrying across the living room she shares with my father—a sad but satisfied aria speaking to the dreams she loved but passed up. In the evening she is content to share dinner with a husband who loves her beyond this world, so deeply he'd ask twice for her hand. And at night, when she lies in bed, her creativity simmers below her sleep, seeking an outlet that will augment the life she's chosen.

This year I go to my parents' lake house, where they are readying the rooms and grounds for rental. I know the final rush is relentless, with days and nights of cleaning, repairing, and prepping. The sky is blue when I arrive despite the sprinkles that followed me for the full forty-five minute drive. My mother is gardening; I grab gloves and stand next to the flowerbed, not knowing plant from weed… not understanding. She says I don't have to, uncertain from years of my avoidance, my apathy. I want to, and I begin to yank the dandelions from the ground, the only weed I recognize as such. She smiles and points out another weed, explaining its invasive roots run as a vine under the surface. As we work, she tells me of dividing plants and the miracle of yielding four or five from one. She shows me how to loosen the root ball at the base of the plant to encourage it to grow; tells me how you have to release the roots to teach them to spread.

As I watch my mother at home in her garden and mimic her movements, I finally understand. I am the daughter of a master gardener. My mother digs deeply through the soil as she cultivates her spirit, her perfectionism put to bed with the bulbs and blossoms, her desire to nurture fulfilled in the foliage of a variegated hosta. She still sings, accompanied by a chorus of clematis and columbine, of black-eyed Susans and Siberian iris and goat's beard. She is a master gardener and her hands have left her heart in the earth and in the roots—and in me.

~Kathryn Roberts

27

A Promise Is a Promise

A promise is a cloud; fulfillment is rain.
~Arabian Proverb

I am a bald woman. It is frightening but also freeing. It is terrifying but also sensual. In reality, it is just very cold. I feel every whisper of wind. I wore hats and bandannas at first—partly to keep warm but mostly to hide my baldness. Secretly I was afraid and wanted to hide.

We discussed her journey—our journey. We listened to all the specialists tell us what was going to happen during her chemotherapy. They talked about all the different kinds of drugs she would take—thirteen in total. They described the ways these drugs would enter her body—some she could take orally, others would have to be injected into her thigh or directly into her spine. Still others would enter the special port that the surgeons had inserted into her chest. The oncologists and nurses talked about the side effects of the drugs and the possible complications that might occur over the next two years of chemotherapy. Two years? She seemed so healthy. How could she be so sick that she needed two years of chemotherapy?

When I told her she had cancer her biggest concern was losing her hair. "Will all my hair really fall out? Will people make fun of me?"

"Don't worry," I told her bravely. "When you lose your hair, I will shave mine and we will both be bald. We will walk down the street proudly with our bald heads held high. We will swim and go to the park and play at the beach with our bald heads."

She pondered this for a minute before responding. "Promise?" she asked with a very serious look on her young little face.

"Promise," I replied matter-of-factly. It seemed liked such a small sacrifice in comparison to what lay in store for her.

The days and weeks of chemotherapy began to take their toll on her little body. Just as the experts had predicted, she began to lose her hair. It was subtle at first. I began to find strands of hair on her clothes and on towels after she bathed. A short time later, the strands turned into small clumps that I would find on the backs of couches and chairs where she had sat. Before long, there were masses of hair on her pillow every morning as she awoke from her restless sleeps. The time was fast approaching for me to keep my promise. Within a few short days of her pillow being covered in hair each morning she was finally completely bald.

Her head was very smooth and soft as I held her to my breast. Her head felt as smooth as a newborn's skin. It reminded me of that wonderful time when I held her in my arms and marveled at how lucky I was to have such a beautiful and healthy baby girl.

Her bald head was beautiful. Her bald head was ugly, as the tumors had left their marks. It was time.

She helped shave my head. She held the shaver carefully and moved it over my head row after row. Soon, there was a large pile of golden brown hair glistening in the sunlight on the ground. I, too, was now bald. My head was prickly and harsh. It was ugly. It was beautiful.

All in all, it was a good day; strange but good. It was good to see her smile and run her hands over the top of my head, searching for the hair. It was fun to see her laugh at my baldness. It was strange that this moment of levity was temporary and tempered with the underlying reality that we were both bald because of the terrifying disease of cancer.

We returned home still strangely upbeat from the afternoon's event. As night began to fall, she silently stifled a yawn and asked to go to bed. As I tucked her into bed that night, the good day suddenly took an unexpected turn. As she lay under the covers her normal smiling face turned fearful and she began to cry, clutching her blankets.

"Charlotte, honey, what is the matter?" I asked not understanding what had just happened to cause such fear in her eyes.

"Oh Mommy, you look so scary now with your bald head. I wish you hadn't shaved it," she sobbed.

I didn't know what to say or how to reply. Words failed me and my inner core of strength and courage deserted me in that moment. So I responded the only way I knew how. I cried. I sobbed. I cried for the irony. I cried in self-pity. I cried for the toll it was taking on our family and the impact it was having on our son. I cried and I sobbed.

She didn't say anything but just lay quietly in the soft glow of her bedside lamp and waited patiently for me to stop crying. Then with the wisdom of a five-year-old she reached for my arm and took my hand. She pulled my hand close to her face before resting it upon her cheek.

I felt the warmth of her skin against my wet hands. She sighed and smiled at me. "Don't worry Mommy," she said softly, "I still love you. Besides, a promise is a promise."

~Tessa Graham

28

My Mother, My Father, My Everything

All that I am or ever hope to be, I owe to my angel Mother.
~Abraham Lincoln

I t was the happiest day of my life. I was dressed in a long, white gown with a train that filled the room and glass slippers on my feet like Cinderella on her way to the ball. My mother's pearls floated around my neck and an old handkerchief made by my great grandmother resided on my heart. A new veil with scattered pearls to match my dress was tucked into my twists and curls; a borrowed tiara was the perfect accessory and a blue garter was hidden under the layers of fabric, beads and crinoline.

My mother stood where a father should be, beaming with pride. Although I did not have a father to walk me down the aisle, give me away or share the traditional father/daughter dance, I did not feel slighted. My mother had always played both roles as a mother and a father to my brothers and me. She hugged and disciplined us. She helped with homework and shared our joy when we passed a test. She taught us how to love each other even when we were pulling hair or fighting over a toy. She taught us the importance of family. She was, to us, our everything—and still is today.

My husband, Nick, proposed to me when I was twenty-five. My mother asked if I would like my older brother or my uncle to walk me down the aisle. I responded with, "No Mom, you have always been my mom and my dad and you are the only one who can give me away."

The morning of my wedding day passed quickly. My mother never left my side. She was there for hair, make-up, and helping me put my gown on. Once I was ready, my mom and I stood alone. She was dressed in a long pale blue spaghetti-strapped dress that made her look thirty years younger and more like a bridesmaid than the mother of a twenty-six-year-old bride. She was beautiful. She knew all the right words to say to calm my nerves and assure me that everything would be okay. No one else could have taken her place.

The tears did not begin for either of us until my pastor said it was time for her to give me away. At that moment it became real to both of us; I was really getting married. As we embraced, the room full of people disappeared and it was only my mom and me. Silent promises were exchanged. This is not a farewell, Mom, this is not the end; this is a new beginning and I am not leaving you behind.

Since my mom and I broke all the traditional rules, we kept the theme going with our mother/daughter dance. It was a medley of a few songs that told our story. Starting with "Shall We Dance," a song we often danced to in the kitchen at home, moving onto "Girls Just Want to Have Fun," and finishing with "Last Dance."

My wedding, much like my life, was not ordinary or normal. Thank you, Mom, for teaching me how to laugh when I wanted to cry, encouraging me to write even though I was shy, for loving me with the strength of two parents and above all, for being there.

~Natalie Scott

Reprinted by permission of Dan Reynolds
and Cartoonresource.com ©2011

29

Standing Out

Courage is being afraid but going on anyhow.
~Dan Rather

I always knew my mom was different from other moms. It wasn't just her appearance—her petite frame, black hair, and dark almond eyes contrasted sharply with the statuesque blondes who accompanied the other kids to school. Her speech was peppered with extra syllables, and sometimes words would come out in the wrong order. It didn't bother me that she was different—after all, I looked different from my friends, too!

On the outside, our house looked like every other house in the neighborhood. But inside, beautiful dolls dressed in colorful kimonos posed in their glass cases. Our refrigerator and cupboards held foods other kids had never seen. I never thought about the significance of these items. They were just a part of my life.

At lunchtime, other kids asked to trade the cookies and candies in their lunches for the rice crackers I brought. And they asked me to show them how to fold squares of paper into little toys like cats, baskets, and birds the way my mom had taught me. If there was any malice directed toward us, my siblings and I were sheltered from it by our wonderful teachers and the other adults in our lives.

The only thing that bothered me was not having relatives nearby. Other kids went to visit their cousins, and talked about their aunts and uncles. My relatives lived on the other side of the world. I knew I had cousins, but I saw them only in pictures. When Mom talked to her sisters on the phone, she used a language that sounded mysterious and fun. At Christmastime, we got beautiful cards embellished with strange looking characters.

It wasn't until I enrolled in a Japanese language class in college that I realized how great an adjustment my mother had made when she followed her husband to his homeland. Until then, Japan was an exotic faraway place, where people spoke differently and ate food that we couldn't find in most Midwest restaurants. Thanks to the international students on campus, I learned more about the customs and culture. In the class I managed to learn several words and phrases, but there were few opportunities to use them once I began my teaching career.

Later on, I became a mom myself. My children inherited my dark hair and eyes, but they were not the only children of Asian descent. By now there were others — children adopted by Caucasian couples, as well as children of immigrants. They, too, were taught to celebrate their differences. When my older daughter was a toddler, my mother and I took her to visit our relatives in Japan. I loved visiting my relatives, but it was frustrating not being able to communicate with them. On shopping trips, my cousins, even though they were younger, watched over me as they would a small child, knowing I couldn't read the street signs or make purchases on my own. Again, I was different. Now I looked like everyone else, but I stood out because I couldn't understand. Was this how Mom felt when she first came to America?

Now that I'm retired from full-time teaching, I have more time to pursue some of my earlier goals. One goal is to learn to speak Japanese fluently. The single year of instruction during my undergraduate years was not enough to carry on a conversation with my aunts and cousins when they came to visit. I want to get to know these relatives. I want to learn about their likes and dislikes, to know about their daily lives, and share stories about our families.

They say it's more difficult to learn a new language after you become an adult, and since I've been an adult for many years, I'd say it's true. But I'm enjoying this new venture. Four days a week, I sit in a classroom with people less than half my age. Four nights a week, I pore over the exercises and diligently complete the worksheets. It may be more difficult for me to retain the new vocabulary, but I have the time now to do the work and practice. I'm doing this for me, not for a grade. But even more, I'm enjoying the connection to my culture. Every night when I finish my homework, I call my "personal tutor" to check my grammar. She's glad I took on this task. It must have been difficult for her, having to be the interpreter for every visit to Japan, and for each time a relative came to visit. If I become fluent, I can share the burden. But even more, we're building a precious connection to the land she loved and left.

I still think my mom is different. She is different in that she had the courage to leave behind everything she knew and go to a new place and build a new life. She had the intelligence to learn how to assimilate into this unknown society and raise three children, teaching them by example the importance of hard work, perseverance, and respect for others.

I hope I'm different too, and that my kids and grandkids appreciate the difference.

~Patricia Gordon

30

Whatever You Want To Be

Shoot for the moon. Even if you miss, you land among the stars.
~Les Brown

My legs swing excitedly, the momentum enough to propel my body off the seat as my pink sneakers scuff the tile floor beneath me. My toothless grin stretches from ear to ear as she places a book that weighs more than I do on the table in front of me. My chubby fingers can't flip the pages quickly enough. My imagination is running wild, creating new tales and carrying me to faraway places faster than I can process.

I am six years old on an early autumn afternoon, sitting at the pattern table at Jo-Ann Fabrics.

Halloween was an event in our house — an event that began well before October thirty-first and far exceeded the simple walk around the neighborhood, sugar highs, and sibling candy bargaining.

Halloween began with a trip to Jo-Ann Fabrics.

While many classmates wandered the three aisles at a seasonal costume mecca a week before the holiday, deciding between trendy movie character costumes and clichés in a bag, we'd park ourselves at a local fabric store table and spend hours poring over pattern envelopes and flipping through books.

"Can I be this, Mom?" We'd point to a picture of an outfit far too complex to be replicated by machines and mass-produced for the stores.

"Whatever you want to be," she'd always answer.

While our friends donned witch hats and princess tiaras, we were the Queen of Hearts. Maid Marian. Robin Hood. Snow White. A unicorn. Laura Ingalls Wilder. A hammerhead shark.

Whatever you want to be.

Our work was done with the selection of a pattern and a request, but for weeks on end, hers continued. After dinner, we'd troop downstairs to play and Mom would retreat to her sewing machine in the corner. We'd hear the buzzing of the sewing machine, punctuated only by the occasional request to try on a sleeve or opine on the angle of a hat.

One day a year, we were allowed to be whatever we wanted to be.

Without even a hint to naïve children, though, her tagline carried over into everyday life. When I wanted to be an actress, I was one. As I pranced onstage, Dad built the production's sets and Mom sewed costumes. Eleven sequined showgirl costumes by Thursday? Whatever you (and your friends) want to be. When my sister wanted to be a Division One college athlete, we piled into the car for practices across the state and tournaments across several. When my brother wanted to be a high-jump star, they huddled under blankets for hours for a two-second spurt of activity.

Eventually, we moved out of the house and began our own lives. College majors changed daily, and the refrain was always the same.

Mom, I want to major in English.

You've always had impeccable grammar. Whatever you want to be, you'll do well.

Maybe special education is the right choice.

You've always been so good with kids—your patience will serve you well in that profession. Whatever you want to be, your dad and I will support you.

I'm going to be a writer.

We've always said that's your gift. Whatever you want to be, we'll always buy your books.

I'm sure Mom groaned to herself each time we veered off track, gravitating toward the intricate (and occasionally downright bizarre) costume patterns and low-paying (and occasionally dead-end) careers. But she gritted her teeth just the same, and worked her magic.

Hindsight is always 20/20. As I look back on my childhood today, I recognize that mantra as the cornerstone of a remarkable woman. A woman who, despite the ever-blowing winds of change that accompany the rearing of three children, knew that her one task was to love us, unconditionally. Love us—and occasionally, tolerate us—and support us, whatever path or persona we chose. Whether we wanted to be a pink satin unicorn or a black velvet hammerhead shark.

~Caitlin Q. Bailey O'Neill

31

Mother or Daughter?

The doors we open and close each day decide the lives we live.
~Flora Whittemore

The hospital woke me before sunrise and told me that my mother was dying. It was the day my daughter was leaving our home in New York to spend a year in Israel. We had lost her father only months earlier so my being with her was doubly important. My mom was deathly ill in an ICU in St. Louis. I didn't know where to be, who to sacrifice. Was I mother or daughter? I didn't think I could be both.

If we didn't pack, Natasha wasn't going. That much was simple. But while every other kid in the program was awakened with kisses and farewell waffles in bed, or so I imagined, my daughter got, "Get up. We need to pack right now because I may be leaving for St. Louis." It wasn't fair, but as any eleventh grader who's lost her daddy will tell you... life isn't.

It has been a fact of my daughter's life that I have parents who are ill and live a thousand miles away. There are phone calls in the night, missed choir performances, last minute changes to plans, and a mom whose brain is not always fully engaged in what happened today in math class. I love her more than words can express, but sometimes I just have to go. This has always been hard, but even more so in the past year, while we are still reeling from the loss of my husband, her father.

While packing her bags—nine T-shirts, one pair of rain boots, a jar of peanut butter—I took calls from the hospital and tried to decide where I belonged. I agreed to have my mother put on a respirator—two hooded sweatshirts, two sets of sheets, three bottles of sunblock—and weighed the duffle bags to be sure that each one was exactly fifty pounds.

I tried to make Natasha's last day at home as pleasant as possible—blood pressure 50/30, kidneys failing, heart rate plummeting—and worked in a break for iced coffee and brownies. Periodically I went into the bathroom and cried.

By the time my daughter's bags were packed, I realized I had made a decision. It broke a part of my heart but it was crystal clear. I couldn't send my daughter alone to an airport departure lounge filled with mothers and fathers, sisters and brothers, balloons and goodbye banners. I needed to help check her luggage, buy her a magazine, give her a hug—or many hugs—and send her off. I prayed that my mother would be there when I got to St. Louis but acknowledged that she would probably not be. I hoped that whatever happened, I would be able to forgive myself. And I said I goodbye to my mother.

I took my daughter to the airport and said goodbye to her too. A different goodbye—a less permanent goodbye—but in its way, just as jarring. As soon as she was out of sight I flew to St. Louis. And miraculously, my mother made it. She might so easily not have. It takes matters too far to say that if she hadn't, I would have believed unswervingly that I made the right decision. But in that horrible case, I hope that with time I would have come to realize that, in deciding to be a mother first, I was being true to my mom too.

A friend told me once that by caring for my parents I was role-modeling behavior that my daughter should learn. "You're teaching her to take care of your old bones someday," is how she put it. I hope not.

We raise our sons and our daughters, not for our own succor, but to see them grow into loves and lives of their own. And hopefully, having children of their own whom we watch them raise and nurture all over again. And while no person should ever face what my mother did alone, perhaps she took comfort from the fact that I honored everything she has been to me and everything she has taught me, by caring for my daughter first. I learned from her what a mother should be.

~Jacqueline Rivkin

A Mother's Last Lecture

The best way to stop smoking is to just stop — no ifs, ands or butts.
~Edith Zittler

t was the day after winter break when Belinda walked up to my desk, silently handing me a note. It was from her mother, requesting a parent-teacher conference. I quickly wrote her back, setting up a time for the following afternoon right after dismissal.

I was actually anxious to meet her, as she had been unable to attend the initial back-to-school night. Belinda was an excellent student, although the past five weeks her grades had dropped dramatically. The scheduled conference would give us a chance to discuss the situation.

At 3:45, Belinda's mother, Mrs. K., arrived. She was an attractive, although rail-thin, woman who proffered a sad, almost melancholy smile before sitting. When she spoke, her voice was soft, almost hoarse. "Nice to meet you," she said.

"And you as well. I enjoy getting to know my students' parents."

She folded her hands in her lap, a tissue twisted in between them. "I guess you know Belinda's grades have been dropping."

I nodded. "She does seem a bit preoccupied."

"Yes, and I wanted to talk to you about that." She leaned forward a moment, suddenly overcome with a harsh cough. "Sorry," she said, pointing to her throat. "This is the reason for Belinda's change."

Puzzled, I stared back at her, unable to decipher her meaning.

"You see, Belinda's worried about my health. In late November I learned that I have lung cancer."

I sat back in my chair, stunned by her news.

Seeing the obvious shock on my face, Mrs. K. reached out and touched my hand. "The prognosis is poor. But these past few weeks I've truly come to grips with it and I hope—I pray—that Belinda has too.

"For years my family warned me about my smoking, but I just laughed it off. I mean, my God, I'm only forty-one years old! Even the constant coughing couldn't convince me to stop. So when the doctor told me I had lung cancer, this did not come as a total shock to them."

"My sole regret is that I won't see my baby grow up. Belinda's been so supportive of me. Now, I want to do something for her—and her classmates. Mr. Chaney, I want to explain the evils of smoking and I want to include your class."

I sat there a moment, dumbfounded, unable at first to comprehend the courageous deed she had offered to me. This was something that could conceivably be much more effective than having the class read statistical data on smoking from a textbook. I asked her what she had in mind.

"Well, I'd like to talk to your fifth period health class since Belinda is in it. I thought I could come in from time to time and talk to them about my progression. And I'd like to do this for as long as I can. What do you think?"

"I'll need the okay from my principal, but that shouldn't be a problem."

She nodded, stood, shook my hand again and turned to go. "Look forward to seeing you soon."

Having gotten permission, Mrs. K. arrived the following Friday, neatly dressed but looking even thinner than she had at our earlier meeting. I looked at Belinda, sitting in the second row, noting both pride, and weariness etched on her face. I introduced her and explained the reason for her visit. The class gave perfunctory applause as she approached the front of the class. She began her lecture by saying, "Hi, I'm Beth, Belinda's mom and I have lung cancer."

You could have heard the proverbial pin drop. Kids who usually were half-tuned in to what I was saying suddenly sat upright. Mrs. K. paused a moment, stifled yet another cough and proceeded to tell the class about her twenty-six-year history of smoking.

She discussed peer pressure and the need to "look cool." It didn't take long, she said before that stage gave way to lighting up whenever she felt stressed or needed a quick pick-me-up. Finally, all that became immaterial when she realized, all too late, that she was hooked and needed her nicotine fix. Afterwards, she took questions; then she indicated she would be back the following week.

As she left I wondered just how many of my eighth grade students were totally convinced by her straightforward talk.

The following session she brought with her a set of X-rays. Drawing the students out of their seats they approached tentatively, staring at the dark spots that Mrs. K. stated were cancer. This seemed to hit home even harder than her earlier talk. She stayed only a few minutes, as she was not feeling well, but she promised to return the following week. Looking around I noticed the students all appeared quite somber and remained that way throughout the rest of the period.

For the next three weeks, Mrs. K. was forced to cancel her talks, due to ill health and doctors' appointments. However, the next week, she reappeared. She seemed more gaunt than ever, her dress hanging on her, huge circles under her eyes. She spent forty minutes discussing her feelings about family support. This time no one questioned her. It appeared my students were becoming as drained as she, obviously affected by her lectures. Belinda, however, was not. Resolve had replaced her earlier misery and with each passing day, I couldn't help but admire her courageous demeanor.

In April, Mrs. K. brought in another set of X-rays showing how the cancer was quickly spreading. She could no longer stand so she addressed the class from a chair. Her coughing remained consistent throughout the lecture but she discussed how she kept up her daily routine, which, much to our chagrin, meant smoking throughout the day whenever possible.

She came again in May, speaking only in a whisper, and pulling a canister of oxygen behind her. Mrs. K. talked about how she and her doctor had discussed hospice care and pain control. She ended by saying she hoped to be back soon but as soon as she got up, the students rose from their chairs, surrounded her and hugged her. Then she left.

During the end of May, she called to say she'd like to come in one more time, as she wanted to end her lectures by asking the kids how many intended to smoke after what they'd heard and seen. But on the day she was to come in I noticed Belinda was not in class. During my lunch hour I called the house and the husband answered. He informed me that his wife had passed away the night before. Shaken, I offered my condolences.

The next day, as my fifth period health class entered, I informed them of the news. I also told them that Mrs. K.'s last request was to ask how many of the students still intended to smoke. "Class," I said, "after what you've witnessed these past few months with Belinda's mom, how many of you still intend to smoke, either now or in the future? Raise your hand if you do."

Not a soul moved. Belinda's mother had done her job well.

~J.D. Chaney

Unconditional Love

*There came a time when the risk to remain tight in the bud
was more painful than the risk it took to blossom.*
~Anaïs Nin

My mother and I have always had a strong relationship, one of understanding, friendship, and trust. We have been there for each other through the most difficult of times, including our escape from our home to a battered women's shelter where we stayed for three months. In our old home we shared a room; my mother was (and still is) my greatest confidante. Although my mother and I have such a strong bond I had always questioned whether a parent's love truly is unconditional, as many say. Deep in the recesses of my mind was the notion that a parent's love could indeed be conditional if her child were to do something horrible enough—and at the time I was harboring a secret that I felt could be the end of our relationship.

It is safe to say that in the very small northern Maine town where I reside, my secret would not be very well received. The repercussions would be inevitable. Although I feared the reaction of those around me, most of all I feared hurting my mother. You see, for the better part of two months I had been in a passionate romance with someone—another woman. I was elated. I would spend nights composing sonnets and love letters.

In the beginning I had no plans to come out to my mother, a woman who is very strong in her Catholic faith. My girlfriend also had no plans to come out to her parents, who were known to be out-wardly homophobic. However, fate had different plans. On a rainy Tuesday afternoon the summer of my first year in college, we made the mistake of allowing her next-door neighbors to see us holding hands, and of course a prompt phone call was made to her parents.

I went home that night in tears, barely able to form complete sentences. It was then that I knew I could no longer lie to my mother about why I did not have a boyfriend. I could no longer hide from her this vital part of my being. My mom was staying at her friend's house so I called her there.

"Mom, I don't know how to tell you this. I think I might be gay," I attempted to say through my tears.

The silence lasted only a few seconds, although it felt like hours, as I waited for the outrage and disappointment that I expected.

"I think you should be an actress; you're so dramatic. It isn't that big a deal. I love you and nothing can change that," she responded.

Suddenly, years of secrecy, years of feeling as though I were an abomination, an abnormality, evaporated. It was as if my mother's warm words melted the ice that had surrounded my heart for so long.

The road to self-acceptance continues to be rough, however I no longer doubt that a mother's love for her child is unconditional. My mother has been one of my biggest supporters. Whenever negative thoughts about myself creep up, I think back on my mother's words: "I love you and nothing can change that."

~Angel Therese Dionne

The Magic of

Mothers &

Daughters

Chapter 4

The Face in the Mirror

Mirror, mirror on the wall,
I am my mother after all.

~Author Unknown

Generation Gap

And thou shalt in thy daughter see, this picture, once, resembled thee.
~Ambrose Philips

'm five and my mom is everything. She smells good, she makes me great things to eat and she washes my "blankey." She dries my tears and cleans my skinned knee.

I'm twelve and now she is embarrassing; how could she make me wear that dress?

All the kids laughed at me. A tear slides down my face as she intones, "Don't be such a drama queen."

I'm seventeen and all I can manage is an eyeball roll at her antiquated lectures. Tears flow in frustration—she just doesn't understand me!

I'm twenty-one and she seems a little smarter now. I tell her that "things will be different with my kids; I will raise them right." Now she rolls her eyes at me with a slight smile playing across her face.

I'm twenty-four and as I hear my daughter's first cry, tears of joy run down both my face and my mother's.

I'm thirty and my daughter is six. "See Mom, how close my daughter and I are? I really think I understand you better now." There are tears in the corners of her eyes as she hugs me and whispers quietly in my ear, "Not yet honey, not yet."

I'm thirty-seven and my fourteen-year-old daughter yells at me for emerging from the car when I pick her up at the dance. She yelled,

"How embarrassing, Mom." As I cried out my hurt feelings to my mom, she says to me, "You're getting closer, dear."

I'm forty and my seventeen-year-old knows all the answers and they seem to be eluding me. I cry because my mom is dying and I now realize her wisdom.

I'm forty-five and my daughter is off to war. I cannot protect her, and she makes her own decisions now. And Mom, if you can hear me, "I think I caught up and I love you and I'm so sorry!" Tears of sorrow for missing her mix with tears of joy at having had her as my mother.

My daughter calls from overseas. After an argument she tells me, "Things will be different; I will raise my children right!" Are my eyeballs rolling?

I'm fifty and my daughter is expecting. It is a girl. As I hold my hand against her protruding belly the baby kicks. My daughter smiles and says, "I think I understand you better now, Mom."

I smile and think, "You're getting closer, honey."

~Therese Guy

Reprinted by permission of Dan Reynolds
and Cartoonresource.com ©2011

The Lady in the Mirror

As you age naturally, your mother shows more and more on your face.
If you deny that, you deny your heritage.
~Frances Conroy

I rise in the morning and bounce out of bed,
Visions of chores and errands rush through my head.
In jammies and slippers, to the kitchen I shuffle,
Hot coffee to pour, a loud yawn to muffle.

I grope through the dark, to the table I walk,
A sight I must be, much too early to talk.
I reach for my purse, now where did it go?
My cell phone was ringing, but I was too slow.

A second cup of coffee, I'm beginning to see
The dust on the table, the bookshelves, the TV.
I pull up my jeans, and turn on the light,
The zipper is stuck again, could they just be too tight?

Brush in one hand, mascara in the other,
I look in the mirror—Oh my gosh, it's my mother!
She crept in while I slept, tippy-toed in my room,
Her hair sprinkled with gray, crow's feet starting to bloom.

When I smile, she smiles back; she blinks with me too!
She's still there if my hands move, when I play peek-a-boo.
I wonder what happened; I try to focus,
Someone's played a trick on me, a little hocus-pocus.

No matter which way I turn to get back on track,
She's still in the mirror, staring right back.
The more I gaze at her, I begin to recall,
Mother was very pretty, and I start to stand tall.

Shall I pull my hair up? A decision to make.
Mother used to wear it that way, like Veronica Lake.
I swish on some lipstick, some shadow and blush,
And now just like Mother, I'm off in a rush.

As I get dressed and ready to greet the day,
I say my good mornings to my family and go on my way.
But with each new morning I race to the bathroom to see,
My copycat mother staring right back at me!

~Terri Lacher

Full Circle

All women become like their mothers. That is their tragedy.
No man does. That's his.
~Oscar Wilde

I always thought I had a weird mom. Not the type of weird that warrants a visit from social services, but just a little bit off-center, a mom who doesn't seem strange to anyone but her own kid. But I was that kid, and when you're that kid, you're pretty sure everyone is looking at you. Maybe it was that she was apt to send in dried fruit for snack at school. Or that she came into my first grade classroom to teach yoga. Or that she gave out non-candy treats for Halloween.

My mom is mainstream with a hippie twist. She seems normal enough on paper—married young, kindergarten teacher turned stay-at-home mom, suburbanite. But, when I was old enough to notice, I realized she put her own spin on things.

When I was five, I saw that we were different from other families. Why couldn't I watch television? (Too mind-numbing.) What was the harm in a little Count Chocula for breakfast? (Too sugary.) I staged rebellions by sneaking off to my best friend's house across the street to watch *The Jetsons* (too non-feminist) and chow down on some heavenly Hamburger Helper. (Too scary.)

When I was nine, my mom became a vegetarian. Then a vegan. Then she cut out sugar from her diet. Who did this to their kids? Why couldn't she just eat at McDonald's like everyone else? I didn't want to think too much about where my food was coming from or what it might be doing to my body. I kept my burgers, fries, and hot fudge sundaes.

I think she started substitute teaching for the librarian at my old elementary school when I was about twelve. I couldn't decide if this was better or worse (for me) than subbing in a regular classroom. Never mind that I didn't go to school there anymore. What if people saw her?

She became a writer. She had her first children's book published when I was thirteen. I was incredibly proud of her, but then she started writing essays based on her life, which, by definition, I was part of. I worried about which new, embarrassing teenage episodes would make it into print.

She began teaching yoga classes at home when I was fourteen. And meditating. My friends' mothers were taking aerobics. She tried to teach me some poses and deep breathing, but I would start to hyperventilate.

When I was in college, my mom went back to study nutrition to help my younger brother manage his newly diagnosed diabetes. Along the way, she discovered alternative healing practices and applied them liberally. At home for spring break, I conspicuously popped Advil as she tried to balance my chi.

I took her life personally. Like any daughter who didn't yet have confidence in her own being, I saw myself reflected in her every opinion, choice, and action: Was that me? Did I think that, too? Did I want other people thinking that was what I thought? If you asked her, my mom would be horrified to imagine that anyone could take the slightest offense at her escapades. She thinks of herself as just a typical mother. She thinks of herself as somewhat shy, as not wanting to rock the boat. She thinks that everyone else thinks like she does. Or they would if they only knew better. Do not get her started on lax federal water quality standards, revoked stem cell funding, or Republican anything.

So, fresh out of college, I wasn't sure exactly what I wanted for myself, but I set off in a different direction—not a radical one, just not my mother's. I moved to the city, took kickboxing, and lived on cheesesteaks. I watched an obsessive amount of *Beverly Hills 90210* and other television candy. I registered as an Independent and (occasionally) didn't vote in local elections. I hung with questionable friends. I deferred marriage and children.

The years went on. I found that new directions seemed to come to me as the universe stepped in with gentle nudges. A colleague shared an unfortunate piece of animal activist literature with me, rendering me incapable of taking another bite of meat for three years. My friend strong-armed me into volunteering at a local elementary school and I fell in love with teaching. A neighbor recommended her yoga instructor after my back injury and I started taking classes. I moved to Washington, DC, where politics defines relationships, and I began rallying and campaigning. I got married and decided to be a stay-at-home mom. I started writing during my son's naps.

Because all of this personal growth happened so far (geographically, at least) from where I grew up, I saw no connection to any part of my upbringing. I was merely coming into my own. I would call my mom, excited about some new crazy idea I had heard or read about — acupuncture, schools without walls, organic farming cooperatives, whatever. She would hear me out, barely getting a word in herself, and then murmur something like, "Yes, I had heard about that/done that/written a book on that." I would marvel at her arcane knowledge of such a timely topic, pump her for information, then hang up on her to go implement my plans. I was my own woman.

Looking back, I never stood a chance. Somehow, in my decades of mother/daughter rebellion and individuation, I managed to become an elementary school teacher and essay writer who loves yoga, is pretty shy but is willing to give someone an earful if called for, who hasn't gotten around to introducing her toddler son to television or sugary snacks, who touts the merits of organic food and animal rights, and is a heartbeat away from an aneurysm if someone mentions the Republican party. I like to think I put my own spin on these things, but probably not.

Here's to us, Mom.

~Stephanie Wolff Mirmina

Self Defense

Of all the things you wear, your expression is the most important.
~Janet Lane

My daughters criticized my wardrobe, my hair and my make-up. Not that long ago, I could have put my clothes on backwards and inside out and they wouldn't have cared. While I knew someday our roles would be reversed, I never expected it this soon.

My niece's wedding approached and my older daughter asked what I planned to wear. "My brown tweed jacket and black skirt," I said defensively.

Silence greeted my suggestion, but I already knew the outdated clothing in my closet wouldn't pass her inspection.

Before long, catalogs lined my kitchen table.

My older daughter, the fashion bug, pointed to a V-neck style wrap dress with long puffed sleeves and announced, "Mom, this would look good on you."

A wrap dress wouldn't suit me any more than rap music. Her next choice was a brocade dragon-patterned tunic. Looked like maternity wear to me.

My younger daughter stopped by and added insult to injury. Ever since she received her cosmetology license, she'd deemed herself an authority on what was in.

And I wasn't.

"Why don't we all go shopping Saturday morning?" she asked.

I reluctantly agreed.

Before she left, I asked, "By the way, would you have time to give me a perm before the wedding?"

She rolled her eyes and shrugged.

Jeez, I wasn't asking for curls within an inch of my scalp, just a little body and a lot less work. Resorting to pleading, I begged, "Are you busy this week?"

She finally broke the silence. "I can give you a perm, but I don't think that's what you want. I'll trim it a little and show you how to fix it once more."

Oh, she'd shown me the ropes more than once and whenever she styled my hair, it looked great. But when I tried it myself, I ended up with straight, limp hair that accented my wrinkles and highlighted my chubby cheeks.

"While we're at it, I'll wax your mustache," she said laughing.

"Mustache! What mustache?" I shrieked and ran my hand above my upper lip. She handed me a lighted magnifying mirror and pointed to the tiny dark hairs.

"Where'd that come from?" Poor eyesight had its advantages after all.

The following week my daughters were out shopping and found a blouse that would be perfect for me. For what I had no idea, but I halfheartedly agreed the top was a nice change from my usual drab clothing.

When my twelve-year-old grandson saw me wearing it, he asked, "Hey, where'd you get that cool shirt?"

Maybe the girls were onto something.

They used Christmas as another opportunity to add fashion to my life and presented me with a small fuchsia clutch purse.

"You shouldn't have," I said, and meant it.

They'd been making fun of the large, worn black purse that I carried season after season. There was nothing wrong with it; it worked just fine. My keys fit in the front pocket along with my cell phone. The sides housed my sunglasses and dental floss, and the dividers made it easy for me to find my coupon holder or checkbook. The inside of the handbag was so large I could even hide a body in it, if I needed to. I'd show them. My new clutch purse would fit just fine inside my Soprano bag.

Now that I've been forced to change my hairstyle (I'd never admit it, but I am starting to like it), I've been told my glasses have to go—my fault for mentioning that I needed a new prescription.

"Small black frames are in. Yep, that's what you need," both girls chimed in.

"Here, try mine," said the beautician.

"I look just like the girls in my high school yearbook."

"You look ten years younger," my older daughter contradicted.

When I arrived home from Lens Crafters wearing my petite, black, square frames, my husband asked, "Got a boyfriend?"

"Yes. He's standing right next to me wearing worn Wrangler jeans, a wrinkled red flannel shirt, and a dingy baseball cap. When are the fashion police going to start in on you?"

Next on my makeover was designer skin care. So what if the cosmetics cost more than a small appliance? You can't put a price on beauty.

At my age, the expensive products were a must. The purifying mist and toner immediately followed the hydrating wash. Then came corrective eye cream, facial serum and age-reversal transforming lift. A dab of SPF 8 day cream completed my morning beauty ritual, while the ageless night cream needed to be slathered on at bedtime.

"I'm going to have to set the alarm a half hour earlier," I complained. "Look at all the beauty sleep I'll miss."

The girls assured me that in a matter of weeks, my wrinkles would disappear. I reminded them who put those wrinkles on my face in the first place. Two weeks later, the only thing I noticed were the dark circles under my eyes from lack of sleep.

Before anyone could bring up the subject, I announced, "I'll have you know I draw the line at having my nose pierced or wearing a jeweled tongue ring."

It was obvious from their hysterical laughter that body piercing wasn't included in my renovation.

My life was better when they didn't notice my appearance, but this phase won't last long. Soon they'll be too busy defending themselves from their own daughters to worry about me.

Rest assured I'll be more than glad to offer some suggestions of my own.

~Alice Muschany

38

The Pied Piper

Be who you are and say what you feel,
because those who mind don't matter and those who matter don't mind.
~Dr. Seuss

Raised by my father and brother, I failed to develop a feminine view of life. Fishing trips stood in for shopping trips, and my world smelled of motor oil mixed with gasoline, burnt leaves, and grass clippings, rather than jasmine, lilacs, and fresh cinnamon. The only time a Barbie doll graced the house was when one of our G.I. Joe action figures freed her from enemy captivity during a skirmish and, even then, one of her limbs would be missing.

Forget the pretty pink bicycle with handlebar pom-poms, decorative straws on the spokes, and a woven basket in the front to transport glittery and sparkly treasures to a girlfriend's house. No, I jumped on my dirt bike and navigated the rugged backroads, dodging wayward tree limbs while choking on dust from the newly forged trail, on my way to the nearby pond for a day of exploration.

By ten, I shot clay pigeons out of the sky with a shotgun, scored outside the paint while guarded by the tallest neighborhood boy, and reeled a twenty-seven inch pike into the boat after an hour's struggle. Then I rowed the boat back across the lake to the cabin and cleaned the fish for dinner.

At thirty-five, I still hadn't mastered that whole feminine thing when my obstetrician held the ultrasound results and announced, "Looks like it's a girl."

"Are you sure?" I asked.

"Never one hundred percent sure, but I have a pretty good track record."

As the doctor calculated my due date and ideal weight gain, I glanced at the ultrasound again, my chest growing heavy. It wasn't that I didn't want a daughter; I just didn't know what to do with one.

Driving home from the doctor's office, my thoughts wandered to the edge of that gaping hole in my life—the missing mother figure—that had grown in diameter with each passing milestone: graduating from college, shopping for my wedding dress, walking down the church aisle, buying my first home, and giving birth to my son. While my mother's absence resonated long after those life-changing events, her absence at the upcoming birth of my daughter would prove the most difficult. Simply put—I needed a woman's perspective on raising a girl. Sure, I had a grandmother, but she grew up in North Dakota and remained as rugged as the state's terrain.

Shopping for my daughter's room décor was my first clue that I still resided in the realm of men. The comforters with appliques of fluffy bunnies reminded me of my father cleaning his Remington 12-Gauge in the garage. I searched for anything plaid, striped, or flannel amidst a linen department filled with lace, pastels, and satin. After a few hours, I realized why Pepto-Bismol was colored pink. I settled on bold, primary colors and a modern décor of geometrical shapes and abstract designs, which I deemed would make my daughter smarter than if she were forced to stare at doilies and ribbons for those first formative years of life.

And then my daughter was born. Every so often, at the urging of others, I attempted to impart some girlishness to Piper, but it didn't work. Barbie, Strawberry Shortcake, and Polly Pocket commiserated in the corner of the room while Piper constructed puzzles shaped like insects and farm equipment. Make-up kits and dress-up trunks remained untouched while she donned hiking boots and hoodies.

"What's the point of make-up and nail polish?" she once asked.

I paused, lacking a good answer, and said, "I'm not really sure,

Piper." Then we smiled at one another as if we had discovered a secret.

Each Christmas, the moment her piano recital ends, she claws off her pantyhose and formal dress, wads them up, and tosses them into the corner before slipping into jeans and a T-shirt. I'm guessing it's an indication of how she'll feel about the prom a few years from now.

School picture day still brings about stress as my daughter and I inspect the decorative barrette, frilly bow, or bedazzled headband that we impulsively bought the night before, continuing to try to sprinkle her with an occasional dose of femininity. After wresting with the dazzling accessory—twisting and turning it—unsure of where it goes, we toss it aside and laugh. She shoves her hair behind her ears and says, "That's good enough." And I agree.

While Piper's friends attend American Girl doll fashion shows or shop for handbags, she identifies various species of arachnids in the backyard. Holding a huge, hairy spider in her hand, she once asked, "If this is a wolf spider, why isn't it howling?" I tried not to jump while answering her insightful question.

On our yearly pilgrimage to the Smoky Mountains, Piper totes *Bugs & Slugs Pocket Naturalist Guide* and the *National Audubon Society Field Guide to Insects and Spiders* to help us decide whether a family member needs to seek medical treatment after suffering a bite or a sting. At least that's the excuse she gives for carrying the books, but I'm guessing it's more out of curiosity about the outdoors. When hiking in the mountains, Piper stops to point out the difference between bear scat and deer scat, and I smile at my husband, knowing he helped impart such wisdom to her. During a recent cave exploration, she was the first to notice the bat clinging to the side of the limestone and the snake that slithered into a crack in the cave's wall. She pitched forward to get a closer look while I tugged at her jacket sleeve.

Piper doesn't have to leave the house to explore. On any given day, she buries herself in the latest science fiction or fantasy book, reveling in the slaying of mythological beasts and the exploration of forbidden lands by brave protagonists. I delight in Piper's never-ending sense of adventure and her lack of fear of the unknown.

There may come a time when Piper attempts to conform to what society believes she should wear, buy, or read. I tried to live in the land of the frilly and dainty for nearly five years, but it felt forced and unnatural. Like me, Piper may slap on a pair of strappy sandals, get a French manicure, or try to read a fashion magazine in order to impress a guy. I know it won't last long, since strappy sandals aren't conducive to a wilderness excursion and a French manicure can't withstand the demands of backyard gardening. When she returns to the comforts of the wild, I'll stand firm in the belief that my daughter is all that a girl should be — her own person.

Someone once asked me if I had named Piper after the Pied Piper of Hamelin. I said, "No," and admitted she was named after the glamorous actress Piper Laurie, an attempt to make my daughter more feminine at the time of her birth, hoping to avoid raising a tomboy like myself. In hindsight, Piper would make a great Pied Piper since she isn't afraid of rats and her girlfriends who aren't afraid to leave the safety of their mother's sides would follow her anywhere.

~Cathi LaMarche

Reprinted by permission of
Steve Barr ©2011

39

Here Come the Brides

*Once in a while, right in the middle of an ordinary life,
love gives us a fairy tale.*

~Anonymous

"How do you feel about a winter wedding, Annie? January 14th is the only weekend I can get away," he said.

"January 14th?" I said.

"Well, if that date doesn't work I'm afraid it will be another six months before I'll be able to take time off."

In those days the United States Navy had the last say in any plans that we made. But this one time, it didn't matter a lick to me. My parents had gotten married on January 14th, 1948, while my father was in the Marines, and now I would marry my Navy man on January 14th, 1984. I liked the idea of that and I knew my parents would be honored by it as well.

"Annie? Are you there? Is January 14th okay with you?"

"Yes, Joe. January 14th sounds perfect."

"Okay Annie, I'll fill out the request. I'd better go, long distance is expensive and we have a wedding to pay for now."

I laughed and we said our goodbyes. With Joe in San Francisco and me in Philadelphia, three thousand miles separated us but in my heart the miles started shrinking away as soon as the date was set.

The next day I went over to my parents' house bursting with my wonderful news. I expected my parents would be happy for us and get a chuckle out of the date, but it never occurred to me that Mom would be so touched.

In 1948 circumstances dictated that a traditional wedding was not in the cards for Mom and Dad. The priest performed the service at three-thirty in the afternoon on a Wednesday at the parish church. My father looked dashing in his dress blues and Mom's ensemble included a winter white wool suit with brown suede pumps, brown gloves and a smart winter white felt hat trimmed in a braided gold cord.

The guest list included my grandparents, the best man and the maid of honor. Directly following the service they went across the street to a photography studio and had their wedding portrait taken. Then it was off to a local restaurant where the reception dinner was served to a group of twelve. By eight o'clock that same evening the party was over and the marriage well on its way to a fifty-two year run until by death they did part.

My mother recounted the events of their wedding day and their two-day honeymoon at Haddon Hall in Atlantic City, New Jersey many times over the years. Never once did she utter a lament that it was not the fairytale wedding most brides dream about. They had the wedding they could afford and found their pleasure in building a home and raising five children.

"Yes, Mom. You and Daddy are going to get all dressed up and go to a big party on your next anniversary!"

"I can hardly wait," she said. "It will be a first." And I saw in her eyes just the tiniest glimmer of excitement that she would at last experience a bit of a fairy tale even if only from the sidelines.

"Let the planning commence, Mom!"

Joe and I decided from the start to keep the wedding small and affordable. We had no intention of asking anyone to help us pay for anything. Our guest list totaled sixty in all and with Joe three thousand miles away I had nothing but free time to shop for the best prices, from the caterer to the wedding dress, and every item and service in between. Mom's nose for sniffing out a bargain came in mighty handy too. It was such a comfort to have her there to help plan. Goodness knows the groom wasn't available and she was so tickled to be a part of making decisions.

We looked to save money in every way that we could. When it came time to shop for my wedding dress just by chance we found a beautiful gown marked down from nine hundred dollars to ninety-nine because it had been altered and the bride never picked it up. When I tried it on it fit like a glove.

"Mom, maybe it's a bad omen that the bride didn't pick it up. Maybe it would be bad luck to buy it."

We stared at each other in silence for about ten seconds and then we both burst out laughing.

"Don't be crazy," she said. "That dress has your name written all over it."

It did too, from the Queen Anne neckline to the leg-o-mutton sleeves, clear to the beautiful train trimmed in lace with floral appliqués.

We joked about the fact that her lovely dusty rose chiffon gown cost more than twice the price of my wedding dress. And she looked stunning in it too. It turned out that she was the one who went to have her dress fitted, not me. Mine didn't need so much as a hem. It was such a pleasure to see the seamstress fuss over her. My mother spent a lifetime making do with what she had so that one or the other of us could have a new dress or new shoes or whatever was needed. It was her turn to be a princess and my pleasure to watch.

When we arrived at the church on the big day I stood in the vestibule with Mom, Dad and the bridesmaids as the last of the guests were seated. Mom's panicked expression was priceless when she saw my fiancé Joe standing at the altar with the groomsmen by his side ready for the ceremony to start.

"What are they doing? Who is going to take me to my seat?" she said.

"I think it should be your handsome groom, Mom."

Daddy stepped toward her and she slipped her hand around his arm. Though he wasn't wearing his dress blues, Daddy cut a fine figure in his white tie and tails.

"I feel like Cinderella, Annie," Mom whispered.

"Cinderella was just make believe, Mom, and for us this day is a dream come true."

Down the aisle they went, the handsome groom and his beautiful bride in her dusty rose chiffon gown thirty-six years to the day after they were first wed. Every eye in the church was upon them as Mom had her moment in the sun. It was our little secret though. Mom and Dad insisted on no fanfare regarding their anniversary. Once Mom was seated Daddy came back for me and we followed the bridesmaids up to the altar where Joe was waiting to take the hand of his own bride.

Joe and I shared eighteen wedding anniversaries with Mom and Dad before heart disease took my father from us. Two years after that my mother was gone as well.

Flipping through our wedding album it's easy to see the bride, but whenever I look I always see two.

~Annmarie B. Tait

Crashing into Grace

The heart of a mother is a deep abyss at the bottom of which you will always find forgiveness.
~Honoré de Balzac

'll never be like her!" I slammed my bedroom door with all the angst of a seventeen-year-old girl and collapsed on my bed in a crying heap. After yet another tussle with my mother, I vowed I would be different when I had children of my own.

My list of grievances against my mom ran long. She worked too much. She demanded too much help around the house. She impatiently snapped her fingers at me and gave me the stink eye if I cut up with my older brother during her phone conversations.

"She never listens," I complained to my friends. When I had children, I would hang on to their every word.

The emotional chasm between us widened with her criticism of me.

"Stop primping so much!" she reminded me when I got up early to use the curling iron.

I grew up in the 1980s. It took time to tease each strand of my bangs to the height of Mount Everest. It wasn't my fault she was out of touch with my generation's grooming habits.

"That's a sexy ensemble," I retorted sarcastically. She was wearing a sweat suit for crying out loud. I swore, as I slipped into my fashion jeans, that I would never wear elasticized pants. Or Grandma shoes. Or carry a purse the size of a suitcase.

"This room is a pigsty!" she nagged. "Clean it up or you can't go out with your friends!"

It looked okay to me. So there were a few clothes on the floor. And it would only take five minutes to pick up the books and records scattered around. When all the glasses from the kitchen found their way to my room, I always returned them. Why did she have to be so uptight?

At the crux of it all, I believed she didn't understand me.

In truth, the vast gulf that lay between mother and daughter usually had a stream of compassion flowing through the abyss. A few months before I left for college, I discovered my mother's mercy.

"I don't want you taking the car today; it is supposed to storm and you could hydroplane," she told me early one spring Saturday morning. My heart sank. I had planned this trip to the mall all week. "Worry wart" went on my mental list of gripes.

In my mind, the idea that my mom was unreasonably anxious justified my next action. In a totally uncharacteristic move, I sneaked out of the house and into one of my parents' cars. I slowly drove away from the curb, not wearing my seatbelt, of course. When I was out of sight of the house, I accelerated away from my unfairly imposed bonds. Freedom!

Of course, the chances of having a wreck increase exponentially when you don't have your mom's permission to drive the car in the first place. I never saw the dark blue hatchback coming as I turned in front of it. My parents' 1975 Buick Skylark, a tank in its own right, suffered only minor damage, but the other car was totaled—in the mall parking lot.

Dazed, I didn't notice the cracked windshield or the blood dripping from my chin. Even if I had, it wouldn't have mattered. I feared more for my life. I trembled in the police officer's car while I waited for my parents to arrive at the scene of the wreck. What was to be my fate? Jail seemed like a safe option. Maybe I could talk the nice officer into booking me downtown before my mom got there. My imagination ran wild, but what actually happened still shocks me to this day.

She was next to me so quickly she must have been out of the car before it came to a complete stop, rushing to the police cruiser and gushing all over her misguided teen.

"Don't worry about the car; I'm just glad you are okay," she said. She hugged me and smiled encouragingly and insisted I go to the emergency room to have my chin treated. Had I suffered head trauma from the wreck? Maybe she was just being nice in front of "the law" and would lower the boom in the privacy of our home. I shuddered.

I was wrong. My mother never made me pay the auto insurance or medical deductible and never punished me in any way for the wreck. In the twenty years since that crash, she has never even mentioned it. Some might say she was too lenient, but I look back now and realize it was the kind of gesture that our relationship needed. Maybe she understood that I learned my lesson from the wreck alone. I was the picture of responsibility from that day forward.

Now I am a stay-at-home mom to Andrew, four, and Gracie, ten months. Most days my husband comes home from work to find me juggling kids, a part-time writing career, and laundry that breeds in the hamper. I no longer wear fashionable jeans. I wear strained peas. The baby thinks I look great with spit all over my T-shirt and velour drawstring pants — the same ones I wore when I was nine months pregnant with her.

Sometimes I tune out my son after he has asked me for the hundredth time, "Are dragons extinct, Mama? Are they? Are they?" Sometimes I nag him to pick up his toys or snap my fingers at him when I am on the phone, giving him my best, "You-just-wait-until-I-get-off-this-phone look." With each snap I sober up with wide-eyed alarm. I have become my mother.

"Please don't ever let me wear orthopedic shoes or carry a purse big enough to hold the baby," I plead with my husband. I have already eaten so many words, I don't trust myself.

I do trust what I have learned. Mother/daughter relationships can be complicated. My mother wasn't the perfect mother, and I wasn't the perfect daughter. It's hard to walk around in this life sharing the same genes as someone else while discovering all the differences that make you unique. That's why it is a good thing grace exists. God must have created it with mothers and daughters in mind.

Sometimes I wonder how I will react when my own sweet baby girl smart-mouths me about my clothing choices or wrecks my car. I think about my own mother, who chose to forgive rather than forsake. Hopefully, when those days collide with me, I will be just like my mom.

~Janeen Lewis

When I Wasn't Looking

Thou art thy mother's glass, and she in thee
Calls back the lovely April of her prime.
~William Shakespeare

I looked up the other day just in time to see my eighteen-year-old daughter walk by in my body.

Shocking, to say the least. Disillusioning, to say the most, because I've lived the last twenty years thinking I still had it. I don't.

I snagged my husband with that outfit, and I wore it proudly for quite a while. Now she's wearing it, and bless her heart, rather than leave me exposed to the elements, she left me with my mother's body.

I know because I caught a glimpse of it in the mirror. The face is mine, but the body is definitely Mom's.

I'm not sure when my progeny made off with my property. Most likely it was when I was sleeping, or cleaning, or grading papers after school in front of the television and not paying attention. Or it could have been a couple of summers ago when I let her borrow one of my denim skirts—those generation-bridging standbys you can dress up with heels and pearls or down with sandals and a T-shirt.

She took the black slingbacks, too, as I recall, and that old red formal with the matching shoulder wrap that somehow came back into style.

It doesn't seem fair that an eighteen-year-old would be allowed to sneak up and steal something I had worked so hard on for so long. And I really object to the exchange: jelly-filled arms and thighs that don't tighten when I flex the muscles I know are in there somewhere.

Not to mention pasty skin. She got the tan, too. I suffered for that tan. And the flat stomach and long, soft hair.

What ingratitude! I carried her inside that body for nine long, anticipatory months. And her brother, too. I carried them both around on my hips for a couple of years after that. In fact that's what's wrong with the hips I've got now. They still look like I'm carrying something around on them.

You'd think she'd show a little more consideration than to run off with what nurtured her so lovingly for so long.

But then I noticed something else she's nabbed. Something deep inside of her dark eyes that twinkles when she teases and flashes when she's angry. Especially when someone strong is mean to some-one who isn't.

I see it when she looks at a certain young man, or when she picks up her nieces and nephew, unruffled by their sticky fingers and slobbery kisses. I see it when she lands a yearned-for job or a sucker punch on her brother's arm.

And secretly, I'm glad she found a few things worth taking. I guess it's not so bad after all. Sharing, that is. It means she'll carry on where I left off.

Unless I can find a way to get my body back.

~Davalynn Spencer

Family Fusion

Man cannot remake himself without suffering,
for he is both the marble and the sculptor.
~Dr. Alexis Carrel

"Beautiful sisters," the barista complimented, handing us matching black coffees. "My mother," I corrected, smiling at her deep blue eyes, vanilla-colored hair and tiny frame. I loved when people thought I looked like her.

"Good genes," he said. He couldn't see the long ragged scar hidden beneath her sundress, the splinters along my own hips or the secret pain we shared with each other.

It was June again: National Scoliosis Awareness month and the thirteenth anniversary of my final visit to the Children's Hospital orthopedic wing.

She'd been my sole support and mirror for as long as I could remember. I'd deferred to her to make my decisions, having never learned to trust myself. Even at twenty-five years old, I wasn't ready to let go and face adulthood—graduate school, career and marriage—pushing me toward an independence I wasn't ready to handle.

Growing up, my mother told me she'd thought she was a freak. When my spinal deformity was diagnosed at age eleven, there were two of us connected by humiliation.

I stood in the Gap dressing room, tall and lanky in white Hanes underwear, as my mother strapped the enormous, plastic brace around my curved back. "Suck in," she said, securing the casting from behind with thick Velcro bands.

It took all of her body weight to fasten the brace shut around me. It covered my torso from just under my breasts to above my thighs. As I looked down at my expanded body and protruding plastic hips, I couldn't breathe.

"Try these." My mother held up a pair of loose-fitting overalls in an adult size six.

At five feet tall, I was well under 100 pounds. My soccer coach had nicknamed me Olive Oyl because I had long dark hair and a thin frame like Popeye's cartoon crush. But the pants wouldn't squeeze over my new artificial body, the one I was now confined to for twenty-three hours a day.

My vertebra was quickly twisting into the adolescent scoliosis my orthopedic surgeon father had first spotted, threatening to leave me looking like Quasimodo and crushing my internal organs.

Stuck in my rock hard shell, unable to get out on my own, my mother brushed my hair out of my eyes murmuring, "Beautiful face."

I shoved her off me. "It's your fault," I screamed, tears running down my cheeks.

She stared at the concrete floor and crossed her thin arms, help-less. She must have known what was in store for me—a distorted reflection. I'm not sure it's possible to spend puberty covered in plastic and see your body as anything except big. At least it wasn't possible for me. In that moment, I wanted to hate her for giving me the gene that was ruining everything, but as she wrapped her arms around me, I could feel her crying.

When my mother was the same age they had no choice but to fuse her spine together, inserting a metal Herrington rod in her back. The surgery left her bedridden in a body cast for six months. My mother lived in a small ward crammed with thirty other children. As the cold wet casting hardened in layers around her, she was aban-doned in a dark room shivering and screaming so the others wouldn't hear her.

When I got my first period, a month after I went into the brace, she tucked me into bed, and shared her war stories with me. She was the only person in my world who'd lived through this embarrassment. "I got mine in my body cast using a bedpan," she told me.

Every time she shared a piece of her private world I felt terrible for complaining about mine. But she seemed to understand my anger. Our normal mother and daughter symbiosis became even more intertwined because of scoliosis.

My clunky brace smelled like preteen sweat from sticky summer days outside. It left bruises and gashes along my underdeveloped hips, splinters in my soft skin. At night, as I chanted the Torah portion in preparation for my Bat Mitzvah, my mother soaked my sores in rubbing alcohol so they wouldn't leave permanent scars. It burned as she held white cotton balls against my pale skin. But no amount of rubbing alcohol could prevent the scars forming beneath the surface.

I started hiding the brace under her hand-knit blankets in my closet. In the winter, covered in a bulky North Face ski jacket, I'd leave it at home while I went to school, hoping my curve would stay the same and I'd prove I didn't need the brace. When it got worse, the doctor lined the plastic with metal "enforcers" that protruded from my stomach like Pez dispensers.

Despite my defiance, she attempted to ease my pain, perhaps wishing she could rewrite her own history. For my first school dance, she gave me two hours out of the brace, instead of my usual sixty minutes, so I wouldn't have to dance with boys in my solid casting, in case anyone ever asked.

"Promise I don't look big," I begged her. When I looked at my reflection, all I saw was wide. I became reliant on my mother as my mirror, to tell me what was really there, even after the brace came off.

"You can't look big if you aren't. It's only the brace," she replied, pinning my long dark hair off my angular face.

While the rest of my world looked at my awkward appearance with pity, my mother treated me with the truth even when it wasn't nice. "That shirt is too small. I'm sorry to say it but it just doesn't fit over that thing," she said, sending me back upstairs to change.

My mother was the only person I trusted to be honest with me.

In front of my friends, I pretended it wasn't there. At her suggestion, I developed a confident coating to protect myself outwardly from the undercurrent of middle school ridicule that loomed around me. When I overheard my peers referring to me as the arcade game Feed Big Bertha, I relied solely on my mother for emotional support.

"Don't let them see you're hurting or it will be worse. We are giving you the gift of great posture. Use it," she advised.

As long as she loved me, it didn't matter that I couldn't stand myself.

I spent three years in the brace before I stopped growing at five feet seven inches and thirteen years old. Even though the doctors had straightened me out, I was uncomfortable with my body and in need of my mother's approval.

While most teenagers rebelled, exploring their own style and identity, I relied on Mom's blessings, sometimes blindly. I majored in English instead of Theatre because she thought it was practical. I didn't wear red. She said it was for prostitutes. Even now, I've never tried crème brûlée because she once told me I'd hate it.

Even after college, Mom continued to act as my anchor. I called her incessantly for her opinion on my choice of outfit, my weekly grocery list and my own feelings. "Is it okay that I am upset, or am I being ridiculous?" I asked, needing her to gauge my reactions.

My mother was the last brace I hadn't taken off.

The day I realized I was willing to let go of Mom, I was waiting for her to tell me if I should get back together with my boyfriend of three years. She'd listened to every one of my tearful thoughts during our month-long breakup, traveled between Boston and New York all summer to hold my head up, and moved my belongings out of the apartment we had lived in together, and into a downtown studio she'd selected.

For thirteen years, I'd relied on her to gauge reality and tell me what was good for me. But when I called her earlier that day, she'd drawn the line. "I don't know what to do," I sighed into the receiver.

"This is your relationship. I can't decide for you. I am sorry, but I can't."

"Why not?" I screamed.

"Because I love you," she yelled.

I knew she did. I could hear it in her voice — the pain of wanting to pick for me, of wishing she could take the hurt away, but knowing that loving me really meant forcing me to decide alone, even when I was desperate to hold on to her.

As I stood up, ready to face myself, the phone rang. For the first time, I ignored her, out of love.

~Alyson Gerber

When I Laugh

A good time to laugh is any time you can.
~Linda Ellerbee

Everyone gathered at my house after the funeral and I just wanted them to go away. I wanted to stay in bed with the covers over my head and not move or think or see or hear or... even be. She was dead and they stood around laughing and socializing and even fighting (albeit under the radar). All I wanted to do was sleep, but instead I was playing hostess and it overwhelmed me.

I left my guests and got into bed. Now I lie here trying to shut out every noise and every voice and trying not cry. I think about my mother, whose voice will be forever missing from family gatherings. I keep coming back to the one attribute of her personality that was always overlooked. Humor. It was my father who was the funny one (and he was funny!). But it was my mother who had to put up with his antics. It was my mother who had to be able to laugh.

I think about her first surgery, which left her with a large open wound that had to be attended to multiple times a day. I volunteered to clean the wound and change her bandages. It was then that I learned how awful a "large gaping wound" could be. As I would change her bandages she would lie on her bed willing herself not to laugh at the look on my face.

"Don't make me laugh," she'd chuckle. "It hurts when I laugh."

"Just don't look at me because I can't do this without making faces! Ugh!"

Finally she would turn her head and squeeze her eyes shut but still have a big grin on her face. I smile, in the dark under the covers, remembering. My mind drifts to more laughter at another serious time. I think back to her reaction to a conversation I had with my seven-year-old son when she was in the hospital for a different surgery.

"I asked Jonathan if he wanted to come with me to visit his grandma. He wanted to know if you were still in the hospital. I told him 'yeah.' He was quiet for a few minutes." I looked at my mother, whose eyes were gleaming as she waited for the punch line.

"Then he said, 'Tell her I said get well soon.'"

My mother threw her head back and laughed loudly. I laughed too. Here was yet another male relative afraid of the hospital.

I realized that my mother gave me a lot of laughs even when it wasn't her intention. She was fiercely protective of her children even after we could clearly fight our own battles. Once at a department store, a clerk was extremely rude to my sister. My mother found out just as we reached the escalator. As we stepped on the down escalator, my mother hesitated at the top, and then with her hands on her hips, she yelled across the store to the rather large, overweight clerk.

"You need to lose weight, honey!"

I looked at the clerk and could see, as if in slow motion, her head along with many onlookers' heads, begin to turn in our direction. Immediately my sisters and I sat down on the escalator stair and out of sight of the onlookers. As I looked up at my mother, who was standing tall, with chest out, hands on hips and round stomach, I thought I saw a superhero cape blowing in the wind. Yet again she had come to the aid of a child in need. Then my mother turned away from the clerk and gave her daughters, who were still sitting on the escalator going down, a nod of victory. The fact that my mother was overweight too, or that her daughters were sitting, embarrassed by her actions, on an escalator (which was causing a lot of our own curious stares) never concerned her. Even as we told this story over the years, my mother would laugh and the twinkling in her eyes always told me she would do it all over again.

I laugh out loud, now under the covers in the dark, and I again hear the sounds of my family coming from downstairs. The clinking of dishes, the loud laughter and the voices from multiple conversations are what I had, only moments before, successfully tuned out. I laugh harder, thinking that my mother would find it funny that I am giggling to myself under the covers in the dark. Throwing off the blanket, I get up and I see myself in the mirror. For a moment I mimic my mother's pose on the escalator. I can't help but giggle as I look at myself and think of her. Everyone says I look just like her. And I do… especially when I laugh.

~Nina Guilbeau

The Magic of Mothers & Daughters

Chapter 5

Family by Choice

Simply having children does not make mothers.

~John A. Shedd

The Jacket

You can't live a perfect day without doing something for someone who will never be able to repay you.
~John Wooden

She looked younger than her fifteen years. Her white face stood out against the blackness of her hair. She was a child of the foster care system. We had received a call from the Ministry that a home was needed for a young girl immediately, and of course we agreed.

There was a lot of hustle and bustle to get her room ready. We were not expecting a child for another two months. The day was filled with a mixture of apprehension and excitement. Our own children kept asking questions such as:

"What is she like?" and "How long will she stay?"

"We'll just have to wait and see," was all I could answer.

We had four children of our own: Margaret and Joanne were seventeen and fifteen, and Rob and Jeff were twelve and nine. That afternoon, Susan arrived with the social worker. She hugged the wall. Her eyes had the look of a hunted animal. At this point, I stepped forward and said, "Welcome to our home, Susan."

"Kids, please go downstairs to the family room, so Dad and I can talk with Mrs. Kline." We sat at the kitchen table, and Susan was very quiet. Her eyes darted back and forth like a creature looking for a way out. This was her fifth foster home since she turned eleven. I wanted to put my arms around her and tell her she would be safe with us. I didn't want to scare her.

For the first two weeks Susan was quiet. She came into the kitchen while I was working. We discussed school and what she would like to do in the future. Mrs. Kline gave me all the information about Susan's past. I never mentioned the terrible things that had happened to her.

Her so-called mother placed her in very strict religious homes. Punishments were harsh—cruel acts like putting Susan in basement closets or forcing her to kneel on rice in the corner.

I wondered if, in trying to help Susan, I had taken on too much. Her life had been one crisis after another. Would she be able to put the pain behind her and get on with her life? Would I fail? Self-doubt overwhelmed me.

It was Friday night and Susan had been with us for only one week. Margaret and Joanne were getting ready to meet their friends. Susan was watching television.

"Aren't you going out with the girls?"

"You mean I'm allowed to go with them?" she asked in amazement. Her question took me by surprise.

"I was never allowed to go out at night at the other house," she continued.

"Well," I finally responded, "it's different here. Friday and Saturday you can go out but the curfew is eleven o'clock." When she heard my words, she jumped up and hugged me. I was so surprised that I almost fell backwards.

As the days went by, Susan became a pleasure to have around. It seemed like she had always been with us. To my delight, the girls would sit in each other's rooms and giggle like typical teenagers. It was a sound that warmed my soul.

Susan had been with us for about a month when I decided Joanne needed a new jacket for school. Susan asked to come with us. She wasn't used to shopping in stores other than discount outlets. The process of buying involved filling out receipts and sending them to the Ministry; she found it all very embarrassing.

Joanne was trying on a green suede jacket with a fur collar. It was expensive but she pleaded and said she would give up her allowance and do extra chores, anything to have it. Susan chose a jacket she liked and was promenading in front of the mirror. As I watched her, I realized she was not the same girl who had entered our home only four weeks earlier. She stood taller and held her head higher. The tightness in her face had softened. She was able to look me in the eye when she spoke.

She walked up to Joanne, modeling the jacket for her, and sighed. "Isn't it beautiful?" Joanne agreed as they both preened in the mirror. Susan replaced the jacket on the rack. I watched the two.

"That coat looks so nice on you, can I borrow it sometime? Alex will love you in it!" She teased. I hadn't seen her face so animated before.

While they were busy I quietly asked the salesperson to wrap up the jacket that Susan had tried on. "Please don't let her see; it's a surprise." For the next few minutes I kept Susan busy while the salesperson rang up the sale and wrapped the treasure. Then we formally bought the coat that Joanne had loved. The salesperson had placed the parcel containing the jacket where the girls couldn't see it. I told them I was going to the ladies room and managed to sneak it out to the car without being caught.

When we arrived home, Joanne proudly modeled her new jacket for Margaret. Susan was still talking about it and how Joanne would lend it to her.

"Susan, would you please go to the car and bring in the parcel from the trunk?" She happily complied and when she returned, laid it on the table.

"Open the parcel for me while I put on the kettle?" I could hear the sounds of ripping paper, and then I turned, and saw her reaching out to touch the jacket.

Her hand recoiled as if she had touched something hostile. I walked towards her and put my arms around her. Susan looked directly into my eyes, unable to speak. Anxiety and concern for this newly acquired sister showed in Joanne's face.

I held Susan's face and asked, "Isn't this the jacket you were trying on?" At that, Susan started sobbing.

"In all my life no one has ever bought me a beautiful jacket like this. Why did you do it?" She held the jacket and stared at it with disbelief. I was on the brink of tears myself and my voice shook as I managed to say, "Because you deserve it."

I left the kitchen and went to my bedroom. I couldn't stop crying. My heart ached for this child, who didn't feel she was worthy of a new jacket. As I was sitting there deep in thought, a knock came on the door.

"Come in." There in the door way stood my five children. Susan was standing at the back holding the jacket so tight. Their faces told me they needed to say something. Margaret stepped forward and spoke for them:

"Mom, thank you for bringing Susan into our home. We hope we can keep her forever." The rest of the heads bobbed up and down in agreement. My eyes welled with tears again.

"We love you, Mom." I looked at the faces of my treasures and whispered, "I love you too. I'm the luckiest mother in the world."

Susan stayed in Vancouver with us until she was twenty-three. She returned to the province she was born in but wasn't accepted back by her mother. I now call her my daughter and she calls me her angel.

~Carol Sharpe

Mother by Proxy

A bit of fragrance always clings to the hand that gives roses.
~Chinese Proverb

My relationship with my mother did not begin in the usual way. I was not born of her womb. Her blood does not course through my veins and I didn't inherit her soft green eyes or her slender frame. Nor was I the result of someone else's poor planning, later to be adopted by my mother. She became my mother by proxy.

She came into my life at a time when I truly needed a mother. At first I resented her, even disrespected her. I saw her as an intruder in my life and I wanted nothing to do with her. But one hot summer afternoon, all that changed. As I was playing in the yard, she brought me a glass of ice water. I began to gulp it down and unwittingly inhaled a large ice cube. It became lodged in my throat and I began to panic. My mother saw my distress and immediately ran to my aid. She helped to dislodge the ice cube and then pulled me into a gentle embrace as I cried. All my resentment for her immediately disappeared and at that moment I knew that she was truly my mother.

Throughout my childhood, we did the kinds of things mothers and daughters are supposed to do. We went shopping, did errands, read books, and watched movies together. She taught me how to cook and clean, tend the garden and do household chores. She savored little moments with me — times when it was just the two of us and we could do something special. Money was always tight, but she found creative ways for us to have fun. She was strict but fair and I adored her.

When I was a teenager, we had the usual ups and downs that girls and their mothers have. We fought and made up. I hated her and loved her. I pushed her away but always came back to her. She encouraged me to join extra-curricular groups at school and to pursue a college degree. She reminded me how difficult it had been for her to earn her degree so much later in life. And when I finally went off to college, we both experienced a loneliness we never anticipated. Somehow, through all the ups and downs, triumphs and tragedies, she was no longer just my mother; she had become my best friend.

Today, as an adult, I am forever grateful that this woman who did not give birth to me, who did not adopt me, and who had not planned on having me in her life, has given so much of herself to me. She is the one I call when I've had a bad day. She's the one I long for when I'm sick in bed. She is the one who can comfort me, reassure me and support me when I need it most

Now that I have children of my own, I know how strong and how beautiful the bond is between a mother and her children. I understand the responsibility to put my children before myself. I ache when they hurt and I smile when they are happy. But could I so unselfishly provide for and love a child who was not my own? I would like to think I could; I would like to think I have learned by example.

As I watch her with my children now, I am amazed at her patience and understanding. I am touched by how deeply she loves them, and reminded of how blessed I am that she came into my life.

Had our paths never crossed, I have no doubt that I would not be the person I am today. My life most certainly would have disintegrated into a downward spiral. The moment she entered my life, she changed the path I would take. She steered me in the right direction and stayed with me until she was certain I wouldn't lose my way. Then she entrusted me to continue on my own, and became a beacon in the distance, a presence to let me know she was always there if I needed her.

My mother does not fit the negative stereotypes associated with her role. She was never cruel to me. She never put her birth children before me. She has given me nothing but unconditional love.

She is the single most influential person in my life. She is my stepmother and I am proud to call this beautiful woman "Mom."

~Kathryn A. Rothschadl

46

That's What Moms Are For

There is… nothing to suggest that mothering cannot be shared
by several people.
~H. R. Schaffer

It nearly broke my heart when he told me his secret. It was four years ago and just two months before our wedding. I knew something was wrong as soon as he walked in the door. After he came inside, he didn't take off his shoes or coat. He greeted me with, "I have to tell you something." We sat on my couch. Instead of looking at me, he stared from beneath the brim of his Minnesota Gophers hat at the space between us on the couch. "My God," I thought, "He's breaking up with me. Two months before our wedding, and he's breaking up with me." I held my breath as he continued talking in a low, tight voice. He told me he had kept a secret from me because he was afraid I wouldn't love him if I knew. His secret's name was Savanha.

Savanha, I learned from my fiancé, was his daughter. She lived with her mother in a city about thirty miles away. How could he have kept this from me? Silent tears slipped down my cheeks. He said shortly after he graduated from high school he began dating a co-worker. She was very much in love with him; he was very much in love with having a good time. Then she got pregnant. He felt over-whelmed and trapped, and decided he wasn't ready to be a father.

"She's fifteen now, and I only see her on her birthday and holidays." As he finished his story, I realized he was crying, too.

Then he looked at me and said, "I understand if you no longer want to marry me." A moment passed. I hated what he had done. My mind was racing: could I marry someone who had left a woman who was pregnant with his child? This means my first child won't be my husband's first child; could I accept that? Did I want to be a stepmom? Then I did something I have never regretted since. I reached over to him, held his face in my hands, and said, "Of course I still want to marry you. You made a mistake many years ago, but I still love you."

By the time we exchanged vows, thoughts of Savanha were far from my mind. I was a happy, busy new bride and didn't spend much time dwelling on my husband's former secret. The reality of the situation finally sunk in at my sister-in-law's birthday party a few months later. Minutes after we arrived at the party, my mother-in-law pulled me aside. "Savanha is here, and she really wants to meet you." My stomach dropped, yet somehow I was able to keep my cool. "Sure," I said with forced enthusiasm, "I want to meet her, too!"

We walked over to a girl who looked much older than fifteen. Besides being short, she didn't look like my husband. Her face and body type were rounder and her nose was smaller than his. She had pale skin and auburn hair like I did. She actually looked more like me. I remember being both surprised and oddly comforted by this observation. I noticed she stood like a lot of teenagers: shoulders a bit slumped, arms across her stomach in a self-conscious way. She was wearing a black T-shirt with the name of a garage rock band I had never heard of on it. Her eyes were thickly lined with black eyeliner. Her serious make-up seemed in sharp contrast to the shy smile that spread across her face when I went in for a hug. "Nice to meet you! I'm Joan," I said, smiling. "I know," she said and hugged me back. That was the moment I realized… I was a stepmom.

As a newly married twenty-four-year-old, getting used to the idea that I was the stepmother of a teenager wasn't easy. However, it became easier over time, especially after I spent more time with

Savanha. It helped that she was a mature, good-humored, creative young woman who was forgiving of her father's mistakes and easy to get along with. We began inviting Savanha to all the Oen family functions. The enthusiasm I felt for her was no longer forced, but it still didn't feel completely right. When, I wondered, would I start to love Savanha?

Two summers ago, my husband and I decided to visit his hometown in Minot, North Dakota. More importantly, we decided to take Savanha with us. She had never seen where her father grew up, and it was long overdue. The eight-hour car ride to Minot provided us with plenty of time to get to know each other better. We laughed, listened to music and munched on snacks from gas stations. Once we arrived, we stayed with my husband's grandmother. On the Sunday of our stay, something happened that forever changed my relationship with my stepdaughter.

It was morning and we were getting ready for church. Once I was dressed, I went into the kitchen for some coffee. Savanha called out from the bathroom: "Joan? Can you come help me?" Curious, I walked down the hall and pushed opened the bathroom door. Inside I found my stepdaughter standing in front of the mirror. She looked as if she was about to cry. "It's my extensions. After I took a shower the glue started coming off; I can't get it all off." It was true, her long auburn hair was spotted with globs of white glue from her home-done extensions; it looked like she had a bad case of dandruff. I grabbed the comb from her hand, "I used to do my sisters' hair all the time," I said. "Let me see what I can do." I started pulling out globs of glue. Then I began to put her hair in a loose bun, using bobby pins to cover her glued-in extensions with her real hair. It was time to leave for church before we were finished, so we took the hairspray and bobby pins with us. As we rode in Grandma's Cadillac to church, I continued strategically placing bobby pins and spraying Savanha's hair with enough hairspray to withstand the strong North Dakota winds. I finished just as we pulled into the church parking lot.

Later that day, Savanha and I returned to the bathroom so I could touch up her hair. While adjusting her bobby pins, our eyes met in the mirror and I admitted I enjoyed helping with her hair crisis. She smiled and replied, "That's what moms are for!" That's what moms are for; her words echoed in my head. She was telling me she valued me as a mother. My eyes welled with happy tears. It was at that moment I felt something I had never felt for her before: I felt a surge of maternal love. I smiled and breathed a silent prayer. "Thank you God for this great weekend with Savanha! Thank you for the chance to be a stepmother!"

~Joan Oen

47

Hope for the Future

*…suffering produces endurance, and endurance produces character, and
character produces hope and hope does not disappoint us.*
~Romans 5:3-5

When I was born they named me Hope. Don't ask me who "they" are—I don't know. It could have been the college kids who had an "oops" one night and knew they couldn't keep me. Or maybe a secretary at the Department of Welfare who had to fill out my paperwork and figured I would need all the positive energy I could get. Maybe it was a foster parent. Obviously, my beginning wasn't the norm.

The way it all went down was very non-traditional. My adoptive mom, Patricia—Pattie for short—had given birth to three adorable young boys, all healthy and full of personality. Light-skinned, blue-eyed, towhead to mousy brown, and ages two to ten. Sam, the oldest, was named after a long line of Sams in the family, fifth in line to be exact. Andy was sixteen months younger than Sam, more fair-skinned and with a slighter build. He had an artistic eye and loved to perform. The youngest, Greg, was still toddling around at two years old, charming folks with his "gregarious" personality and his spontaneous nature.

Happily in love with these three boys, my mom had always wanted a girl. Really, what is the experience of having a baby without the ruffles and lace? Or playing dress up with the sassy, pink, little girl outfits and combing shiny smooth hair into ponytails and adorning it with ribbon? For my mom, the family would not be complete without a little sugar and spice.

Interestingly, and for many reasons, Mom was drawn to the idea of a bi-racial baby. First, she knew there were a lot out there who needed homes and she liked the idea of being able to share that and give one of these children a second chance. She also knew if she wanted to have a fair-skinned Caucasian child, she and Dad were capable of taking care of that themselves. And third, she had recently taken a course at the local women's college on black history and found herself fascinated with the trials, tribulations and strengths of the African American culture.

At this time, in the late sixties, there was an abundance of mixed-race children up for adoption. It was still a period when people of different races weren't encouraged to be together, when these relationships could even be considered taboo. When a child came along in one of these relationships, sometimes, in certain circumstances, the only choice was to give the child up for adoption. There were so many of these cases that the Department of Welfare ran announcements in the newspaper about particular children who needed caring families and a stable home.

And this is how my mother fell in love.

She found an article in the *Rocky Mountain News* about a little girl, Rene, who was available for adoption. The headline read "Alone in the World." It stated, "Rene is just six weeks old, but she already has a winning personality. She loves to be cuddled and shows curiosity about her surroundings. Because Rene is of Negro-Caucasian descent, it is difficult to find a home for this baby. She is one of about fifty children of special needs who have no prospects for adoption according to Denver Department of Welfare social workers." There was an address and contact person at the bottom of the article. My mother clipped it out of the paper and made up her mind. She was going to adopt a mixed-race baby girl. (Race never was an issue for Mom. Years later, when my brothers were teenagers, she put them on a bus to send them to high school in a predominantly black neighborhood.)

So my mom and dad began to fill out the forms, went through family interviews with social services and put in their request for the type of baby they wanted. Mom's only stipulation was that she wanted a baby between two and six months old. My father, an obstetrician, stipulated a healthy birth mom.

The application and interviews helped the social workers approve the candidates and match the babies with the families. But it was a process, and by the time the Downing clan was approved for a new addition, little Rene had been adopted elsewhere.

After starting the process in the heat of the July sun, six months later, in the dead of winter, my parents received the call. They had a five-and-a half-month-old baby girl, just waiting to be taken home and loved. My family packed up a blanket and clothes, and the five of them piled into the car, knowing their lives were about to change.

It wasn't a ceremonious exchange, but more like, "Here's the little girl you ordered." The cost of the entire adoption was about twelve dollars. This was something my brother Greg used to like to tease me about when we were growing up. One of his favorite insults was to remind me that I wasn't even worth as much as a twenty-dollar bill.

My mother instantly fell in love. After she dropped my father back at the hospital to work, she took my brothers and me first to the hairdresser and then to the church to show me off. I had an olive skin tone and chocolate brown eyes, with a little tuft of curly black hair standing straight up on the top of my head. I looked nothing like anyone in my family, but if you really wanted to stretch the association, my father had black hair and brown eyes too.

You could say that I was my mom's birthday present. I arrived six days after she turned thirty-two. Although I had a name, Hope, which was fitting for my circumstances, my mom wanted one that would fit my new life. Even though I was never physically part of her, she wanted me to be an everlasting piece of who she is.

She is Patricia Carolyn. And since that day she picked me up at social services, I have been her second half. My name is Tricia Lynn.

~Tricia Downing

Loving Her Through the Fear

[A] mother is one to whom you hurry when you are troubled.
~Emily Dickinson

I was busy in the kitchen when the phone rang. I smiled as I recognized my stepdaughter's phone number.

"Hello?"

"Hi." Came the hesitant response. I could hear all the unspoken fear in that simple word.

I put my knife down and pushed the vegetables and cutting board aside. Wiping my hands on the ever-present dishtowel, I sat down and quietly asked the question, "So, what's up?"

Two days before, she and her new boyfriend had come by our place for coffee. I could tell something was bothering her but we didn't find the right time to talk.

I heard her sigh on the other end of the line, and before I could even brace myself, she blurted it out: "I'm pregnant."

"Wow. How are you doing?"

At that very moment I heard the break in her voice and could feel the sting of tears on my own cheeks to match hers. "Pretty scared," came the difficult reply.

All I could think about was holding her as she cried over past hurt and future trials.

I had to ask: "Does Dad know yet?"

"No." She sighed. "I was hoping you could help me tell him."

While her upbringing may have been fairly strict, she certainly had all the love a father could possibly bestow upon his little girl. I knew he would love her through this without question.

"Of course."

Through her crying, I heard, "He's going to be so disappointed in me."

My arms ached to hold her. "Your dad loves you dearly, sweetheart. He may be disappointed in choices you've made, but you know he would never be disappointed in you. We're here and we love you."

After more tears and encouragement, we said our goodbyes and she prepared to call her dad. Tears warmed my eyes once again as I prayed a quick prayer for the beautiful, scared girl whom I had come to love so much.

Today, as I look back and wait to hold our tiny bundle, I wonder how things could have ever been any different. I look forward to the day when I can hold our wriggly wonder and whisper, "Welcome little one. We love you."

~Chantel Friesen

Learning to Trust

Patience is also a form of action.
~Auguste Rodin

"Mom, meet Alicia." My son smiled at the young woman by his side. I instantly embraced her and she returned the hug. I sensed that her inner beauty matched the outer beauty of her heart-shaped face and exotic blue eyes, and that she would become my fourth child—the one I had longed for since a miscarriage many years before.

I was thrilled when Alicia asked if she could call me "Mom" after she and my son were engaged. After all, Alicia had received little nurturing growing up. Her mother had been married seven times and had preferred alcohol and tobacco to her spouses and children. Now she had cancer, but when she was well enough to go out, she went to bars, not to visit Alicia.

Ben and Alicia married and settled in Seattle. Alicia entered a triathlon, a real challenge since she hadn't previously been a runner, biker or swimmer. My husband and I drove up from Portland to watch. We applauded wildly when she pulled herself from Lake Washington after her half-mile swim and when she finished her thirteen-mile bike ride. When she entered the home stretch, I burst from the crowd lining the street to run with her.

"I can't believe you came," she said, as we ran. "My mother never would have."

"I'm so proud of you," I repeated over and over.

Surely the triathlon would cement our mother/daughter relationship. But it wasn't that easy. After her tough childhood, Alicia was cautious. The next time we visited, when we were preparing to go to breakfast, I looked for my cell phone on the table where I was sure I had left it. "Did someone move my phone?" I asked.

"I didn't touch it," Alicia snapped.

I flinched. "I didn't mean…"

Ben found my phone, ending the exchange. I remembered Alicia telling me she sometimes felt like the world was out to get her. To her, I'd sounded accusatory, and I vowed to be more careful how I said things in the future.

As we got to know each other better, communicating became more comfortable. Alicia never snapped again. In fact, she was delightful whenever we got together. We talked about everything from husbands to home décor. She delighted me with a witty commentary on everything around her from dogs to fashion, and she punctuated our conversations with her hearty laugh. When Ben and Alicia moved to Portland and bought a small house fifteen minutes from us, I was thrilled. Now we'd see them often.

I forgot to temper my enthusiasm with an awareness that Alicia had left her father, a half-brother she was close to, and a lot of friends in Seattle. She would need time and space to adjust to a new place and a new circle of friends. "Can you come to dinner?" I'd call or e-mail.

"We can't. I'm sorry," Ben would tell me.

I tried to cover my disappointment with a cheerful response. I definitely had my own issues to factor in, oversensitivity being a prominent one.

Over the months, family gatherings became more frequent and Alicia always asked what she could bring. At Christmas she gave us all beautiful gifts she'd made herself—handbags, neck warmers, scarves. I grew comfortable again.

Then Alicia got pregnant. She had morning sickness and felt miserable. She wasn't used to a mother tucking an afghan around her and making her a cup of tea. She had to take care of herself in her own way, the only way she knew, which was to withdraw and spend time alone. I so wanted to pull that afghan up around her chin and put a steaming cup of chamomile on the nightstand by her bed. But I had to step back.

I was excited about my coming grandchild so I took Alicia the things I had loved most when I was pregnant—books on development of the baby in utero. I envisioned sitting on the couch together admiring tiny fingers and toes, eyes and ears. Alicia was courteous, but distant. I was hurt and disappointed, forgetting entirely how I had not wanted my own mother around much when I was first pregnant; I was afraid she would start giving advice when I desperately wanted to have this new experience my way.

When Alicia told me she planned a home birth I further strained our relationship. I told her how I would have lost Ben if I hadn't delivered in a hospital, because I had needed an emergency forceps delivery and oxygen to save him. Alicia sounded cool and detached as she talked about the statistical safety of home births. I realized that she had made a careful, well-informed decision, whereas I'd read nothing about that birthing option.

"We'll call you when you can come see the baby," my son told me.

When would that be? When the baby was first born? After a few days? A few weeks? I held back tears. What kind of relationship did we have?

Alicia's due date came. A week passed, and then another. I tried to keep quiet, but I asked about an ultrasound. Alicia reassured me that she and her midwife weren't worried because the normal range of gestation periods was actually two weeks beyond the theoretical due date. Once again, I looked like the meddling mother-in-law and Alicia the one who was fully informed. Not only did she need to trust my good intentions, but also I needed to trust the way she made examined choices based on careful research.

My granddaughter was born eighteen days past the supposed "due date," weighing in at eight pounds, two ounces, the healthiest, most beautiful baby I had seen since my own three were born.

We were invited to see Anais hours after her birth. I thought again about how defensive I'd been with my own mother, and checked with Alicia to make sure I held the baby in a way she felt comfortable with. In the following weeks and early months, I never dropped by to see the baby without calling first and scheduling a time convenient for Alicia. I never stayed very long, remembering what a tiring time it is for a new mother. Later, Alicia told me, "The way you handled it made me feel really understood and respected, and it warmed my heart." Alicia swung her doors open both physically and metaphorically after she had Anais. Short visits turned into weekly two-hour stretches.

When Anais was a year old, and our relationship was blossoming, Alicia's mother died. I was glad Alicia and I had become close and I could support her in her loss. A second mother to her, my daughter... my fourth child.

~Samantha Ducloux Waltz

A Little Bite of Love

Give what you can. To someone, it may be better than you dare to think.
~Henry Wadsworth Longfellow

After months of planning, prayer, and preparation, my husband Bob and I could hardly wait to fly to China to welcome our new little daughter. In fact, we had already named our eighteen-month-old angel "Amy" (meaning "love"). We three would be the perfect little family and live happily ever after.

But as soon as we picked Amy up from her Chinese foster mother, our dreams of snuggly joy went terribly wrong. Amy missed her "Amah" so intensely that she would barely look at Bob and me. Instead, she'd stand at our hotel room door and scream for the only mother she had known. Many times I tried to speak to her, but she would avoid eye contact with me and continue to grieve for her beloved foster family. How would we ever make it back to the U.S. with her in such misery?

At this point I was so distraught and embarrassed that lunch in a restaurant was out of the question. I was afraid people would think I was being a "bad mother." So I gave up and ordered our meals from room service.

One time I chose the noodle plate. When the noodles arrived, I put my plate on the bed and decided I would try to use chopsticks for the very first time instead of a fork. As the noodles slithered off my chopsticks, Amy's screaming and crying suddenly stopped.

Peeking out of the corner of my eye, I saw her sitting in the corner of the room watching me intently. Again and again I tried to pick up the noodles with the chopsticks, but not a single one made it into my mouth!

A tiny hand came into view, took the chopsticks from my big American hand, and tapped the ends expertly on the edge of my plate. As I looked up, Amy—with the chopsticks professionally arranged in her chubby little fingers—began expertly feeding me noodles, without dropping a single one.

I looked at Bob, who was wide-eyed with amazement. He ran to get the camera and took a picture of Amy feeding me. (It is our dearest photo!)

"Do you think she would feed me?" my husband wondered hopefully.

So, trembling with excitement, I asked, "Amy, will you feed your daddy now?" and pointed to Bob. She nodded "yes" with a big smile on her face!

As she fed Bob, I grabbed the camera and took a picture of them together. That meal was definitely a bonding experience. I think Amy felt sorry for us and figured that we would surely starve without her assistance!

At age nine, back here in the U.S., she continues to be a real caregiver—especially to her younger sister Bonnie, also adopted from China. In fact, Amy has even promised to drive us to our favorite restaurant on Sunday afternoons some day when we are "too old to drive ourselves." You can't ask for more than that!

~Mary Ulrich Jackson

A Second Chance

Biology is the least of what makes someone a mother.
~Oprah Winfrey

I had been in foster care since the age of eight. By the time I was in the eleventh grade, I was in my second foster home and had been there for five years. Although I was surrounded by a warm and caring family, something still pained me deeply. I felt "out of place." I wasn't her birth child so I kept a distance from my foster mom, not allowing myself to love her as much as I could.

One day, things changed for the better. I was working on homework, waiting for the rest of the family to return home from their events. It was a daily routine. I would spend most of my nights by myself finding things to do to keep me busy. As I was reading a paragraph for English I heard the back door close and my foster mom called for me. Quietly, I walked upstairs and into the kitchen where she was holding a hardcover children's book. "I want you to read this," she said excitedly. "It's absolutely wonderful." She handed me a book and I glanced at it with curiosity: *The Kissing Hand* by Audrey Penn. She smiled at me. "Trust me," she said. "You'll love it."

Reluctantly I grabbed a stool, made myself comfortable at the counter, and began to read the book. It was a touching story of a raccoon mom who places a kiss in the palm of her child's hand to remind him that if ever he should get scared he just has to press his kissed hand to his cheek. By doing so, he will always remember that his mommy loves him.

Later that night, I was talking with Mom when suddenly she did something totally unexpected. She, ever so gently, took my hand and put a warm loving kiss in the center of my palm. Then she quietly closed my hand and held it between hers and spoke the words that I had dreamt of hearing for so long.

"Whenever you get scared or sad remember that your mommy loves you." As tears began to form, I understood and I smiled from the very depth of my wounded heart. At that moment I knew... I truly did have a mother. No, she isn't biological, but she is mine just the same.

~Cynthia Lynn Blatchford

52

Redemption

Forgiveness does not change the past, but it does enlarge the future.
~Paul Boese

I was twenty-three years old the day I met ten-year-old Amber. She was my fiancé's daughter and it was the night before our wedding. The minute Amber looked at me I knew I was in trouble. She spread her feet, cocked her head, raised one eyebrow and looked me up and down. "You don't look like your picture," she said, and walked straight past me into the church. I wondered if it was too late to cancel the ceremony.

• • •

My first real memory of my stepmom was sitting at a piano in the church. I was overwhelmed with meeting so many new people. I had spent the night at my dad's house and Aunt Judy did my hair and made me wear a white fluffy dress. It was early in the morning and I wanted to be in bed instead.

My grandma took my brother and me from California where I had been living in a foster home for over a year. Before that, I was living in a meth house with my mom and three brothers. My stepdad beat us every time he was high.

I wanted to be anywhere other than the wedding. I wasn't about to get pushed around by a bunch of people I didn't know, so I put my boxing gloves on. I did like carrying the flowers down the aisle.

•••

Amber and her little brother Tyson lived with us full-time. My husband Ed and I were in for a rude awakening. We didn't truly know each other and the children needed constant attention. Most days, I felt like our household was a bad science experiment. We were four highly combustible chemicals abruptly combined.

My walk with the Lord at that point in my life was weak. I had been sober for only two years and although I prayed, I rarely attended church and never read my Bible. I remember most of Amber's middle school years as a giant black cloud. I cried frequently and wished I could heal her little heart. Her pain was so visible; I just wanted to undo her past. She reminded me of a wounded wild animal.

•••

I had always prayed to meet my dad and now I was going to live with him. I didn't trust anyone, so I lied about everything. I had to steal food when I was younger in order to eat; when I moved in with Dad and Danika, I continued to steal. I used to open packages of food in the cupboard and try to hide the evidence by taping them shut.

I hated middle school. In fact, I still hate that school today. I got swept up in the drama of people who didn't really even care about me. I said and did what everyone else did just to survive. I stole, swore, tried smoking and never did my homework. I was sure Danika was out to get me and that she didn't want me around. I felt like I caused most of Dad and Danika's problems. I was depressed.

•••

By the time Amber entered high school my marriage was a wreck. I had a baby, I was pregnant and the tension in our household was thick enough to swim in. All my efforts to control Amber's behavior, my husband's anger and Tyson's constant arguing only made the situation worse. Early one Sunday morning I tied my baby's tiny hiking boots on his little feet, grabbed my keys, and eased my pregnant belly behind the steering wheel of the car. Ten minutes later I sat in the back pew of our neighborhood church and listened to a woman give her testimony.

"My mom and stepdad were meth addicts," she said quietly. "After dragging my brother and me around in the back of their car for years, my mom sold me at a swap meet." I sat in the back of that church with my baby in my arms and wept. Near the end, she looked over the audience and tearfully said, "...that's when I finally understood that when no one else loved me, God did."

That day God broke into my heart. I wept over my own broken childhood and I wept over Amber's. That was the day she became my daughter.

Amber began attending church with me. I drove her and my niece Holly to youth group each week. I attended Bible study and a preschool moms' group. God worked a miracle in my marriage and my husband and I slowly stopped fighting. I was the mother of four kids and we finally felt like a real family.

Until the day Amber set her school on fire.

• • •

I quit caring about myself or anyone else. I didn't feel like I could live up to what anyone else wanted. I was a great liar, but I wanted to get caught. I hated how I felt, but I was too stubborn to ask for help. I started burning my skin with lighters, skipping school, and sneaking people in and out of my room in the middle of the night. I was fascinated by the occult. I let people use me. I didn't care; I was too numb. In May of my sophomore year, I set the school bathroom on fire.

When Dad and Danika confronted me, I was relieved. It had taken them a long time to figure it all out. I finally felt like I didn't have to keep walking alone.

I was expelled from school and I spent my summer with Danika. I took aluminum off the side of the house, gardened, went to the zoo, visited the fire marshal and went through counseling.

My eyes started to open; I let other people love me. I started to feel happy. I could see life from a better angle. I started to feel like I could do whatever I wanted to do.

• • •

It's been eleven years since I met that angry, hurt little girl one rainy evening in front of a modest country church. Amber and I have fought, ignored each other, wounded each other, wept together and healed together. Today I am so proud to call her my daughter. What a wonderful young woman she has grown into. She is always helping the wounded and defending the defenseless. God allowed me to grow up alongside Amber. She has made me strong and given me empathy. It's been quite the journey.

• • •

I'm glad I met Danika. I'm glad God gave me a strong mom. I spent years fighting her, but I finally appreciate all she's done for me. I have been given the skills to live life on my own. I couldn't have done it without Dad and Danika.

~Danika Cooley and Amber Nocole Vanderzanden

53

Towel Folding

That best academy, a mother's knee.
~James Russell Lowell

With a flip of her head, my daughter cast her beautiful copper-colored curls over one shoulder. She grabbed another towel from the laundry basket and folded it into thirds, then in half, the way I had taught her. She and her husband of less than a year took advantage of our invitation to bring their laundry along when they came for dinner.

Feeling a bit impatient, her husband grabbed one of the towels to help with the folding. He doubled it over twice and tossed it onto the pile.

"That's not how you fold a towel," she told him.

"Well, how do you fold it then?" he asked.

She picked up his towel, did the triple fold and then the double, and replaced it on the pile as I watched and tried to hide a smile.

As she picked up the next towel, she sat taller and with more authority. Her blue-green eyes flashed.

"That's how you fold a towel."

"Oh yeah," he answered. "And who taught you how to fold a towel?"

She jerked a thumb over her shoulder at me. "My mother did."

Now I was not only fighting to hide a smile but tears as well. Several weeks earlier my husband and I had accompanied our daughter to meet with her biological parents for the first time since she had been removed from their home at age three. At age six, she was available for adoption and we fell in love with her. The agency gave us quite a bit of background when we adopted her, including the names of her birth parents. The plan had always been to allow her to meet them when she became an adult.

When we met her birth mother, I found myself staring at an older version of my daughter—the same copper-colored hair, blue-green eyes, pale skin, and dimpled cheek. My dark hair, brown eyes, and olive skin emphasized my status as the adoptive mother. I wondered what other traits had been passed on to her by her birth parents. Was there anything of me in her?

With a jerk of her thumb on that afternoon of towel folding, she gave me the greatest gift—the answer to my question. She may not have gotten her hair or eye color or her curls from me, but she did learn how to fold a towel. Hopefully there are many more lessons learned, qualities shared, love infused that will not desert her. Although not genetic, little bits of me will stay with her forever.

~Karen Robbins

To My Other Mother

I would maintain that thanks are the highest form of thought, and that gratitude is happiness doubled by wonder.
~G.K. Chesterton

When you married my dad, I was twelve. We didn't meet then, you and I, for I lived with my mother. Dad emerged occasionally, a shadow from the past—a smiling face in a photo in Mom's cedar chest.

You made no difference in my life. You and Dad inhabited one corner of the earth, Mom and us kids another. We still ate peanut butter sandwiches for lunch every day, and wore holes through the soles of our shoes.

That first year, the shadow I knew as Dad visited; you waited in the car outside. For a long time afterwards, I cherished the memory of Dad's hug as we sat together on the sofa. Soon after that first visit, black patent leather shoes appeared in my closet. At first I wondered where they came from… until Mom said Dad had sent them. How special those shoes were! No laces to tie; instead, small pearl buttons decorated the clasps on the narrow straps. I thought of Dad whenever I wore them.

Six months later, when Dad visited, he took my face in his hands, studied my smile, and concluded that I needed braces on my teeth. Embarrassed, my smile shriveled; then Dad tickled my lips again, and I giggled. Once again, you waited in the car outside. That was the day we met. Mom practically dragged me to the car. "Can't you say hello?" she prodded. I dropped my head in adolescent shyness, and squeaked, "Hi."

You turned into a smile with a name that day, not just a lady in the car. As you and Mom chattered away like old friends, I wrestled with the problem of what I was supposed to call you.

Several weeks later, Mom made an appointment with the dentist. That dreaded dentist trip, a weekly worry, stretched into a two-month ordeal, but at least I didn't need braces.

Then there was the coat. Dad had never given me an Easter present, but shortly after I met you, a large box wrapped with brown grocery bags and string was delivered just in time for Easter. When Mom lifted the lid, I squealed with delight. There was the prettiest, softest, pink coat I'd ever seen—and it was mine. With the cool satin lining caressing my skin, I buried my hands in the deep pockets, and twirled around the living room. As if that wasn't enough, later that same day the florist delivered a pink and lavender corsage of flowers, which was also from Dad. It's funny that Dad had never thought of these things before marrying you.

Mom said this called for a celebration, and we went shopping together. Now that Mom didn't have to buy the coat I needed, she used the money instead for my very first new Easter outfit—a navy blue dress with a white lace collar.

Time passed. I graduated from high school, got my first job, married, had children, and eventually pursued a career. Contact with you was sporadic during these years. Although you didn't know it, I enjoyed the occasional times we spent together. I'm not sure why—perhaps I was curious about you back then. Of course, Mom was first in my life as always, but you never seemed to mind.

You were patient. Because you understood Mom's need to be my only mom, you waited behind the curtain, and whispered the cues to Dad. Many times in the midst of trouble and turmoil in my own home, Dad appeared on the scene just in time to make a difference. I remember the urgent financial crisis that resulted from my husband's incarceration, and Dad's help. About this time, God stepped into my life, bringing peace to quiet the storm. When a special delivery letter arrived from Dad with a generous check enclosed, my faith surged. Knowing you now, I can't help but wonder what role you played in each intervention.

My faith was shaken when my brother died, but I had to be strong for Mom's sake. When we gathered at the funeral parlor to stand at the casket, you stepped back again. Yet we were on one level. Grief only crawls; it cannot climb. You stood among the backdrop of my friends that day, waiting to help if you were needed.

Seven years later, my mother died. We stood together at the grave to mourn my loss. This time you were at my side.

Eventually, my own nest had emptied and I was alone. Because of my growing relationship with God over the years, I didn't mind the solitude so much. But you and Dad were there for me. I watched you shower gifts upon my grandchildren; if I tried to refuse the folded bill that Dad slipped into my hand, you protested. It didn't take long for me to discover that the "care packages" containing groceries, favorite junk foods, and treats for my doggie were your idea, and not Dad's. I could always depend on you for licorice and cheddar cheese crackers when I attended an out-of-town conference.

Dad and I grew closer in recent years thanks to you. You urged him to call if we hadn't been in touch; you planned your vacations to coincide with mine. In a way, you were still whispering the cues, right up to the time of his death, when again you and I stood together at a gravesite. I no longer stumble over the word "stepmother." You're my friend, and you have made a difference in my life.

~Penny Smith

The Magic of Mothers & Daughters

Away We Go!

*And that's the wonderful thing about family travel:
it provides you with experiences that will remain locked forever
in the scar tissue of your mind.*

~Dave Barry

The Great Navigators

Laughter is an instant vacation.
~Milton Berle

Barbara is my mother-in-law. Many mothers and daughters-in-law don't like each other. But not us. We love each other! We get along better than most mothers and daughters do. One thing we are great at is helping each other navigate our way through everything. Almost.

One summer, Barbara, my father-in-law Frank, their son (my husband) Mike and I went on vacation together to visit the Opryland Hotel and Resort in Nashville, TN. The hotel offers fourteen places to eat, many stores, three lounges, over a quarter of a mile of artificial waterways and over 2,800 hotel rooms, all under one huge, climate controlled glass roof!

This hotel was by far the largest I had ever seen—a miniature city all under glass! I loved how big it was. The four of us went to the reservation counter to check in. We were given our keys, our room numbers and two maps, with directions to our rooms. "To get to your room, simply follow the highlighted directions on this map," we were told by the sweet, smiling woman with a southern drawl who worked behind the counter. "Y'all can't miss it!"

After a quick stop at the nearest bar to keep ourselves hydrated in the Nashville summer, it was decided that the guys would go park the cars, get our luggage and meet us in the rooms. Barbara and I said we'd see them there shortly. We headed straight for the rooms, thinking we'd have plenty of time to freshen up before they got there. Before parting, we asked the guys if they wanted one of the maps, so they wouldn't get lost. "No," they said in their best southern drawl. "We can't miss it."

Off they went. Barbara and I headed toward the rooms, referring to our highlighted maps. First we walked passed the magnificent fountains and waterways, noticing the plants and flowers as we strolled. We happily noted where the stores were so we could return to shop later. We passed several of the eateries, browsing the menus along the way. How great it was to be at such a huge place that had absolutely everything.

On we went, finally finding the massive expanse of hotel rooms. "Whew, that was a long walk," Barbara exclaimed. But no worries, we were almost there. We looked at the room numbers on the doors as we passed, trying to see if they were getting bigger or smaller. "Uh-oh. I think we made a wrong turn somewhere," I said, giggling. We turned around and began walking back the way we had come, down what had to be the world's longest hallway.

After chuckling and walking for a long while, we looked at the numbers again. How did we keep missing the room? "Oh! We're on the wrong floor," Barbara said, laughing. We found the elevator, went up three floors, and turned left towards our room number as the arrow directed us to do. We glanced at the maps. We were back on track. We walked to the end of the world's second longest hallway and realized, much to our chagrin, that we had again missed our rooms. The numbers weren't even close.

Okay, we thought. It's time to get some help. Just then we passed by a house phone. I picked it up and told the operator the number of the house phone, so she could determine our location and asked her to please explain how to find our rooms starting from where we were currently located. "Sorry, I have no idea where those rooms are," she said, and hung up. Was she kidding? She worked at the hotel and she couldn't help us find our rooms. Were we doomed to walk the halls of Opryland... forever?

A little farther down this long, long hallway, a nice couple stopped us, showed us their highlighted map and asked if we could help them find their room. Barbara took one look at me and we both laughed so hard we were practically crying. The couple gave us a very nervous look and walked away from us as quickly as possible, probably thinking we must have escaped from the nearest loony bin.

Off the two of us loony birds went, continuing our walk through this never-ending, God forsaken hallway. Thirty minutes later and just when we were about to give up, we saw our dear, sweet husbands, down the hall, walking OUT of our hotel rooms!

"Where in the world have you been?" they asked. "We have been waiting for you for a long time." Barbara and I took one look at each other, doubled over and laughed harder than I think either of us has ever laughed before. We tried explaining, but we were laughing too hard to get any words out. Our husbands gave us the same look as the nice couple in the hallway but Barbara and I just kept laughing. We're still laughing about it today. And we're still loony!

I've been in Barbara's family now for twenty-two years, and while we may not be able to find our hotel rooms, we can navigate our way through just about everything else in life together!

~Crescent LoMonaco

A Changing
of the Guard

The best things in life are unexpected—because there were no expectations.
~Eli Khamarov

I am planning a trip to Greece," I told my daughter Alice on the phone. "I'm sitting here surrounded by guide books and getting more and more confused. I need to make some decisions and get this done before my frequent flyer miles expire."

"I wish I could join you," she said.

"Why don't you?" I exclaimed. "I'm pretty sure I have enough miles for both of us."

This was going to be my first trip since my husband died and I was nervous about traveling alone. I also was proud to be able to offer my daughter a grand vacation. Still in her twenties, she hadn't the means for much travel. I looked forward to showing her how to navigate in unfamiliar cultures. After all, I was a seasoned traveler, the perfect one to usher my neophyte daughter into a larger world.

Alice read my guidebook and decided we should island hop, using ferries between several Greek Islands. In her reading she discovered that locals with rooms to rent met every ferry and we could choose from among them when we got there, no reservations needed. I'd never traveled that way before. My husband and I always liked to have everything well planned beforehand, but Alice assured me it would all work out, especially if we traveled light.

I had to smile at her naïveté about packing. We were going to be gone for three weeks. We'd have to pack quantity and variety, since we didn't know what might be needed. My explanation did not impress her.

Alice was not pleased to see my two suitcases when we met at her place for our flight to Athens. She began to re-pack for me, eliminating items. In short order, I was down to one carry-on suitcase. I reminded her of how many days we'd be gone and she pointed out that a different outfit was not required for each day. If there weren't any laundry facilities, we could use the bathroom sink to rinse things out.

Rolling only one suitcase along as we queued up for boarding planes and ferries was so easy. Why had I never thought to travel that way before?

Our first stop was Crete. We roamed about, discovering ancient sites, new foods and scenic places. Alice heard of a tiny secluded island nearby with a fabulous beach and decided we should have a day of rest, basking on the warm sand and cooling off in the Mediterranean Sea. It was only a short hop by powerboat to get there. I readily agreed. What my daughter didn't mention was that this beach was not up to American standards of modesty. I admit to wobbling at the sight of the totally naked man who pulled our craft onto the sand and gallantly steadied me with his hand on my arm as I stepped out of the boat. I made a mental note to tell my daughter to gather more details before arranging to visit non-tourist places.

It didn't seem to bother the locals that I wore a bathing suit so I stopped caring that they did not. I lost myself in the endless stretch of soft sand and gentle sea. I could not remember having a more glorious day.

Back in our room, relaxed and refreshed, I thanked Alice for finding such a beautiful beach. It wasn't until much later that I remembered I'd meant to lecture her about knowing more before visiting places off the beaten path. The thought seemed so close-minded and silly now. Why travel if not to experience new things?

We didn't encounter the usual room-renters at the dock in

Santorini when our late afternoon ferry arrived. Earlier tourists had snapped up all of the rooms. We waited alone as long as we dared, but no further room hawkers appeared. Evening was approaching. We were tired and hungry. Now what?

Alice walked away from the dock and found a taxi. She talked to the driver and motioned for me to get in. He drove until we reached an old street, too narrow for his cab. He pointed to a tall, skinny building further up the road. "You go there," he said, asked for his fare and was off, uninterested in staying long enough to be sure there was a room available.

We pulled our suitcases over the cobblestones to the place he had indicated. The old woman who handed Alice a key pointed outside the building. Old, stone stairs wound endlessly up the right side of the structure. "What floor?" I asked my daughter, hoping she'd say the second. She shrugged and began climbing. "Key says ten. Watch for room numbers as we pass doors." I followed her up the stairs, my bag bumping behind me. I started counting as round and round we went. It seemed endless. I was getting dizzy from the constant turning. Up, up, up we went, until finally, as I reached the 110th stair, Alice called out, "We're here."

I stood stewing as she worked the key. What a ridiculous place. 110 stairs! Before I could tell Alice she shouldn't have relied on a cab driver's choice, she was inside and calling, "Mom, come look!"

She was on the balcony, staring down, her arms stretched wide. I trudged in and joined her. Our room was perched directly over the caldera, made luminous by the slowly setting sun. We settled into the balcony chairs and sat there transfixed for a long time, saying nothing.

Once the sky went dark with evening, we turned our thoughts to dinner and trotted down our 110 steps to find a restaurant nearby. We enjoyed a good dinner and congratulated ourselves on what a treasure of a room we had. Well fed and still feeling the glow of the caldera, I hardly noticed the trip back up to our room. I forgot about telling Alice how foolish she'd been to accept a room recommendation without knowing more about it. Instead I suggested we stay an extra day. I loved gazing into the caldera from our little nest above the world.

We were nearing the end of our island hopping adventure and would soon have to plan our return to Athens for the flight home. We had stopped for a cool drink at an outdoor café after a day of exploring Mykonos. Alice was explaining to me what she had planned for our final few days. As she talked, I remembered that this trip had been my idea, my chance to broaden my daughter's horizons. After all, I was the mother and that's what mothers do: guide their children and open new vistas to them. Yet here she was, taking charge again and deciding where we would go and what we would see.

"Whoa," I said. "Since when did we switch roles?"

Alice leaned back in her chair and gave me a patient smile, as one would a small child. "Oh Mom, that happened years ago. You just never noticed."

It's true. I don't know when or how our relationship changed. But it did. I'm not complaining though. I'm grateful for the switch — now that I'm used to it.

~Marcia Rudoff

High Five

There are only two emotions in a plane: boredom and terror.
~Orson Welles

"Hey, Mary, do you think the fact that our flight number adds up to a five means we're in for a dilly of a ride?" I asked my daughter as we entered the seating area for our flight home. Being the anxious flyer that I am, I'm always looking for ways to reassure myself that everything will be okay. I had learned in my numerology class that numbers are believed to have a certain energy; fives being change in some form. I looked to Mary for some reassurance.

"Nah, we're good; fives just mean change. As long as there's no turbulence," she added confidently. "I just want to get home safely to Gary and Boogie," she said referring to her husband Gary and her cat.

I was eager to see my husband too. This was the first time I had been apart from him since our younger days when he travelled for his job.

We had gone to Silverdale, Washington for a week to visit my oldest daughter Jennifer. She was experiencing some health challenges and was also going to be without any adult company on her birthday. She is a military wife with just her young daughter living at home while her husband is stationed in Bahrain. Mary and I had decided she needed cheering up, so we decided to fly up and visit. A little "girlie" party might help.

Now, we sadly said goodbyes to Jennifer after our week of good times, and headed off to the security check area. Upon boarding our plane, we settled into our seats, me by the window and Mary on the aisle. I have always been an anxious flyer and experienced panic attacks on several flights. Having Mary along helped allay my fears. I hoped she could cope with me if they got the best of me. Usually that entailed talking to me non-stop to distract me. As we buckled up, Mary pulled out her headphones and plugged into the TV jack by her seat. I tried to get comfortable and pulled out my crossword puzzle.

Wind and rain pelted the jet as it started taxiing down the runway, and as we lifted off, Mary grabbed my hand and squeezed it until my rings hurt.

"Why the death grip?" I asked her.

"Oh, I hate this part," Mary responded. I noticed her face was white as a sheet.

"This is my favorite part," I commented. What had happened to my pillar of strength? She was supposed to be the one I leaned on. I chalked it up to a momentary lapse of confidence and settled back to enjoy the ride as best I could.

The flight attendant proceeded with her "if we have to ditch or crash" lecture, which I usually ignore, as it makes my anxiety worse.

"Anyone flying with us for the first time today?" she asked. My ears perked up.

"Oh, I see several hands back there. Me too," she replied. I whipped my head around to Mary.

"Is she kidding?" I asked with a tinge of panic in my voice.

"I sure hope so," Mary replied, appearing a little ruffled.

We flew on for about forty minutes when I heard Mary say, "Damn television."

"It says it's looking for a signal," I said.

"Mom, it's been a long time. We should have a signal by now. This happened last time too. The flight attendant just needs to reboot the system," Mary said knowingly. She rang for help and proceeded to tell the flight attendant what needed to be done.

Ah, I thought, now that's my girl. Taking charge and in control again. I relaxed a little.

The system was rebooted, and just as Mary tuned into a channel she liked the plane shuddered. We dropped a little and the seat belt sign lit again.

"Oh, oh, we're going to crash!" Mary said louder than she realized. She just kept repeating this mantra and I yanked her earphones off.

"Mary, not so loud. We're fine. Just a little turbulence."

"Oh no, I hate turbulence," she repeated with a look of terror on her face.

"Mary, just breathe deep. Here," I said, placing my hand on her tummy.

"Breathe from here, feel your breath slowing going in and out."

"I need a drink," she replied.

"No you don't," I said, taking charge. "You just need to relax. Keep breathing and think of a happy place. Picture yourself in a nice place with Gary. Try Hawaii."

We continued this technique for a while. As I talked Mary down from her anxiety, we climbed to 38,400 feet, according to the map on the screen, and the pilot finally found a spot that was smooth.

"Wow," I said. "That was some experience."

Mary smiled weakly. "Thanks, Mom. I should have known you, of all people, would know what to do."

"Just a little trick I learned," I said, smiling warmly at my daughter. I was the mom in charge again and I felt closer to my daughter than I ever had.

In no time we were touching down in Long Beach and walking through the airport towards the passenger-loading zone in front.

As we stood there waiting for our men to arrive, I wondered if we would ever find an opportunity to fly together again. Our husbands showed up and we reached out and hugged each other goodbye.

"Been nice flying with you," I said with a lump in my throat.

Mary hesitated as she hugged me back. "Mom, if you're not busy, let's go back to Jennifer's for your birthday next February."

"I would like that a lot," I said as I mused… maybe fives do mean change… the good kind.

~Sallie A. Rodman

Tent Lessons

It always rains on tents. Rainstorms will travel thousands of miles,
against prevailing winds for the opportunity to rain on a tent.
~Dave Barry

When my daughter and I planned our backpack trip through Britain and Ireland we debated taking a tent. Maryellen thought it might be too late in the year for camping out. And why carry around all that extra weight when youth hostels provide a perfectly adequate roof and a bed? Yet I clung to the image of the two of us falling asleep under a full moon as gentle waves lapped on grassy shores. While confident that after one idyllic night she'd see it my way, I promised, if it didn't work out, we'd visit our friends Sella and Bill in Northumbria to drop off the tent and related camping gear.

Our mother/daughter project arose from conversations around the kitchen table. We were both at a crossroad and we agreed to put our lives on hold for three months, hoping a physical challenge in a different environment would provide the space we needed for introspection. For nineteen-year-old Maryellen it was college and a need to discover what she wanted from the experience. For me, a faltering marriage, stale job, and the breast cancer I'd been living with for three years.

We pitched our tent for the first time in late September at the northernmost tip of Scotland. Having missed the last ferry across the Pentland Firth to the Orkney Islands, we set out from the ferry dock in search of the local youth hostel, only to run into the perfect tent setting—a park and campground on the cliff above the docks, complete with island vistas.

"I'm afraid it might be awfully windy so high up, Mom."

We could nearly touch the stars when we crawled into the tent and zippered it closed. But sleep came to an abrupt halt when howling winds shook our "bedroom."

"Mom, I'm going out to tie down the fly before it blows away."

"Want me to come with you?"

"No! Stay here. You're the ballast."

The next day, while all ferries were canceled due to high winds, Maryellen adjusted lines, prepared new ones, and pounded in sturdier stakes to keep us grounded for another night on the cliff. If we lived through it, I'd never again suggest pitching a tent on a rise above the sea.

The next day we moved south and joined a group of hikers camped at the foot of Ben Nevis. I believed the red sky at night forecast a fair morning hike to the summit.

"Don't get your hopes up, Mom. I heard those guys next to us say rain's coming in."

It poured. Before daybreak we gave up plans for climbing Britain's tallest mountain, lit the alcohol stove and shared a cup of tea.

"Next time, at the first mention of rain, I vote we pull up stakes and head for the nearest shelter." A feeble smile from Maryellen acknowledged my suggestion.

In late October western Ireland was still enjoying mild air from the Gulf Stream. "How many more opportunities like this are we going to have?" I asked as we approached a tent and caravan park near the mouth of the Shannon River. The wind was calm, the skies clear and we had the place to ourselves.

"There's no privacy here, Mom. Doesn't it look too exposed to you?"

After setting up camp, we sat reading at our picnic table when a motorcycle gang roared into our space. Beer bottles crashed and broke against the metal refuse containers separating our tables. Despite my disappearing glares, overtures were made. Would my daughter like to go for a ride?

At her signal I followed Maryellen into our tent where she unsheathed her Swiss Army knife. I mimicked the move and together we froze in attack position until midnight when the mob thundered off, leaving me alone with my guilt. "I should never have let us stay here. I'm sorry I put you in danger."

"That's okay. You're learning."

By mid-November we were in Wales where it was dark at four o'clock. The night before our visit to Tintern Abbey we planned to stay at a youth hostel in the village of Chepstow, leaving only a short hike the next morning to the river valley of Wordsworth's romantic ode. The map pinpointed our hostel directly across the street from the Chepstow Downs, a racetrack on the outskirts of town. Intermittent neighing suggested we were in the right place, though the hostel clearly was not. Despite fatigue and the late hour, we'd have to trudge more than a mile back to town in search of a bed and breakfast.

If I hadn't been desperate to get the load off my back and lie down I never would have spotted the large hole in the track's chain link fence. Without hesitation I dropped my pack. "I'm going through. Hand me our stuff. We can put up the tent on the grass in the middle of the ring."

But Maryellen stood her ground. "I'll do this on one condition, Mom. Tomorrow we take the train to Sella and Bill's and dump the damn tent."

"Yes!"

~Ann Barnett

Broadway Follies

I never make stupid mistakes. Only very, very clever ones.
~John Peel

The smell of popcorn permeated the air. Bright yellow cabs honked as they whizzed down the streets. The sights, sounds and smells of the Big Apple overwhelmed me as I walked into the Ambassador Theater on 49th Street. I could hardly contain my excitement. I was going to see *Chicago* on Broadway! I had seen the film version of the musical four times in the movie theater. I bought the DVD the day of its release, and watched it so many times that, if it had been a VHS tape I would have worn it out.

My friends had chipped in to buy me a ticket for my nineteenth birthday. They also bought an extra ticket so that my mother could go with me.

Standing in a long line to enter the theater, I could hear the music coming from inside. I was clutching the white envelope that held our tickets in one hand, and grabbing my mom's arm with the other. I felt more like a kid entering Disney World than a college student about to have a sophisticated theater experience.

We finally arrived at the front of the line, a large man dressed in a security uniform looked at our tickets, ripped them and gave them back. We went into the clean, expensive-looking building and elbowed our way through the crowded lobby. Before we entered the theater, an usher looked at our tickets again and directed us to our seats. We went up a flight of red-carpeted stairs to the upper level.

My mom found our seats easily. They were in the first row of the balcony section. Even more excited than I was before, I reveled in the fact that we had an outstanding view, and then became engrossed in my *Playbill*.

A few moments later, an elderly couple approached us. The woman, who was barely five feet tall and had huge glasses and a big pearl necklace, was clinging to her thin, sickly-looking husband.

"You're sitting in our seats!" the man said, waving his tickets in our faces. The veins in his forehead looked like they were going to explode as he yelled at us.

My usually calm and polite mother jumped up and told the man that these were definitely our seats. The usher had even seated us, my mom said. The elderly man just shook his head and said again that these seats belonged to him and his wife.

In the meantime, a different usher came up and asked what the problem was. We told him that we both had tickets for these seats.

"Let me see both sets of tickets," he said in an authoritative voice, crossing his arms over his chest.

My mother and I gave him our tickets, as did the elderly couple. After examining them for a few moments, the usher laughed and shook his head.

"Yeah, you all have tickets for these seats, but yours are for tomorrow," he said, turning to my mother and me.

I slapped my hand to my forehead, horrified. It was then that I realized that I had never really looked at the tickets, and neither had my mother. I had somehow confused the dates and was sure Tina had told me the show was on Saturday. But sure enough, after we got our tickets back we saw that they did say "Sunday" on them.

We were mortified. My mother explained to the usher that we were from Pennsylvania, had taken a bus to get there and would not be able to come back the next day for the show. The usher told us to speak with the house manager.

After explaining the situation to her, she told us we could stand at the back of the theater, on the orchestra level. So I stood in my uncomfortable heels for the first ninety minutes, not even able to tap my feet to "All That Jazz" because I was so embarrassed. Not only was I sure that blisters were forming on my feet, but I couldn't see a thing from where we were standing. Roxie Hart looked like a little blond blur to me. I longed for the view we would have had from our seats in the balcony.

But our embarrassing mishap had its benefit. Surprisingly, during intermission, the house manager came up to us and said, "Two people in the second row never showed up. Feel like sitting down?"

We couldn't believe it as an usher took us to the second row of the orchestra level. We sat in the comfortable red seats, turned to each other and laughed at our bizarre luck. A heavy man sitting next to me turned and said in an excited voice, "Guys, you missed the first act! It was amazing!" I had to stifle my giggle and resist the urge to tell him about my mistake.

~Amanda Koehler

A Better View

Rule number one is, don't sweat the small stuff.
Rule number two is, it's all small stuff.
~Robert Eliot

As my two-year-old daughter and I arrive at the airport on a cold January morning, I am thinking that in the next ten hours practically anything could happen. If ever there is a time to fear one's own child, it's at the outset of a full day of air travel.

She could play quietly with the tantalizing distractions I've packed. She could be so mollified by going up in the air, in an actual airplane, that she sits quietly, eventually slipping into a nap. Or she could refuse her toys along with any of two dozen snacks I carry, become over-stimulated, and begin to scream and flail and cry.

Traveling with children takes some getting used to. After nearly three years as a mother, I don't think I've adapted yet.

Up until I gave birth, I believed that a vacation was supposed to be easier than regular life. The first time I traveled with Miss Libby, however, I instantly found myself wanting to sprint back to the tiresome simplicity of my own home, where the outlets were covered with safety protectors and the sleeping arrangements were blessedly segregated. As my sister puts it, vacationing with children is your regular life, only harder... but with a better view.

If there is one thing I know after nearly three years of living, loving and traveling with this small person, it's that on this journey, as on all others, I should expect the unexpected. Most everything I've planned for won't occur, and things I'd never been able to imagine, will.

So, once we're in the air and my daughter refuses to take a nap, I am not surprised. When she chooses to eat only cookies, I hand them over. When, a thousand miles west of the Oregon coastline, she starts hitting me on the head with her open hand I tell myself I saw that coming. After all, the high fructose corn syrup has just kicked in and we're strapped into 24A and 24B. I feel like having a little tantrum myself.

As the blows rain down, it occurs to me that perhaps my greatest challenge on this journey is also my greatest teacher. Aren't the secrets to a successful vacation welcoming new experiences and doing whatever one wants? And aren't those the two mantras that Libby daily embraces, right down to her tiny red polished toes?

In terms of Libby's search for the fresh and the indulgent, today hasn't been any different. When the plane started taxiing out of Redmond, she was doing her very favorite thing: watching my parenting godsend, the portable DVD player.

So what can I learn here? I am determined to succeed at this vacation. I haven't visited Hawaii in years, I've left Libby's eleven-month-old sister (and my doting spouse) behind, and we're destined for Grandma's (and plenty of help for me). This is the closest I'm getting to "time off" for quite a while.

Embracing the new will mean rolling with the punches (even the literal ones). Doing as I wish will require letting Libby do as she wishes, because pleasure does not result from wars waged against one's own progeny. Also, I will have to stay alert to the arrival of the easy moments, remembering to enjoy them.

I realize that Libby's attention has reverted to *Finding Nemo*, and therefore one of those easy moments is now. I crack open my mystery and sit back with my seltzer water and lime.

An hour before landing, Libby purposefully shuts her movie player, announces, "I want to take a nap," plops her head in my lap, and falls asleep.

The unexpected and the pleasurable. These shall be our themes for the week.

Once we're settled at Grandma's, Libby refuses the fancy stickers and ABC puzzle I packed for her and instead plays with my mother's turkey baster, refrigerator magnets and calculator. Her special vacation T-shirts never leave the suitcase; instead she wears pajamas at all times and everywhere, including the zoo. Her new sunglasses are tried on and discarded. The bright new cherry-speckled swimsuit—which, incidentally she wore for three straight days back home where it was twenty degrees Fahrenheit—will be worn exactly once before the superior appeal of the beach in one's birthday suit wins out.

I paste a dazed grin on my face and acquiesce. I become that mother whose child runs barefoot at the aquarium and consumes cereal for every meal. In exchange for these slovenly standards, I get a child stricken with delight at her mother's leniency and therefore, the opportunity to collapse in a pool chair, one eye cracked, while she picks all of the flowers off the bougainvillea.

When she naps, I don't do the dishes. I don't do the laundry. I don't read an important novel. I don't write. I read trashy fiction. I stare stupidly into the middle distance.

It's the best vacation we've ever had. We are two girls, far from home and feeling frisky. At the beach, on our last night, I drink two Mai Tais while Libby holds the hem of her tie-dyed dress up around her head and spins, singing, "The sun is going down! Down!" And it does, and it's better than any romantic sunset I can recall.

Eventually, the good times come to an end. As Libby launches a full-throttle meltdown because I won't let her get on the airplane in her pajamas, I glimpse the messy habits I now have to overcome. A week ago, this fit would have sent me into a panic. Now, I take a breath and wait for whatever will come during the fifteen-hour journey in front of us. I bet that, somewhere in there, I'll be able to find the pleasurable and the unexpected.

~Kim Cooper Findling

My Travel Companion

A daughter is a gift of love.
~Author Unknown

Our son, Senior Airman Matthew J. Rompca, and his wife Sunny had recently had a baby—Azriel Jadyn—in Germany where he is stationed at Ramstein Air Force Base. He has been stationed there almost a year and we had not seen him in all that time. He desperately wanted us to come for a visit. I am by nature a homebody and very reluctant to fly. The prospect of flying alone on a journey of this length was mind boggling, as my husband, Len, was unable to get away due to work. I finally relented and made my travel plans.

About two weeks before I was due to leave, Len and I had the opportunity to visit our daughter, Annemarie, at Indiana University. Annemarie, our only daughter, was the last bird to leave the nest. It seemed like only yesterday that I was tucking her into bed with her favorite teddy bear. Being the only two girls in a house full of men, we learned to stick together. And now she was a lovely young woman, off on her own.

We had a great parents weekend. We cheered at the football game, ate at marvelous restaurants and hung around together laughing and teasing each other. We met several of her new friends and it was fascinating to observe the young woman we had raised relish her new environment.

Annemarie is very intuitive and she knew the journey to Germany was weighing heavily on my mind. Not only am I a nervous flyer, but two weeks away from Len and home would be a first for me.

After the weekend, it was time for us to make our drive back home. Annemarie presented me with a gift bag and told me I could not open it until she texted me in the car. I reluctantly left her and we started home. After about a half hour of driving, the following text finally came:

> *Tuck me in your arms so tight*
> *While you travel through the night*
> *Across that great blue sea*
> *To visit AJ, Matt and Sunny.*
> *Please take me to the ones I dearly miss*
> *And bring me back a hug and kiss.*
> *So I'm yours to borrow*
> *To keep you from sorrow*
> *As you travel alone, so brave*
> *To make the memories you will save.*
> *Open!*

Inside the gift bag, was her (and my) favorite stuffed bear, Kiki. It was the only stuffed animal that made the cut to go to college with her. Kiki has been on Annemarie's bed for as long as I can recall. I remember holding Kiki while I was sitting in her room chatting with her while she would be getting ready for a date. Or Annemarie would hold Kiki while she bared her soul to me about friends or boys and the trials of life.

Kiki traveled in my arms to Germany. This "stuffed expression" of Annemarie's love and support sat on my bed for the entire trip, reminding me of the importance of family and the connections that are made and never broken. I was able to share this bear with my new granddaughter, creating even more memories. Annemarie's selfless-ness in lending me her bear and writing me the poem was one of the most heartwarming, loving things I have ever experienced.

~Patricia M. Rompca

The Stormy Cape Cod Day

If you don't like something change it; if you can't change it,
change the way you think about it.
~Mary Engelbreit

You're going on vacation together? But you work together. If I worked with my mother I would need a vacation away from her."

This remark came from a very nice woman who was a regular customer at my book and gift shop. Her facial expression revealed complete bafflement that I had my mother working with me several days a week and chose to spend the only week I had off each year going on vacation with her.

"We live in the same house too," I added. "I live downstairs from her."

The customer's eyes bugged out and her mouth gaped open. I was afraid if I revealed any more about the close relationship I had with my mother, the poor woman would have a seizure. Mom was standing beside me, grinning with pride.

I truly felt bad for the woman. I had known quite a few women who dreaded being around their mothers. I couldn't imagine that. Mom and I certainly had our differences but we enjoyed each other's company.

This would be our second visit to Cape Cod. On the two and

a half hour drive down, Mom and I reminisced about the previous year. The weather had been picture perfect. Our room overlooked the ocean and the sand dunes, which had patches of tall grass that swayed in the breeze. The effect had been hypnotic, calming and relaxing.

This year the weather report indicated rain. The rain was intermittent during the drive down so we held out hope for sunny skies. When we arrived at the motel, the rain stopped long enough for us to unpack the car. We interpreted that as a favorable sign. After all, weather reports have been known to be wrong.

We woke up the next morning to the sound of rain—not the gentle pitter-patter of raindrops but the pounding noise of a deluge combined with the roar of the ocean. I opened the drapes and confirmed what my ears already knew; there was a torrential downpour, whipping winds, and ferocious waves battering the shoreline. According to the local weather report, the downpour would last the entire day.

Mom and I were both disappointed but we decided to enjoy our vacation despite the weather. "Let's open the drapes all the way and move the table and chairs in front of the sliding glass door," I suggested. "Then we can watch the waves."

"After we go out for breakfast, let's stop somewhere to pick up some snacks," added my mother. Mom had a notorious sweet tooth and as for me, well, I am my mother's daughter.

After our excursion into the wild weather, we returned to our motel room, soaked to the bone. We changed into dry clothes while laughing and giggling about how drenched we got while successfully protecting our precious survival supplies from getting wet too. Our supplies included cheese and crackers, sodas, and assorted pastries and candy. We also bought an Italian grinder for me, and a ham and cheese grinder for Mom. We stored the grinders in the small refrigerator in our room. This was our backup plan for supper if the rain didn't let up.

Mom laid out some of the snacks and two sodas on the table and we each took out a paperback book. We settled into our chairs, books in hand, snacks at the ready. We had a close-up view of the powerful waves smacking the shore and the torrents of rain. It was glorious!

Between reading, snacking, and enjoying the view, Mom and I talked. Oddly, though most of that day is clearly etched in my mind, I don't remember what we talked about but I know that our conversations deepened our mother/daughter bond. Rather than developing cabin fever by suppertime, we were relieved that the rain kept pouring down, giving us an excuse to stay in and continue to share this special time with each other.

The following morning, we woke to find that the rain was slowing down. We went for breakfast and replenished our survival supplies despite the weather report predicting a sunny afternoon. This included a trip to a bookstore as we were nearly finished with our books and wanted to stock up on a few more. By the time we got back to our room and unloaded our supplies, including two more grinders, the weather was clearing. We spent the rest of the day visiting favorite places, shopping, walking along the beach, and having supper at a very nice restaurant famous for its seafood. The grinders became a late-night snack.

Mom and I made our annual Cape Cod trip a tradition and we have now gone six times. The only time that we have had bad weather was that second year. But it was that stormy day, stuck inside a motel room, that we both agree was one of the most beautiful experiences we've shared as mother and daughter.

~Dianne Bourgeois

To Russia, With Mom

Anything I've ever done that ultimately was worthwhile...
initially scared me to death.
~Betty Bender

My mother walked behind me, clutching her thin, white sheet close to her body, covering her front. I was carrying mine loosely over one arm, naked apart from a stretchy pair of slippers the staff from the Sandunovskiye Baths had provided in the changing room. Through small windows cut into the wooden doors of the main sauna room, we could see half a dozen elderly Russian women paired up and hitting each other with bunches of birch sticks.

"Cool," I said, mentally comparing it to the public baths I'd used in Japan, or the bath I'd dipped into in Budapest. This Russian version was certainly not as pretty, but it made up for it with interest: sweet old babushkas thrashing their hot skin with sticks were something you didn't see every day.

"I don't think I'll go in the sauna," my mother said, squatting down on a small stool.

"Come on, we have to experience it!" I said, and started scrubbing my arms in a sink.

My mother sat firm, not letting the sheet fall from her chest. "I'll come with you into the pool afterwards."

"Whatever." I grabbed my sheet and went over to the sauna. An older Russian woman looked at me without smiling and then ignored me. I let the heat of the sauna sweat out my frustration with my mother, who didn't seem to be making the most of our trip so far.

I had been living abroad for about five years when I had the idea of taking my mother on a trip to Russia. It was partly her fault that I'd fallen for the country in the first place. When I was a kid, she'd finally acted on her lifelong dream of trying to learn the Russian language, and she used to teach me basic phrases while she did her homework. Her fascination with Russia didn't have an obvious cause, but once I'd traveled across the country on the Trans-Siberian Railway while moving between jobs in Asia and Europe, I was determined to take her there sometime. Moscow and Saint Petersburg were two of the most captivating cities I'd ever visited, and I was positive my mother would love them too.

It was on our second day in Moscow that we'd decided to head to the Sandunovskiye Baths. I hadn't made it there on my first trip, and I wanted my mother to experience this aspect of culture that was missing at home. As I sat in the sauna, I reflected on my first public bathing experience in Japan, when I had felt quite nervous about being naked in front of strangers. I guessed that was bothering my mother now, but she was in her sixties, and normally didn't care what people thought, so I was still a little annoyed.

We didn't talk much on our way back from the baths. Our accommodation was a homestay arrangement, spending four nights with a Russian woman who spoke a little English, and gave us pancakes for breakfast each day. We had bought some bread and cheese to prepare a light evening meal, and not long after, I went to bed.

The next day, we had planned a trip out to the Golden Ring town of Sergiev Posad. The month before, my mother had sent me the link to a website offering guided bus tours that would take us there, but I'd told her we could just get there on a local bus for a fraction of the cost and have a lot more fun. Following my guidebook, we took a metro ride out to the All-Russian Exhibition Center, a kind of permanent trade fair, where there was also a bus station where we would find the bus for the hour-long trip out to Sergiev Posad.

Guidebooks are great at giving advice that is difficult to follow.

We wandered up and down the row of buses and checked every sign for a mention of Sergiev Posad. I was a lot slower at reading the signs in Cyrillic than my mother, but even she needed a minute or two at each sign to see whether the name of our destination was there or not.

"I'm going to start asking people," my mother told me.

She'd practiced a few Russian sentences on our friendly home-stay host, but just the same, her Russian was fairly limited. I meekly followed as she walked up to people waiting at various bus stops and asked them something; the only bit I could understand was "Sergiev Posad." The first couple of people just stared at her, and it wasn't clear if they couldn't understand the question or simply didn't know the answer. That didn't put her off; my mother just marched along to the next bus stop and asked again. By the time she got into an animated conversation with a middle-aged Russian man, I had lagged behind and caught up only as I heard her saying "spasiba," thank you.

"I think there's a bus at stop five, leaving at eleven o'clock," she told me. "Well, I'm pretty sure that's what he said."

I checked my watch, and it was ten to eleven. "Worth a try then," I said, and we walked down to the fifth stop. When the bus pulled up, my mother used her basic Russian skills to ask the driver if he was headed for Sergiev Posad, and he nodded. We headed off into the Russian countryside.

Our day out in Sergiev Posad was fantastic. Apart from experiencing a typical Russian country town, a lot different from Moscow, we also walked out to the Holy Trinity church complex, an utterly photogenic collection of buildings where the highlight was the Assumption Cathedral. It had bright blue onion domes decorated with large gold stars, as though they'd been awarded by a teacher for good work.

Thanks to my mother's abilities, we easily got the bus back to Moscow late in the afternoon, and splurged for dinner at a restaurant recommended by our homestay host. I held up my glass of red wine and toasted my mother. "To your great Russian skills, which got us to that beautiful town today." She smiled.

Our trip went smoothly after that. When I thought about it, probably none of my friends had mothers who would take a low-budget backpacking trip around Russia with them. My mother might not have been brave about being naked in public, and she hadn't backpacked across half the world, but that didn't mean she wasn't the perfect person to travel with.

~Amanda Kendle

The Magic of Mothers & Daughters

Chapter 7

Learning from Each Other

Remember, we all stumble, every one of us.
That's why it is a comfort to go hand in hand.

~Emily Kimbrough

Fearless

There are two lasting bequests we can give our children.
One is roots. The other is wings.
~Hodding Carter, Jr.

will never go whitewater rafting or skiing. I won't even go on amusement park rides that leave the ground. But I have a daughter who will do all of that and more. From the time my daughter, April, tumbled off the furniture and gave herself a black eye as a preschooler, she has possessed a fearlessness that I admire.

When she was four years old, I took her and her cousins to an amusement park. I'm the person who holds the jackets while everyone else goes on the rides. I let my niece and nephew take April on the teacup ride, which throws a person around a little too much for my taste. April staggered off the ride with a big grin on her face. "That was fun," she gasped. "I have to do that again." A daredevil was born.

I put her in gymnastics classes about that same time because I was tired of her leaping and tumbling off the furniture, especially after giving herself that black eye. She excelled on the trampoline and her instructor said that she could be a real champ. She excelled at swimming, skiing, tennis and anything else she put her mind to. She has been a dancer all of her life. When she started going to camp during the summer, I had to sign a "special" permission slip that allowed her to climb mountains and go on difficult obstacle courses.

I often wondered, as she grew up, where her adventurous streak came from. Her father was a businessman, very traditional. My career as a social worker and sometimes writer provided little adventure for my life. We were not talented athletes.

Being the mother of an overachiever, I was one of the moms chauffeuring the kids to practice or school events. My daughter was growing up in a different world than I had. When I was a little girl, black children didn't swim or ski or play tennis. Those opportunities weren't available to us. My child embraced all of these new opportunities and took me along for the ride.

In middle school, April was recruited for a prep school, the Phillips Academy, a prestigious boarding school in Andover, Massachusetts that everyone calls "Andover." I went to the Andover meeting with April, listened to the representative and gathered the written materials. April was very excited. I said nothing, but my heart was sinking. I could not lose my only child at fourteen. Who would guide her through her teen years and tell her about boys and dating? Fortunately, peer pressure won out. All her friends were going to high school locally and eventually she decided that was what she wanted too.

High school was a busy time. April got good grades, never missed a dance and was on Cass Tech High School's winning tennis team. She was also very active in her church youth group. Initially she talked about wanting to be a journalist, a foreign correspondent so that she could travel all over the world. My mama mind was saying, "Don't go overseas. I don't want you to get hurt or arrested," but again I kept quiet. April finally settled on public health and talked of going to foreign countries to help the poor and the sick. Again, I said nothing.

When it came time for April to make a decision on a college, staying in Michigan was not an option. She went on the Black College Tour and came home raving about several schools. I finally spoke up and vetoed Texas and Florida as options. "Those are too far away," I told her. "If you get sick or hurt, I need to be able to get to you right away." April acquiesced. She finally settled on Howard University in Washington, DC, only an hour and fifteen minutes away by airplane.

My family was so proud. She was the first one in our family to go to a school out of state.

That was ten years ago. April just bought her first home, in Maryland. She never came back to Michigan to live.

I was talking to a participant at a writer's conference recently and we were comparing notes on our daughters. Her daughter was just entering college and I was talking about how adventurous April was. I told her about April going whitewater rafting last year and how she had gone to a spa in Arizona recently by herself. She was telling me about how fabulous the spa was and how she was going horseback riding and hiking the next day. I told her to have fun, but then my mama mind kicked in. "Don't go out by yourself at night and make sure you lock your door," I warned. April just laughed and told me she would be careful.

"I admire her fearlessness," I told my companion. "I would never have had the nerve to do the things she's done."

Knowing my background, my companion said quietly, "That's because she has a safety net. She knows that you'll be there if she falls. You didn't have that growing up." She was referring to the fact that my mother died when I was eleven. Despite being raised by very loving grandparents, there was always a void in my life.

My friend's observation wowed me. I had never thought in those terms. I could think of myself as an anchor, not a scaredy-cat. My cautiousness had given April roots and wings, what we all want for our children. And who knows? That spa thing sounds pretty good. I just might give that a try — by myself one day.

~Sharon M. Stanford

The Strong One

What do girls do who haven't any mothers
to help them through their troubles?
~Louisa May Alcott

am the strong one. I'm the daughter who made it through the news that her baby had suffered a stroke at birth; hypothyroid disease followed at age eleven, and type I diabetes at age twelve. My daughter is now a college freshman with a sense of humor, excellent grades, a job, and a kind, compassionate nature.

I am the strong one. At age forty-six, I can run a mile in fifteen minutes, regularly walk five miles, help my dad get firewood, work a forty-hour week, plus keep house, do yard work, give blood, care for family and pets, and lecture at church.

Then one day I stopped being the strong one. The flu hit me at the end of October. November brought pneumonia and less than two weeks later a mass was found on my kidney.

The alien thing inside me was assessed on a scale from one to four, one being a cyst, four being cancerous. Mine was a four. I was okay. I couldn't control what was inside me, but I could control my attitude. After all, I am the strong one.

Of all the people in my life—husband, daughter, dad, siblings, friends—I dreaded sharing the news with my mom the most. Mom's a champion worrier. She sports high blood pressure as a result. She's also plagued with other health issues. Mom's always been there for

220   Learning from Each Other : The Strong One

me in the past, but I've never really given her much cause for concern. Would she be strong enough to handle my bad news?

I knew she would cry and she did. But what I forgot was where I acquired my strength. Mom's a five-year survivor of breast cancer. It was Mom who taught me to believe in God, to believe in miracles, to believe in others, and to believe in myself. Her tears weren't a sign of weakness, but a sign of love—love that made our whole family strong.

After the removal of my kidney and the subsequent biopsy, I was found to have an abscess... not cancer. Thanksgiving this year was truly for the giving of thanks.

When I needed help during my recovery, there was Mom, the strong one. My mother taught me that being strong doesn't always mean standing by oneself, alone. Strength is asking and accepting help, too.

~Jackie Allison

"Seriously...how well do we really know Mom?"

Reprinted by permission of Dan Reynolds
and Cartoonresource.com ©2011

Thunderstorms

A mother's arms are made of tenderness and children sleep soundly in them.
~Victor Hugo

I've been afraid of thunderstorms since I was seven and a tree fell into our house during an afternoon storm. After that, a flash of lightning or a rumble of thunder would send me running to the one person I knew would comfort me, my mother. As soon as I would step into her room, she'd move over, giving me half of her bed. I always wondered how, even in a deep sleep, she knew I was there. She said, "What kind of mother would I be if I couldn't sense my child's presence?"

It had always been just the two of us. I was a rarity in my neighborhood—an only child. Of course there were those that pitied me, but I never felt like I got the short end of the stick... I had my mom. She would build snowmen with me during the winter and have water fights with me during the sticky New York City summers. She taught me how to jump double-dutch, had flashlight wars with me during blackouts and "drank" the "penny tea" I served at my tea parties. Over the years, we'd become so comfortable with our duet that becoming a trio seemed unnecessary. Who needed a younger sister when I had her?

That all changed when I was seventeen. I had just finished my junior year of high school with almost straight A's and was preparing to send those grades to my dream colleges. I would be eighteen soon. My dreams of learning to drive, getting out of New York and finding freedom were about to come true and I couldn't wait. Then one day I came home from work and as I was settling in, my mom said two words I had never expected to come out of her mouth: "I'm pregnant."

I could barely comprehend what she had just said. Our lives were just returning to normal after the sudden death of her long-time boyfriend. And she was planning on bringing a baby into the world?

I could see my future changing before my eyes. I was going to become an eighteen-year-old babysitter, still taking the train, having to attend a city college and not an out-of-state college I had worked so hard for. My confusion turned to anger when I found out who the father was. He was a few years younger than my mom with children of his own. He immediately proclaimed that the baby wasn't his.

"How could you do this?" I yelled. "After years of telling me not to get caught up with an immature guy, you went and did just that and brought a baby into the mix!" As I saw the tears fall from my mother's eyes, I knew I had gone too far. So I walked out of the room and for the next two days, I barely said two words to my mother.

Then a thunderstorm blew into New York City. I jumped out of bed, as usual, and headed towards my mother's room. Then I remembered our fight, but after some hesitation, I walked into her room and she instantly slid over in the bed. I climbed in and as I lay there listening to my mother breathe, it dawned on me that my mother's heart was even bigger than I thought because she was able to comfort me even when I was being a selfish brat.

There I was thinking this baby would take away my freedom and adulthood but in reality, my actions showed that I wasn't an adult at all. An adult would never act so selfishly toward the person who raised her. I had never thought about what my mom might be going through. Carrying a child whose father was already proving to be a deadbeat, wondering how she would pay for my education and the many expenses that come with a newborn. I needed to stop thinking about myself for a change. My mother had taken care of me my entire life and now it was my chance to return the favor to her and the new baby. If there was any time to claim my adulthood, now was the time. Sure, things were going to change but no matter what, my mom would always be the woman who would slide over whenever she sensed my presence.

I began to realize the joys that a new baby would bring. Now there was going to be another person who knew how great a mother and friend my mom could be. We could handle this. Staying at home for college was something I could sacrifice, if it meant seeing my little sister take her first steps.

No sooner had I come to terms with my new sibling did the news change. It had been a false positive. And as we mourned in our own ways, I made sure to hold onto what I had learned. Being an adult is not something obtained through age but rather maturity. This experience had taken me to a new level of maturity and adulthood that no driver's license or out-of-state college could ever help me reach. Acting like a child was no longer acceptable; but even now at twenty-two as I write this, with a storm brewing outside, I know that when I'm done, I'll be able to walk into my mother's room and she'll instantly slide over because at that moment I will still be her baby.

~Tiana Lawson

67

Magic Baggies

If you want others to be happy, practice compassion.
If you want to be happy, practice compassion.
~Dalai Lama

I pushed open her bedroom door, just a crack, and almost threw up. I wasn't the neatest kid—back in the day—but this was crazy. Board of Health crazy. Her floor was covered in clothes, her garbage pail overflowed with tissues, and her desk seemed to pulsate beneath mounds of dusty clutter. At fifteen, Leah was in her own world, and I often wondered what went on there.

Moments later she was downstairs with her rainbow-colored hair and worn-out camp bag. I guess I looked at her hair a little too long. "What?" she asked, giving me her special look.

"Nothing. I just miss your dark hair," I responded, knowing I was taking a big chance with that one.

"I don't!" she said. And that was that.

We drove in silence to the bus stop, and I delivered her to the mounds of kids running in circles around water jugs and rolled up towels. Leah was a volunteer CIT at a local Y camp, and she spent eight hours a day working with those little balls of energy. I watched her walk toward the kids, remembering clearly when she was just like them—little, lively, and easy to read.

There's something about girls, the way they suddenly step out of childhood. Conversations with their friends become a foreign language of inside jokes. Text messages are erased instantly. And life is veiled in secrecy. I backed out of my parking spot and headed home.

Beep. Beep. Beep. How did anyone ever manage without a cell phone? I grabbed mine and read Leah's text. "Worst day ever. Wish I were home."

I texted back. "What's wrong?"

"Tell you later."

That afternoon at pick-up, it seemed to take forever for Leah to emerge from the crowd of bouncing campers. She walked expressionless to the car and got in. "Are you okay?" I asked. Instant tears.

"I saw the biggest spider I've ever seen in my life—on the dock at the lake! It was bigger than my hand. I couldn't even get out of the water. My whole body felt tingly. I threw up. I never want to go near the lake again."

"I'm sorry," I answered. "You know they're harmless though, right?" I knew how empty my words were. I just couldn't find any others. What do you do with a girl who has real issues with bugs and is working at an outdoor camp? Leah's fear of spiders had stopped her in her tracks for years. My tough girl could crumble in an instant, and logic played no part in this. She gave me the death glare; I deserved it.

"I am not going near the lake for the rest of the summer." And she meant it.

Later that evening, a few of Leah's friends came over. They were sitting on the deck, and bits of their conversation blew in through the screen of the open kitchen window. "OMG, there's this little kid at camp named Jimmy. He's like the cutest kid, but he's sooooooo high maintenance. He has OCD, and he's really difficult," Leah explained. "The counselors have no patience with him. He's really rude, and they blow him off. But I think he's just miserable."

"You think that's bad?" asked her friend Mandi. "My boss fired a kid because he forgot to put onions in someone's sub."

"Jimmy won't even go to the waterfront with his group, because the sand is too dirty! The other kids laugh at him."

"Well, I had a customer who almost poured her coffee on my

head, because it was too light," said Alexa. And so their chatting continued... a mix of summer tales and solo adventures.

The next morning I walked into the kitchen as Leah quickly zipped her camp bag shut. She closed the cabinet and hurriedly walked away. "What are you up to?" I asked.

"Nothing."

"What do you need from the cleaning cabinet?" I really wanted to know.

"I'm going to be late," she responded. Case closed.

It's not that I didn't trust her — okay, maybe I didn't always trust her. I watched her climb into the car in her multi-colored tights, short shorts, bright gigantic beads, and clashing shoelaces. I just wasn't always sure who she was under all those colors.

When I returned home, I decided to check out the cleaning cabinet. It was messy in there, and there were a bunch of extra large Ziploc bags stuffed carelessly into their box — a box that seemed emptier than I had remembered. What on earth would she be doing with large plastic bags at camp? And why wouldn't she have just explained when I asked her?

It wasn't until later that evening that I understood. Leah came downstairs and joined me on the couch. "So Jimmy played with the other kids down by the water today," she said mysteriously.

"You mean the little boy who won't even walk on the sand? Really?"

"He will now," she said. "He just stepped into his magic baggies. They have superpowers, and they protect him." She smiled.

"Is that what you did with the bags?" I asked.

"Yeah. He just sits by himself every day and acts mean. It's heartbreaking. But I told him he could be a part of all the games on the sand, and he should just try the magic baggies. His counselor told me I was wasting my time. But I guess I wasn't."

"So you were down by the water too?"

"Yes." She paused, and I knew she was fighting tears. "There was no way Jimmy would go if I didn't. I didn't have much of a choice.

You should have seen him. He kept those bags on his feet all day. He was laughing! Now all the kids want them."

I looked at her face — the way the light illuminated her colorful hair and rainbow eye shadow — and I soaked up the beauty of her colors.

~Carol S. Rothchild

68

Be Careful What You Tell Your Children

Blessed are the flexible, for they shall not be bent out of shape.
~Author Unknown

"Om," I chanted along with twenty or so others as we readied our minds and spirits at Friday's yoga class. The others sat cross-legged, while I crouched on a block to lift my sore sixty-five-year-old hips off the floor. Arthritis wasn't something I ever planned on getting, but it snuck up on me when I wasn't looking.

"Just do what you can," the teacher had said earlier. As a retired dancer, I wanted to do more than I could, but hearing her gentle words helped me to be easier on myself.

"Om... om... om." Beautiful tones swept across the wooden floor and bounced up against the high ceiling and white stucco walls. My body vibrated with the lovely music our voices created. The black velvet headband I wore to keep my shoulder length hair out of my eyes pressed hard against my forehead.

After the "oms," the strong, lyrical voice of our teacher led us through a song of self-acceptance, love, divinity within and appreciation for life. The words were Sanskrit.

As I struggled to follow her lead, the memory of my daughter at age ten, dressed in a pink gingham skirt and white blouse, flashed through my head.

"I can't sing in front of all these people. It's too scary," she said. Her little chin trembled as we stood in the wings waiting for her turn to perform at Wonderland Avenue Grade School.

"Just try," I replied. "Do what you can."

When we were deep into the hour, the teacher said we were warmed up enough to do handstands. Handstands! I hadn't done handstands since I was eighteen years old and a paid dancer at Ben Maksik's Town and Country Club in Long Island, New York. That was forty-seven years ago. I tugged nervously on my long purple T-shirt and twisted my fingers around the loose bottom.

Our teacher demonstrated how to get into position. "Put your hands on the floor, fingers facing forward. Raise your hips as high as you can. Walk forward until your knees rest on your elbows. Plug your shoulders firmly together. Then, lift one leg at a time off the floor. When you're ready, lean forward and balance both feet above the ground." I watched in envy as she gracefully lifted herself up.

I tried to jog my memory. Wasn't this listed as a "basics" class, one suitable for beginners? It didn't say anything about group preparation for the Cirque du Soleil. My stomach tightened into a knot. That thing called karma was coming back to haunt me. How many times had I told my little girl that she could do a walkover if she just kept trying? A walkover is a combination of standing on your hands, going into a backbend, and then standing up. That's three moves, not just one. I didn't pay attention to the fear on her face back then. "You can do it. I know you can. Just try," I said over and over.

When I was a young, physically fit woman, it didn't seem that difficult. I mean, she was little and close to the ground—how hard could it be? Guilt pangs shot through my chest. "Sorry," I muttered to her and this memory.

We were encouraged to find a partner to help us get the "feel" of lifting off the ground. I watched as the others paired up. Excuses raced through my head. Should I go to the bathroom, wash my hands, or go downstairs and get a drink of water?

As I was trying to figure out my next move the teacher walked back to where I'd set up my mat. In the back of the room, of course. "You can do it, Mom. I know you can."

"I don't think so," I said.

"Just try. I'll help you. I think you can do it."

I shook my head, bent down, walked my feet forward, strengthened my shoulders and with everything inside of me screaming, "I can't do this," I kicked as high as I could. And my daughter, the teacher, was right. I could do it. It felt exhilarating. My heart beat wildly at knowing that I could still do something as physically challenging as a handstand.

I didn't stay up for very long that first time, but now, after a year, the screams are fainter and the knots in my stomach have lessened. I know that when I think I can't do something, if I try, I often succeed.

You have to be careful what you tell your children. The words come back to haunt you.

~Judith Morton Fraser

Her Own Person

We cannot direct the wind but we can adjust the sails.
~Author Unknown

I had known since I was a little girl that I would one day have a daughter and her name would be Elizabeth. I anticipated my love for that little girl. We would laugh and cry together and I would share all of life's treasures with her. I would teach my daughter from my mistakes and life experiences. We would enjoy everything that I had enjoyed — walks in the woods, quiet weekends watching Christmas movies by the fire in baggy sweatpants and slippers, planting flowers in the spring, and hot summer days spent relaxing by the pool.

Indeed, my husband and I were blessed with a daughter, and yes, her name is Elizabeth. As my Elizabeth grew, it wasn't exactly as I had envisioned. Don't get me wrong, Elizabeth is a joy to all who know and love her. But somehow as she grew up and became more and more her own person, that person became somewhat the opposite of me. While I relish throwing on jeans and a sweatshirt, Elizabeth is obsessed with fashion and dearly loves getting all decked out just to go grocery shopping. She is very high energy and prefers to be on the go instead of watching movies by the fire or relaxing by the pool. So, as a loving mom should… I adapted.

Elizabeth wanted to dance and so she danced. I found myself enthralled with watching her talent, while I had difficulty following the routines on simple fitness workout tapes. Elizabeth wanted to twirl baton and so she twirled. I found myself up at the crack of dawn to drive her to a competition hours away, on snow-covered roads, yet being elated as Elizabeth was awarded trophy after trophy. My planned walks in the woods didn't happen since Elizabeth could not stand bugs of any kind. Ironically, while I have a fear of birds, Elizabeth has a fear of worms. Her ideal walk involves the mall.

Then there was figure skating. Personally, I can't make one loop around the rink without falling on my rear. I have never figured out how to actually stop so I simply slow down and plow into the boards surrounding the rink when it is time to do so. Yet there I was at eight o'clock each Saturday morning sitting on ice cold aluminum bleachers sipping hot chocolate and watching Elizabeth gracefully glide and twirl on the ice.

I had often heard that men should carefully evaluate their future mothers-in-law as their wives will eventually become just like them. Based on my experience, there just is no way that will be possible for my daughter.

It was sometime during all those dance recitals, skating lessons, and baton twirling competitions that I realized that Elizabeth was teaching me as much, or more, than I was teaching her. I was concentrating on teaching her the basics of life—the reading, the math, keeping a clean home, baking, cooking, laundry, and yard work—all of life's responsibilities. Elizabeth was teaching me how to actually live and love every aspect while doing so.

I've learned from my daughter that the true beauty in life is not finding someone just like you, but someone who can show you wonderful things that you might have missed otherwise.

~Lil Blosfield

Hair

A daughter is a little girl who grows up to be a friend.
~Author Unknown

The first traumatic experience for most children is typically something along the lines of getting lost in the grocery store, having a terrible nightmare or even being forced onto Santa's lap for the family Christmas card photo. Mine was when my mother came home from work with a perm. It wasn't that it was an unflattering style, but rather, it was simply not consistent with the image of my mother that I had at age four.

On the way home from the sitter's I examined her from the back seat. I saw her familiar blue eyes in the rearview mirror and her gentle hands on the steering wheel. But there, at the nape of her neck, peeking through the bottom of the headrest was the back of another mother's head. She didn't even smell like Mom, the stench of the chemicals temporarily masking her hair's usual sweet, floral scent. I was mad.

Fortunately for me, the perm era was short-lived and my mother, with the chin-length, face-framing chestnut brown hairdo, returned. Like most mothers, mine rarely changed her cut. Unlike most mothers, hers was never outdated. Mom was simply an evolved beauty who didn't need editing.

Somehow, she managed to keep up with my hair-related demands without letting her own style suffer. She pinned my hair away from my eyes during the awkward phases of growing out my bangs, finding clips to pull together my "look." When they finally grew long enough, I began wanting my hair braided into pigtails each day. Despite how badly I wanted to resemble Amy from *Little Women*, I still whined as I sat on the edge of the bathtub while she pulled my braids tight. Although sometimes this gave me a "nine-year-old with a face lift" look, I was never the one running in after recess looking disheveled in my Catholic school uniform with frayed braids or missing bows.

Over the years, she curled my hair for birthday parties, Christmas, Thanksgiving, my First Communion and random Tuesdays. She rubbed baby powder on my swim cap so it wouldn't pull when I shoved my thick ponytail into it. She braided beads and thread into it when I was jealous of a neighborhood girl who had just returned from the Caribbean. Once, in an experiment, my little brother ran his remote control truck over my hair and when it got caught, my mother untangled my hair from the wheels—all eighteen of them. I shrieked and sobbed while she untangled me. Eventually, she sorted through each strand and somehow my hair survived the incident intact, but it wouldn't be the last time she detangled me in life.

Much like that day, I would often come home throughout my teen years a hysterical, hormonal mess and she would calm me down while she sorted through my problems. I experimented with things much more damaging than a toy car running over my hair. Still, she was patient and gentle as she fixed the problems of her crying daughter, problems that she adopted as her own.

My sophomore year of high school, I was angry at her reaction to my desire to go blond. It was a ridiculous idea, since I have always had such dark, thick hair—the kind that makes you the first girl in school to start shaving your legs. But I saw the way boys looked at girls like Britney Spears and Jessica Simpson and I thought that maybe they would look at me like that too. My mother wasn't having it. At the time I couldn't recognize that she was trying to instill a sense of confidence in me, not letting me conform to the so-called attractiveness of Hollywood stars. So I did it anyway. I am not sure what horrified her most when I emerged from the shower, unveiling a tiger-striped orange mane from the towel on my head. Was it the fact that I had deliberately gone against her wishes or simply the brassy chunks of pumpkin-colored hair sprouting from my scalp? One very expensive trip to a professional colorist later, I looked human again. Mothers know best, even when it comes to cosmetic decisions.

Two years ago, as a sophomore in college, I sat in a small salon above a wig shop and reverted to my four-year-old self. My mother was changing her look again, and I was mad. Mad that I didn't recognize her, mad that I felt like I was looking at someone else's mom. "Okay Mary," the woman said, "I'm going to just cut it a little at first, before I do the whole thing, so you can get used to it." She looked up from her red leather chair, "It's okay. I'm ready… just do all of it." The woman nodded and a shrill buzzing sound filled the room as Mom's hair fell to the floor.

Dark brown hair encircled her chair, while I smiled encouragingly, knowing that this was my chance to repay her for all of the support she had ever given to me. I simply watched the strands she grew over the years fall away as I held on to her new bandana, its pink awareness ribbon print taunting me. The stylist spun her chair around to face the mirror, and my fists clenched as Mom took her first look. She smiled bravely as she rubbed her hairless head. And then I recognized my mother—fearless, resilient, and beautiful.

~Kelly Reidenbaugh

The Second Promise

Honesty is the first chapter of the book of wisdom.
~Thomas Jefferson

I remember the day I had my last alcoholic drink vividly. It was more than two decades ago. I was divorced and struggling with a dysfunctional relationship. I wanted to get married and (luckily) the object of my marital desires did not wish to do so. To get even with him, I bought a quart of vodka and settled in for a night of vengeful drinking. The next morning, I was not able to go to my teaching job in a middle school. One of my teenage daughters was up and ready for her walk to school. I walked slowly downstairs into the family room where she was gathering up her books. She looked at me, her eyes swimming with tears, and said, "Mom, when are you going to stop drinking? You are slowly killing yourself and hurting everyone around you."

I had no answer for her.

It was a Friday in May. It was also the alternate weekend when my daughters had to be at their father's house. As soon as my daughter left for school, I poured myself another drink, and called the school's office to tell them I was home sick with the flu. I was sick all right: sick of the roller coaster ride I called my life.

I began doing what I had done so many times before: I went through the townhouse where we lived and found all the hidden bottles of booze. I emptied them all into the sink. Then I did something I had never done before. I called a friend of mine whose son had a drug problem. She gave me the name and phone number of an organization that specialized in alcohol and drug addictions. I called their office and made an appointment for an evaluation. One month later, after school was on summer break, I was admitted to a treatment center for thirty days. It was the worst/best experience of my life. At the end of my stay, my daughters took me home. I promised them I would do everything I could to stay sober. So far, I have been able to keep that promise.

Five years later, my older daughter married a young man who was intelligent, educated, and very personable. Two years after that, she gave birth to my only grandchild. Unfortunately, my son-in-law's penchant for good times led him to become an abusive binge drinker. There were many nights when my daughter came to my house carrying my granddaughter in her arms in order to escape her husband's violent behavior.

His downward spiral into chronic alcoholism cost him his teaching job, his driver's license, and eventually, his family. My daughter divorced him, as did his second wife. Despite many visits to many treatment centers, AA meetings, and therapists, he was not able to commit to a life without alcohol.

As my daughter struggled to build a life for herself and her daughter, I tried to help my former son-in-law become a decent father to my granddaughter. All my efforts were ineffective. He lacked the desire to do whatever it took to stay clean and sober.

Eventually, my daughter was able to obtain the necessary certificates to get a job as a special education teacher. I took care of my granddaughter when my daughter was working or out on a date. And, often, when they were sick, I cared for both of them.

After ten years of my fervent prayers, my daughter met a wonderful man and remarried. He became the perfect stepfather to my granddaughter. If I had had a son, I would have wanted him to be like my new son-in-law.

My former son-in-law had a profoundly negative effect on my granddaughter's emotional state of being. It became apparent that she needed therapy. After two years of weekly sessions with an excellent psychologist, my daughter asked me when I was going to tell my granddaughter that I was a recovering alcoholic. "Never!" was my immediate response.

My daughter gently sighed and said, "Mom, the therapist thinks it would be good for her to know that it is possible for someone to get help and maintain a sober way of life. Why don't you want her to know? It's been such a long time for you. She's about the only person in both families who doesn't know about your experience with drinking."

It took me a moment to express an honest answer. "I just don't want her to associate me with all the agony her father has put her through. I don't want her to know that I put you and your sister through a lot of miserable times. I can't bear the thought that she could love me less after she learns about me."

"This isn't about you. This is about a thirteen-year-old girl who is struggling with an alcoholic father and who needs the understanding and wisdom only you can give her." My daughter's words struck home. I agreed to share my secret life with my granddaughter.

We decided to tell her just before her next therapy appointment. It was a bright and shiny Tuesday in May, the same month as my Alcoholics Anonymous birthday, when I sat across from my granddaughter and daughter in their living room. My heart was beating wildly and it was difficult for me to breathe as I told my favorite person in the whole world my history as an alcoholic.

She began to cry. I left my chair and took her in my arms. We both cried together as my daughter quietly watched us. After a few minutes, my granddaughter left the room to get ready for her therapy session.

My daughter said, "Thank you, Mom. I know that was hard for you."

My granddaughter returned and sat down next to me. She took my hands in hers and looked at me carefully. "Grandma, I want you to know that I don't think any less of you for being an alcoholic. You have beaten the disease. I am so proud of you. Will you promise me that no matter what happens, you will always be the person you are right now?"

I had no choice but to answer, "Yes, with all my heart."

I think God knew that it was time this old lady needed another reason to leave the "demon rum" alone. After all, the first promise lasted more than twenty years.

~Linda J. Hinds

Mom's Sage Advice

The best advice is this: Don't take advice and don't give advice.
~Author Unknown

I was having dinner with my mother the other night... Chinese. Actually, she was having dinner and I was pouring my heart out to her over a plate of crab puffs—comfort food.

My heart had been broken and I was looking to her for support the way a daughter does in times like these. You have to understand that my mother is a pillar of strength when it comes to love and all that entails. The woman is a rock so it's not always easy for me to reveal my more vulnerable side to her. I know that she expects a lot from me as a daughter, as a woman and especially as the mother of her grandchildren.

But this was a significant turn of events for me and she had always been my touchstone. Besides I couldn't keep it to myself anymore. I needed to bend her ear and to perhaps get her to offer up something prophetic.

My mother's great about always knowing the right thing to say, especially to me, her only daughter. That's not to say that I always agree with her. As a matter of fact, over the years we've come to terms with our differences of opinions.

But I do, however, value her perspective. So I spilled the broken pieces of my heart onto the table like one of those 1,000-piece jigsaw puzzles. Trying not to choke up, I leaned in towards her.

"What do you think I should do, Mom?" My eyes zeroed in on

her while she took the time to swallow a bite of her almond chicken. Her face grew pensive as her eyes zeroed in on me. She took a deep breath. I could feel my heart beating inside my chest as I waited for her pearl of wisdom.

She leaned in closer, as if to breathe a secret to me that would make it all better. "Nat, I think you need to tweeze more off of the inside of your eyebrows," she whispered.

"What?" I gasped. That was it? That was her great pronouncement in the midst of my despair? I was hoping for something a little more profound, perhaps something more along the lines of what Confucius might say.

It just goes to show that when it comes to mothers and daughters, you should expect just about anything. But maybe Mom was just pointing out, in her own way, that life goes on.

~Natalie June Reilly

Ripped Pants

He that respects himself is safe from others;
he wears a coat of mail that none can pierce.
~Henry Wadsworth Longfellow

"Honey, do you have to wear those ripped pants?" I looked at my youngest daughter, shaking my head.

"But I like these pants, Mom. They're comfortable." She proceeded to pack her backpack for school, ignoring my exasperated sighs and rolling eyes.

"The teachers are going to think you don't have any good pants."

"But I do have good pants, Mom. They're just not as comfortable." She walked into the bathroom to pull her long hair up into a ponytail.

"What will your friends say? They are going to make fun of you because you have a big hole in your pants."

"But I don't care what my friends say. If they make fun of me, then they weren't friends to begin with." She turned on the water to start brushing her teeth.

"What about the dress code? I don't want to be called to school to bring you a decent pair of pants." I was running out of objections, but I didn't want her wearing those pants to school.

"The dress code says you can't have holes on the butt of your pants. They don't want us showing our underwear. It doesn't say anything about holes in the knees." She rinsed her mouth and headed for the front door.

"But honey, I just don't want you wearing those pants!" I knew my voice had gotten forceful, but I couldn't help it.

"Why, Mom? Are you worried about me, or are you embarrassed for yourself?"

I stopped dead in my tracks and looked at my daughter with different eyes.

"Mom, these pants are comfortable. I'm not wearing them to make a statement. I'm not wearing them to upset my teachers. I'm not wearing them because of my friends. I'm not wearing them to go against the dress code. And I'm certainly not wearing them to make you mad. You're a great mother! You shouldn't worry so much about what other people think of you." With her speech complete, she kissed me on the cheek, threw her backpack over one shoulder and headed out the door to the bus stop.

I was dumbfounded. I suddenly realized I was more worried about what people thought of me. I was afraid her ripped pants would be a bad reflection on me.

Out of the mouths of babes.

~Bobbi Dawn Rightmyer

Choices

Children have more need of models than of critics.
~Carolyn Coats

"I don't want to move." Tami, my ten-year-old daughter, blinked back tears. "I want to stay here with my friends."

"We have to, sweetie." I knelt and put my arms around her, rocking her gently as I had when she was little.

"I won't even have a bedroom."

My heart ached for my daughter. My husband was moving us to ten acres outside Portland so he could create a self-sufficient life-style, a laudable goal. But he was moving us into a decrepit cabin on the property, perhaps the original homestead, without plumbing and with just a single outlet for electricity. He planned to make it livable as we basically camped there, then built a new house a few hundred yards north.

When I asked Hank to wait to move until we had a house built for the family, his exact words were, "I'm going and you can come if you want."

I wasn't about to break up the family so I started packing.

"We'll have your friends for sleepovers," I promised Tami. "They're only twenty minutes away."

"I don't even want my friends to see that place."

Sad, but resolute, Tami gathered her courage, made new friends, and for months climbed the slats nailed to a wall of the cabin to access the loft where she slept. She helped us with house projects with little complaint.

Hank did a Herculean job of building the new house and maintaining his day job, but the pressure took a terrible toll. "Can't you do anything right?" he would snarl at us all when we did our best to help him.

Tami caught much of his wrath. Her skirts were too short, her bangs too long. She didn't sing loud enough in church, talked too much on the phone, and spent too much time with friends. He even criticized her beautiful smile.

At the high school where I taught I was known for creating classrooms where students felt nurtured, yet I couldn't create the same positive climate at home. Sometimes I supported Hank. "Look at your father's beautiful work," I'd say, sincerely praising it. Other times I'd support the children. "It's important for the kids to have their after-school activities, whether you think so or not," I'd tell Hank. Or, "The kids are trying hard to do what you want. Do you have to criticize them all the time?" I'd been raised in a home tense with my father's rage and my mother's tolerance of it, in a church that promoted the preservation of the family unit above all else. Surely I could do something to make the family work.

One night Tami was curled up on the couch with a book when Hank came home from work. "What are you reading?" he demanded.

She showed him the V.C. Andrews novel.

"*Secrets in the Attic*?" He spun into one of the rages that were growing more and more frequent. "You'll rot your mind with that trash!" He grabbed the book and hurled it onto the top of a three-quarter wall that divided the family room and living room.

I couldn't defend *Secrets in the Attic* as great literature, but knew it was just one of many kinds of books that Tami, a voracious reader, inhaled. If Hank was worried about the content, he needed to open a respectful dialog with her. Still, any intervention on my part would make him angrier, so I bit my lip and kept silent.

"It's not rotting my mind," Tami retorted, then retreated to her room, probably to call one of her friends.

Over the next year, their arguments grew more and more bitter. One day, when Tami was a junior in high school, she came to me with tears streaming down her face after yet another fight. "Can I live with Jessica?" she asked. "Her mother invited me. I can't survive here anymore."

"Yes," I said without hesitation. "You shouldn't have to go through this for another minute." I'd heard her on the phone with Jessica night after night crying about the day's encounters with her father.

Then I caught my breath. My mind reeled with the enormity of what I'd said. Was I really going to send her to Jessica's with my blessing? And yet, how could I expect her to stay here, continuously belittled and shamed? We were all belittled and shamed. Everyone in the family had grown depressed from the constant conflict in our home. Although I believed marriage to be a sacred institution, was it time to take the children and strike out on my own?

Sobbing, I made an emergency call to the marriage counselor Hank had finally agreed to meet with. "Tami wants to move out. What should I do?" I wailed.

"Tami needs to do what she needs to do for herself," she said.

I hung up, furious. Was she really recommending that I send my daughter away?

Next, I made an emergency call to the counselor I'd been seeing individually. He asked, "What do you want?"

I poured out a prayer to the Lord for guidance. I'd been praying for months for His help, feeling guilty about even the thought of leaving Hank. Then I drew deep breaths and sat as quietly as I could, listening for His answer.

A feeling of complete peace came over me. I knew without any doubt the right answer. I wasn't about to lose my daughter.

Tami had gone to her room to call Jessica and pack. I knocked on her door. "Can you stand it here for a little bit longer while I make arrangements for us all to leave?"

She sniffed. "How long?"

"I'll start making calls tonight. I have to find a place for us to stay."

"I'm so unhappy, Mom."

"I know. We all are."

Within months I had filed for divorce, borrowed the money for a down payment on a small house, and settled in with my three children. We developed a tradition of gathering around the kitchen table and chatting at night. If one of us was upset, we talked it through. I asked Tami's forgiveness for not taking care of her sooner, and worked in therapy to forgive myself. Hank began the difficult task of rebuilding his relationship with us all.

It's been more than a decade since Tami asked if she could leave the family home and I finally made a firm stand on her behalf. This morning she sent me an e-mail. "Have you been on Facebook lately?" she asked.

I hadn't checked Facebook in weeks. Curious, I brought it up and checked my page, then went to Tami's.

I wish she could have seen a smile broader than the Cheshire cat's spread across my face. I'd seen a variety of Tami's profile pictures: a come-to-my-party face framed in a hot pink wig; a "this is going to be a good deal" business face, her BlackBerry held to her ear; a "catch this style" face, a gray twill derby tipped rakishly over one eyebrow. Now I was looking at a headshot of my precious daughter and me, side by side, temples touching. This was my hands-down favorite. What better toast to an enduring mother/daughter relationship?

~Samantha Ducloux Waltz

The Magic of

Mothers &

Daughters

Chapter 8

Healing and
Second Chances

There is no love without forgiveness,
and there is no forgiveness without love.

~Bryant H. McGill

Hope and Acceptance

I know God will not give me anything I can't handle.
I just wish that He didn't trust me so much.
~Mother Teresa

The happiest day of my life was the day my daughter Danielle was born. I remember every sight, sound, and smell of her birth. As I held her in my arms for the first time, I thanked God for her precious life. I had been separated from my first husband at the time I discovered that I was pregnant. Although, the news led to a temporary reconciliation, I was initially not happy about the pregnancy. However, three days of bed rest during a threatened miscarriage gave me the precious time I needed to think and bond with the baby. As I prayed for the tiny life I was carrying, I promised God that if the baby survived, I would become the best mother possible. He trusted me enough to send Danielle to me.

Danielle was a bright, curious, strong-willed child. There was something special and different about her. From the beginning, her powerful personality tested my patience and endurance. Danielle was only two years old at the time of the divorce and it was a traumatic experience for her. Her brother Michael was six months old and too young to remember the drama and chaos. Over time, she seemed to adjust and we became the three Musketeers... "All for one and one for all."

A few years later, I met and married my husband Matt and together we created a stable loving home for our family. Danielle and Michael spent holidays and summer breaks with their father. Although sharing custody was challenging, we were very happy during the time we spent together. I looked forward with hope and anticipation to all of the wonderful moments we would continue to share as mother and daughter.

Everything changed when Danielle turned thirteen. She was attractive, tall for her age and looked sixteen. She became increasingly restless, moody, and defiant. We thought her radical behavior changes were simply due to adolescence and sought the advice of a family counselor. We set boundaries, drew up family contracts, and prayed that this stage would pass quickly. Unfortunately, it was only the beginning.

Watching Danielle's rapid transformation was like watching a speeding train... derailing. We were powerless to stop it. We discovered that she had become involved with an older boy. There was an angry scene, ending with us forbidding her to see him again. Later that night, we found her bedroom window open and her bed empty. She was gone. As parents, we discovered a new level of terror and agony that night. We called the police and searched for her. I believed that she knew how much we loved her and the only reason that she didn't call us was because she couldn't. I visualized her lying in a ditch along the side of the road, calling my name. In the morning, she was found at her boyfriend's house. His mother had allowed her to stay the night and lied to us about her being there.

We quickly graduated from family counselors to child psychiatrists. The first of these experts explained, "Your daughter is suffering from bipolar disorder." Bipolar disorder was formerly known as manic depression. Symptoms may vary from mild to severe. Danielle's included roller coaster mood swings, fluctuating energy levels, and impulsive high-risk behaviors. Substance abuse is very common in individuals with bipolar disorder. There is no known cure, but treatment with medications and therapy can help many people with bipolar disorder lead balanced and productive lives.

Adolescence had awakened this sleeping giant within our daughter. To outsiders her behavior mimicked typical teenage rebellion.

Ignorance regarding this disorder and a sluggish legal system conspired against our efforts to obtain the level of care Danielle desperately needed.

Her first treatment programs were considered "voluntary" and she could "check out" whenever she liked. Before she was finally court-ordered into a residential treatment program several years later, she ran away from home thirty times and was hospitalized for evaluations at least as often. By this time, Danielle had learned how to manipulate the system and play the joint custody card to her advantage.

One afternoon, I discovered Danielle sitting cross-legged on the bathroom counter, shaving her head. I began screaming hysterically. I believe the only thing that prevented me from having a stroke was catching a glimpse of myself in the bathroom mirror. My face was beet red and my neck veins were bulging. The shock of seeing my distorted reflection silenced my screaming. I did not recognize the woman I saw in the mirror.

I shrieked, "What have you done? I can't take it anymore! Do you have any idea how hard it is to live with someone with bipolar disorder?"

She calmly replied, "You think that's hard… try being the person who has it."

My husband and I were both critical care nurses at the time. We were very skilled at fixing problems for other people. From the onset of Danielle's illness, we went into high gear rescue mode. I was certain that we would find the right doctor, medication, or treatment program to help "fix" Danielle. One agonizing sleepless night, while she was missing, it seemed clear that we were failing in our mission. I felt hopeless and powerless. I prayed, "Dear God… she came from you… she belongs to you… please protect her." Again, my prayers were answered when she was found unharmed.

Love for our children is not based on the awards they win or how successful they make us look or feel. It is a deeper bond that, despite any circumstance, accepts them as they truly are.

Danielle is now a beautiful young woman with a family of her own. Her exuberant vivacious personality is larger than life. She has an oversized loving heart that she freely shares with her family and friends. I have watched in awe over the years as she courageously faces the challenges and setbacks of living with bipolar disorder. My daughter Danielle is more beautiful to me now than the moment I first saw her.

~Laura Wisniewski

I'm the Mom

The central struggle of parenthood is to let our hopes for our children outweigh our fears.
~Ellen Goodman

I am the grandmother of an autistic child. I am the mother of a daughter who has an autistic child. Autism affects everyone who is involved in the child's life. The burden I carry is two-fold. I love my granddaughter dearly. When she's having a good day, she is sweet, charming, playful, loving and a joy to be around. But before I was a grandmother, I was a mom.

This morning, I woke to a text message, sent from my daughter at 5:05. Savannah had been up since 4:00 and was in full tantrum mode. She had ripped apart her room, taken pictures off the wall, and thrown everything down the stairs. The text said: "call me when you get up." I dialed the phone, knowing I had no answers.

It's several hours later, and my heart still hurts. At 7 a.m., my daughter was still struggling to get clothes on her daughter and get her to the bus stop. When I called I asked how Savannah's younger sister was during this. My daughter remarked that Aubrey was crying and looking at Savannah as if to say, "Why are you doing what you are doing?" I know she had to be thinking that, because that is what we are all thinking.

What could be going on within Savannah's mind at 4 a.m. that would cause her to have that type of frustration and rage? She was scheduled to go visit her daddy and his family that weekend. Was she upset about the upcoming visit? Then I remember she has been agitated all week. I wonder if it could it be her diet — did she have sugar this week? Erin had checked with the school earlier in the week, and made sure that Savannah received no sugar.

I feel helpless. For years, it was my job to help my daughter when she hurt. When she was small, I would kiss a bruised knee, dry a tear, and hold her until she felt better. Now I look at my fully-grown daughter, in such pain, and I realize, I can't fix this. I can't kiss it away, eliminate the pain or stop the tears. My daughter's car is in the shop this morning, so we drive into work together. Her younger daughter sits happily in the back seat, seeming to have recovered from the chaotic morning. My daughter, on the other hand, looks as if she has been through the battle of her life… and lost. We drop Aubrey at daycare, and my daughter struggles to switch gears so that she can go into work and function for the day. In the back of her mind is the knowledge that she has a five-hour round trip ahead of her this evening, to deliver the children to their dad for the weekend.

I hate autism. Package it any way you want. It is not a blessing. It's a thief. It robs my granddaughter of the ability to play and socialize. It steals precious energy from my daughter, who is a single parent. Autism causes pain to the entire family as they try to cope with its fury. There is no cure. There is no magic drug that will give back what it has stolen.

At night, my daughter struggles with questions. "Can she meet Savannah's needs? Will she have the strength to go on another day? Will she ever get a full night's sleep again?" She struggles with guilt, anger, self-pity, resentment and frustration. And then she gallantly gets up at four and spends three hours trying to calm her child so she can go to work for the next eight hours.

I can't fix it. I want to. I come up with solutions daily. "What if you move in with us? What if you take her to a new doctor? What if you change her diet? What if she comes to our house a few days a week?" As a mom, I want it to be all better. I want to hold my daughter until the tears stop and say, "It's going to be okay, and Mommy's got you." But I can't. I'm up against something I cannot fix. Just when

I feel as if I will never be enough, I hear a gentle voice calling within me. "My child, she was mine before she was yours." I recognize that as the Lord himself, comforting his child so that I may comfort mine.

~Cindy Gore

She Never Stopped Loving Me

Mother, the ribbons of your love are woven around my heart.
~Author Unknown

The police officer cleared his throat. "Ma'am — you okay?"

Bent over, I wiped my face on the blood-soaked bandage covering my lacerated thigh. "No." Tears cascaded from my eyes as I pleaded to God with the desperation of a lost child. "I want my mommy." My voice broke. Trying to mimic my mother's hold, I curled my legs up and clung to them, then rocked myself back and forth. Never before had I understood how much her love meant.

I hoped she would still love me.

"You can call her once we get to the station."

A guttural sound loosed from within, and my weeping increased. "No. I can't. She's in Haiti."

"Oh," he said. "Sorry."

Was this really happening?

My mother always told me she'd love me no matter what, but I didn't believe her. Convinced she'd be disappointed and stop loving me if she knew all the terrible things I did, I hid myself from her. My life was full of secrets and lies.

Would she stop loving me now that she would know the truth?

At the station, I gave a false statement to the detective. Promising myself I'd be honest if he questioned my story, I searched for signs of disbelief, but receiving only assurances, my lies continued. I couldn't even think the truth, let alone say it out loud.

A knock interrupted us. "Her attorney's here," a voice said.

"My attorney?" Confused, I shook my head. "I don't have an attorney."

"Well, she says she's your attorney," the voice said. "She wants to talk to you."

The detective slammed his hand on the desk. "She doesn't need an attorney."

Startled, I looked up at him. "I don't?"

He furrowed his brow. "Why would you?"

My lips trembled. "I don't know." I thought for a moment. "Maybe I should see what she wants."

The detective scowled as the door opened and a woman appeared. She looked at the floor beneath my bleeding leg and pointed. "Is that her blood on the carpet?"

Looking down, I nodded.

The woman pointed at me. "Don't say another word." She turned to the detective and put her hands on her hips. "She needs to go to the hospital. Now!"

In the emergency room, she explained the seriousness of my predicament. "Your mother insisted you have an attorney."

"My mother?"

"Yes. Your sister called her and she told your family to get you an attorney. It's a good thing—it's very important you don't say another word."

After that, I didn't say anything to anyone. I was afraid the truth, that I shot and killed my husband, would make everyone stop loving me. I worried no one would believe that it was self-defense.

My mother took the first flight home to help me with funeral arrangements. She held my weary body up as I faced the man I once loved in his casket. She helped me clean my house, which had been a crime scene for two days, and never asked me what had happened that night.

It took months, but the phone call from my attorney came.

"You've been indicted for murder. You need to be in court in the morning."

Hands shaking and knees bouncing, I nervously awaited the judge's ruling for bond. Then, with a thundering clang, I was behind bars.

I thought back to years before, and my mother's words echoed in my ears. "Don't get involved with him. He's bad news."

Although afraid she'd stop loving me, I had married him anyway. I loved him and needed his love.

"I'm so disappointed. Why do you make such choices?" she asked.

My heart deflated.

"Well," her voice held resignation, "I'm worried, but I still love you. You made your bed, now you can lie in it."

At least she still loved me.

Then I had a child of my own, and maternal love overwhelmed me. When my mother saw her grandson for the first time, her face lit up. "Oh! Oh my goodness! He's so wonderful." She stroked his head and ran her hand down his body, then wrapped him in her arms and brought his face close to hers.

Her love was overpowering; it flowed from her as she drew him into her chest and held him tight. She looked at me with tear-filled eyes. "He's so precious. He reminds me of you."

"Me?" I grimaced. "How's that?"

She looked at him. "Holding him reminds me of holding you when you were born. I love him, just like I love you."

Could she really love me like that?

As time went by, my husband's extreme jealousy grew into obsession, which evolved into emotional and verbal abuse. Then the abuse became physical. But what could I do? The old mantra danced in my head. Worried the truth would cause me to lose someone I loved, I kept my burdens to myself, even when his anger escalated to daily threats on my life with a knife held to my throat. As my mom said, I had made my bed; I had to lie in it.

One dreadful night, my husband spun out of control. He tortured me with a knife and threatened our son's life. Instinct to protect my child kicked in and I knew I had to do whatever it took. I would die for my son. With that resolve, I managed to get away from my abuser and ran for the hidden gun.

The metallic clatter of enormous keys startled me back to the reality of jail. In a letter to my mom, I mentioned how much joy it brought me to receive mail; after that, she wrote to me every day. With each letter, the realization that she just might love me after all, even though I'd done so many egregious things, began to sink in.

Although my mother lived in another country, she put taking care of my business and visiting me at the top on her list whenever she came to town. She did everything she could while I was incarcerated for over eight months, including managing my bankruptcy filing, hiring a high-powered attorney who got me out on bond, and taking custody of my son in an effort to keep me from losing him.

On the eve of my trial, fear besieged me. My mother hugged me tight and rocked me. "It's alright." She tucked me into bed and kissed my forehead. "I'm here for you, no matter what."

Her presence reassured me during every minute of testimony. At the end of each day, she held me and comforted me. She stayed by my side and loved me through it all. When my jurors spared me from prison, she gave me a thumbs-up and mouthed, "I love you."

A smile crossed my face—I believed her.

My mother loves me, no matter what.

~Leigh Ann Bryant

78

Card Shop Quandary

Love is the ability and willingness to allow those that you care for to be what
they choose for themselves without any insistence that they satisfy you.
~Wayne Dyer

stood in the card shop in my little town. Normally, I took pleasure in picking out cards for celebrations and milestones. Today
was different; it was the first Thursday in May.

The two annual events that I dreaded were Mother's Day and
my mother's birthday. I treasure the cards I receive from my own son,
whether homemade or store-bought. The problem is buying them for
my mother, because it brings to the surface so much cynicism, dread,
sadness and love, all entangled.

I found myself grabbing a card, reading the verses, then putting
it back. I searched for nearly an hour to find a card that said what I
felt. I didn't care about the design or the price. Objectively, the cards
were quite suitable, sentimental and lovely. Subjectively, however, I
felt insincere if I picked up a card that gushed "To The World's Best
Mother" or "You Did Everything For Me."

I needed a card addressing the mother who left me with grandparents until I was nine years old, when my grandmother died. A
verse for the mom who reentered my life for good after that death,
bringing two younger brothers and a sister with her but not bringing
fathers for any of us. A poem for the mother who went through the
hell of alcoholism, abuse, poverty, a brief stint of homelessness, a

bevy of questionable men and many run-down residences, all the while exposing her children to some harrowing situations.

The irony was that the card would also need to address the mommy who would snuggle me on her lap and read Dr. Seuss to me when she was around, thus igniting my lifelong passion for words. A poem for the momma who probably did questionable things just to provide food and keep us from being split apart by the welfare department. A sentiment for the mom who was simultaneously cool and immature, dressing in her teen daughter's clothing and sporting Def Leppard posters on her bedroom wall.

This mom who put her fist through the windows of her rented houses, yet kissed each of us children four times on the forehead before bedtime. The mom who found God only to lose Him again, which is a cycle she continues to this day.

I don't know why I cannot casually snatch up a pretty, lace-trimmed card, breezily sign my name and pop it in the mail. Perhaps it is because I feel that words are too precious to be trivialized and maybe, just maybe, so is my mother.

~Shauna Hambrick Jones

79

Childhood's End

*One thing you will probably remember well
is any time you forgive and forget.*
~Franklin P. Jones

was fifteen years old when my dad stepped on his bathroom scale and discovered he'd lost weight without trying. Soon after that he began waking in the night slick with sweat. I was sixteen when cancer killed him. He was forty-nine.

My mother fell apart during his final year when our lives were about doctors and test results and the antiseptic smell of hospitals. Surgeons cut my dad open and closed him up again. He returned home a bedridden, shrunken, frightened man—not my wise, witty father at all—whispering to me about fun things we'd do, places we'd go when he recovered. He remained at home with visiting nurses coming and going until he was moved to a nursing home to live his last month on a morphine drip, with round-the-clock nursing care. My mother sought relief in prescription drugs, one after the other, to ease her constant anxiety and depression.

She was fifty-five and white-haired when she became a widow. She'd married my dad in her late twenties—before that she'd lived with her brother who'd looked out for her. As a pampered only child, I had no idea that when my dad became too sick to work our family income stopped as well, and our financial situation was precarious. I didn't know how emotionally fragile my mother was, or how frightened she must have felt selling the suburban New York home she loved, and moving near her sister in Manhattan. I didn't know what it meant to have or to lose a life partner—and to deal with menopause at the same time.

But I was a teenager and to me the world was made up of my thoughts, my wants, and my feelings. The dad I adored and admired was gone. My mother—my adversary and nemesis since I turned thirteen and my hormones kicked in—was consumed by her sorrow, vanishing into a perpetual haze of legal drugs.

I felt alone—like I'd lost both parents, even while one still lived. My mom didn't cry when my dad died, or at his funeral or after that—never smiled or laughed again either. Aching for attention I reached out to a neighbor in his twenties and we became lovers. I was happy again, imagining myself in love. I got married and had a son a year later. I was eighteen years old.

My mom and I never fully reconnected after that, although she and my aunt lived only three blocks away from me. Our relationship was so stressed, I was angry when my mother had a breakdown and was hospitalized for a week—angry at my obligation to join the relatives in conferring with her doctors about her latest ailment and escalating depression.

"What's to be done about poor Celia?" the family asked, hands wringing, gathered around her hospital bed—while head hanging, eyes cast down, my mother waited for us to decide. But short of resurrecting my father and restoring him to her side, we had no idea how to help her and the doctors continued to prescribe pills.

My second son was born after we moved upstate. I earned my college degree and then divorced two years after my graduation. I moved with the boys to San Francisco.

Although my mom considered my cross-country move a personal betrayal, I was, given the circumstances, the best daughter I could be. I telephoned often, wrote letters, took my sons to visit her, and had her visit us. She drank us in like sunlight when we were together—but when goodbyes were said and I resumed my life her world went dark again.

She was in her late seventies when her sister lost her mind and was put in a nursing home. Her brother, who lived not too far away in Queens, died a few years later. My mom was eighty-seven, tiny, frail, and swallowed up by dementia when I packed her up and took her to a nursing home two miles from my home near San Francisco, where I lived with my second husband.

There was, at the end, a reconnection. One stormy day in September, the afternoon of my fifty-first birthday, I visited my mom at the home. It was a good one as such places go: clean, and the care-takers were courteous and kind. But I felt my own mortality gazing at the terminally old sitting silently in their wheelchairs, lined up along the hallways like pigeons on a fence.

I exhaled sharply before taking a deep breath and helping my mother to the enclosed front porch, the least depressing spot in the place. After seating her in a comfortable chair, I sat beside her setting out paper plates, the banana bread that she loved, fresh fruit, and chocolate cupcakes on a small table between us. We sat nibbling, looking out the big front window at the trees swaying in the wind.

I sat, as I had all my life, bearing witness to my mother's grief, thinking I could hardly remember back to when I was small and called her Mommy—and she smiled, laughed, gave dinner parties, made me dresses and birthday cakes, and cared for me when I was sick.

And then my mother spoke. "You know I'm not normal anymore, Lynn," she said in her charming Hungarian accent, with her precise, almost formal way of expressing herself. I turned to her, surprised, and she continued. "It can't have been much fun for you being my daughter all these years, since your father died. Honey, I'm so sorry for that."

I stared at her in astonishment. My mother—the mother I loved and longed for—still existed inside this ancient wreck of a woman. I felt a hot rush of love for her and tears slid down my face as I took her wrinkled old hand and stroked it gently. We sat together talking about my childhood, and the life she loved in the suburbs with her fruit trees and backyard garden. She asked if I'd loved my dad and I told her she'd given me the best father anyone could have had. We sat like that until she was tired and I took her back to her room and put her to bed.

When I came the next day she'd disappeared again. I searched her eyes for a sign she remembered yesterday's conversation. There was none. My mom died a week later, silently in the night, at ninety-one.

I was and remain grateful for that brief moment when the veil over her lifted and I heard my mother's voice filled with love for me — and our connection, battered but unbroken, was reaffirmed. It wasn't everything I'd dreamed of but it would have to be enough.

~Lynn Sunday

80

Understanding Lori

A mother's love is instinctual, unconditional, and forever.
~Author Unknown

My daughter Lori stormed through the door after school. "Mom, I don't want you to help in my class anymore."

I stopped stirring. "Why?"

"I mean I like it when you come, but the kids stare at you. They laugh and say, 'Your mom's eyes are weird, the way they move around.'"

"You must have been embarrassed."

"I let them know you're as good as any of their moms and they said the yummy cookies you make are the best."

"Thank you."

Before I could say more, she abruptly changed the subject. "Can I go play with Ann?"

I nodded, worried about what Lori was going through.

The next day the principal called to inform me that Lori had been fighting with a student on the playground.

When I confronted her that night, she became defensive. "Sally started making fun of you so I told her, 'She's my mom and you better not talk bad about her.' Sally wouldn't stop calling you names like 'blind bat.' I had to punch her out."

I managed to remain calm. "You don't need to fight on my account."

"Yes, I do!" She rushed from the room.

I was stunned. What was I going to do? I had to say something to her. After some contemplation, I knocked on her door. "Can I come in?"

"I guess," she mumbled.

I sat on her bed and stroked her hair. "Lori, I appreciate you sticking up for me, but you don't have to prove yourself to anyone. I don't want to be the cause of you getting into trouble."

"You're my mom," she said softly.

I patted her back. "Honey, talk to me."

She stiffened, pulled away from me and got up. "I have a lot of homework to do."

While I stood outside my daughter's door, I thought about how I had always communicated freely about my partial blindness to my seven children, and I believed they could state their feelings if my disability bothered them. What had changed with Lori?

I discussed my concerns with a friend when she and I went out to lunch the next day. "I can't change the fact that I'm sight impaired," I told her. "Still, Lori acts out because I am." I sighed. "How can I reach her?"

"Sounds like a difficult spot for you to be in." She squeezed my hand. "Give her time. She's always been able to come to you."

"With her becoming an adolescent someday soon, I hope this problem gets resolved. "

That didn't happen. More and more, Lori seemed to withdraw from me, closing up, replacing the carefree chatter of childhood with a wall of resentment. Overnight my sunny, spirited daughter turned sullen and angry. I didn't know how to help her.

By the time she entered junior high, she had stopped bullying other kids, but she vented her unhappiness about me in other ways.

One afternoon Lori burst into the house. "Mom, I want to take dancing lessons with Jessica." She hesitated. "How do I get there? You can't drive."

It was all I could do to keep my voice cheerful without taking her irritation personally. "No, I can't drive, but I don't want you to miss out on the opportunity. You have a talent for dancing. I'm sure Jessica's mom wouldn't mind you going along with them."

"It's always the other mothers who can do everything," she lashed out.

Something snapped in me. "I know I'm not living up to your expectations as a mom but you could still go to dancing lessons."

I left the room to gain control of my emotions. When I had calmed down, I convinced myself, "She's not trying to be mean." I knew there was such turmoil and conflict raging inside her. I still couldn't make excuses for her or blame her change of mood on the fact that she might be going through a stage. Her struggle with my partial blindness was real and had affected our relationship and I didn't know how to find a solution. I had lost my perspective. I wondered if counseling would help.

A month later, our church had a dinner to honor mothers. Each daughter gave her mother a gift and told the audience something special about her mom. As Lori presented her tribute, she said in part, "I have the best mom around even if she is blind." This would have been a compliment to me because of the pride in her voice, yet her tone hinted at a note of sarcasm. She deliberately ignored me during the rest of the meal and I felt humiliated.

While we walked home the tension mounted and I couldn't take any more of the awkward silence between us. "Lori, I'm not your enemy. I know you're upset. You need to talk to someone, if not me, then a friend, a trusted adult, or a counselor."

"I don't need dumb counseling," her voice broke. "I used to be able to talk to you."

"You still can," I spoke quietly. I put my arm around her and we cried all the way home.

"You've kept a lot in for a long time," I finally said. "It might help you to share it."

"How can I? It's about you."

"I can handle it a lot easier if you tell me what's bugging you instead of bottling it up inside."

"I feel guilty because I'm so mad," she sobbed.

"Because I'm blind?"

"Oh! Mother, I'm an awful daughter. I don't want to hurt you."

I touched her cheek. "You're not terrible. I know you care. There's no right or wrong with feelings. It's okay."

"How can I tell my mom her blindness is ruining my life?"

"How can you not tell me if it disturbs you that much?"

"But I'm your daughter," she insisted. "I've lived with you all my life. I'm supposed to be kind and show other kids how to treat you."

"Why do you think you have to do all that for me?"

"It started when the kids at school made fun of you. I had to defend you. I haven't been very nice to you because sometimes I'm ashamed to have a blind mom," she whispered.

My throat tightened. "That's what has torn you up inside and made you unhappy?"

"Yes."

I hugged her to me. "I'm sorry, honey. What a load to carry alone."

"It's not your fault, Mom."

"And it's not yours, either. It takes courage for you to say this. I'm glad to hear how you feel. I'm not offended."

We held each other and a weight of pain lifted from me. Lori seemed relieved. It was the beginning of healing and our gaining closeness again.

~Pam Bostwick

81

To the Owner of the Great Gray Dollhouse

*How am I going to live today
in order to create the tomorrow I'm committed to?*
~Anthony Robbins

"To the owner of the great gray dollhouse," my mother began to read aloud from the yellow-tinged, tattered letter. "I do not yet know you, but I already love you. One day, many years from now, this dollhouse will be yours and I can't wait to play in it with you."

Earlier in the day, we had carried the dollhouse down from the attic and, in preparation for the birthday party, gently removed all of its newspaper-wrapped contents: doll furniture and miniature figurines. Tucked neatly in the back of the dollhouse were six letters we had written, more than twenty years earlier, to my future daughter, who would one day be the new owner of the great gray dollhouse. After placing the dollhouse on the coffee table, we gathered around and began to read our letters, one by one. As the letters were being read, the realization that the owner of the great gray dollhouse was no longer a nameless, imaginary face touched me deeply. She was real. She was here. And she was my four-year-old daughter Isabella. And sitting beside her were my six-year-old son Diego and my husband Hebert. While this precious heirloom was being handed down, from mother to daughter, I felt the most surreal sensation. The moment that I had longed for had finally come to pass.

It was on my sixth Christmas that Santa had brought me this beautiful, wooden, two-story gray dollhouse. Over the years, I spent hours rearranging the delicate furniture, acting out imaginary scenarios, and becoming immersed in this little pretend world. In a matter of years, as things tend to happens, I had outgrown the dollhouse as well as my baby dolls and other childhood playthings. Over time, as I imagine most girls do, I began to dream of what having a real little girl would one day be like. What would I name her? What lessons would I teach her? What would she look like? What kind of temperament would she have?

Yet, there were patches of time during my youth when the image of my future daughter vanished from my mind. As the dark clouds of depression rolled into my life, all thoughts of any type of future disappeared. As skewed and flawed as my thinking was during those times, all I could see was my current state. All I could feel was my current sadness. All I could believe was my current condition.

The main turning point in my life came when I was twenty-five. After months of being depressed, my husband sent me from California back home to Texas to stay with my parents. He worked during the day and correctly determined that it was not healthy for me to be home alone without him. My state of mind continued to deteriorate over the next two weeks and I found myself in a moment of crisis one night. My mother sat by my bed and watched me that night so that I could get a good rest before being placed in the hospital the next morning.

Within a few days, my state of mind began to improve. My medication had been regulated, I had been introduced to new coping tools, and the dark clouds, which had impaired my thinking, drifted away. Slowly, thoughts of peace and happiness and a future began to return. It wasn't long before the face of my future daughter resurfaced. And because of her, I poured my heart and soul into becoming well again. The desire to be a healthy mom for my children was my motivation to enthusiastically and wholeheartedly devote myself to my treatment plan.

And so, eight years later, the dollhouse letters were being read. I sat in the presence of my family and a tear fell from my cheek. While listening to my mother read her letter, I watched in wonder as my real-life daughter began to play with the tiny figurines. After a few moments, the new owner of the great gray dollhouse began to giggle with sheer delight, and I couldn't help but smile.

~Michelle Sedas

82

A Mother Is Born

The moment a child is born, the mother is also born. She never existed before.
The woman existed, but the mother, never.
A mother is something absolutely new.
~Rajneesh

"But she's only seventeen!" I cried to the heavens and then I simply cried. My oldest daughter, my over-achieving, headstrong, stubborn, beautiful first-born child was pregnant. She'd gone to live with her dad the year before, but needed to come home now to decide what to do.

As I opened my arms to my errant child on my doorstep, I cried in despair over the loss of her childhood. I wanted to take that burden from her and give her back her teen years. I wanted to take the fear and the hurt from her and send her back in time to a more innocent life. But that was impossible. So I prayed and I cried and I prayed some more. I asked God to give me the wisdom to deal with the anger that burned in her towards me so that we could become a family again.

As she settled in, and joined her younger brother and sister in our home, she started to feel the effects of pregnancy and tried not to become attached yet... just in case. We talked and we planned for one thing and another and we visited doctors and were assured that everything was "normal." I could have strangled every doctor who said that. There was nothing "normal" about a seventeen-year-old becoming a mother. But we adjusted. Weeks passed and we talked about options. Abortion? No. Adoption? Maybe. Keep the baby? Maybe. Where was the father? Would he be involved? Not likely. Where would they live? Who would pay?

One quiet evening two weeks before the birth, she asked, "Mom, could you do it? Could you ever give up a child?" I said I could not. "Guess we better get ready for a baby then." I had just witnessed the birth of a mother as she took the first decisive step toward caring for this unborn baby.

I attended the birth of my granddaughter. I knew with certainty that the right decision had been made for this child. Who could love her more?

Then I watched as my beautiful, headstrong, overachieving, stubborn oldest child became a graceful mature mother. And I watch in wonder as this new child grows in grace. She is beautiful, of course, but also has the heart of a truly good person. I could not be prouder of my daughter for becoming the woman I now know. But it pales in comparison to my pride in my granddaughter. This young girl, Samantha, now twelve years old, loves with her whole heart, is forgiving and generous to a fault, and will become more than we could have ever hoped for.

~Ann Blakely

No More Ditches

A bend in the road is not the end of the road...
unless you fail to make the turn.
~Author Unknown

"G o to the hardware store and get new locks for the doors." That Sunday night the door was locked. Before she even had the chance to dig in her purse for her key, my husband met our daughter at the door and went outside to talk to her.

Where was I? I was sitting in her room, crying.

That evening she found out that she was no longer welcome in the home she had grown up in, and that all her belongings were boxed up and put in the carport. Clothes. Baseball and soccer trophies. Stuffed animals. Framed pictures.

Hearing the front door open and close again, I peeked out the window. There was Virginia walking up the street, away from the house and out of our lives. The only thing she took? Her baseball bat.

Every weekend, for months, it had been the same thing. Friday night, she'd leave. We would not see her again until Sunday evening. We had no clue where she was or what she was doing. Drugs? Boys? Drinking? We weren't sure, but we were certain it wasn't marathon study sessions that kept her away. There were some weekends when the worry was just overwhelming. No way could a teenager could continue to dance with danger indefinitely.

The last straw was hearing reports from neighbors: Virginia and a boy (her boyfriend, we later found out) skipped out on some classes so they could wait at a bus stop for another student. They jumped the kid and beat him up. We were told it was over drugs. Perhaps our daughter could watch her life go down the drain, her potential circling and whirling into the sewer, but we had our son to think about.

For the next five or six years, it felt like we had given up on Virginia, like she had been digitally removed from the holiday portrait… without a trace. Occasionally, she called. During those infrequent phone conversations, we'd talk of only superficial things — how work was for me, what job she currently had — but we never delved into anything deeper. We never spoke of that day.

One time during those lost years, when I guess things were especially tough for her, she called and asked, "Mom, could I come back home?"

There was no way we could go back to battling and worrying constantly. There was no way we could raise our son with rules and expectations, while our daughter did whatever she pleased. There was no way we could go back to preparing ourselves — every weekend — for a trip to the morgue to identify her body. And as much as it broke my heart to hear her swallow her pride and ask the question, it hurt even more to have to say, "No. I'm sorry. There's just no way."

In a quiet voice, she said that she understood, and the conversation ended soon after that. When I hung up the phone, I sat on the kitchen chair and sobbed.

When Virginia was twenty-four, she seemed to settle down a little. We were glad when she broke up with the boyfriend who had been there from the very beginning of her problems. We were glad when she began to make a real home for herself in her apartment. We were glad when she met Jason, who seemed like a nice young man. We were even glad when she called one day to say she was moving to Kickapoo, a tiny Illinois farm town.

"Jason has moved up there to help his mom and dad. They have a little house that needs work, and Jason's dad is sick. I think I can get a job with Cat." (Caterpillar was the major business in Peoria.)

Curiously, Virginia seemed to welcome the idea of living in a place where she could look out the front door and see nothing but cornfields. She was looking forward to being somewhere quiet. Perhaps the isolation, the lack of "city craziness" would help heal what was wrong with her.

Things were going well. We talked often on the phone. She got a job at Caterpillar and worked so hard on her skills that she made herself almost indispensable in her department. Most of her coworkers were men, but she could dish it out as well as take it, so their ribbing and comments had no effect. She worked the midnight shift because that meant a higher pay rate. She went to work every day, instead of allowing parties to get in the way of her job. She and Jason were happy. It seemed like she was really becoming a responsible, mature young lady.

A year or so later, my daughter called; the thing I had worried about for years had finally happened. She was pregnant. And although this was not a planned event, both she and Jason were happy, as was Jason's mother. (His father had died earlier in the year.) It seemed like a positive turn for everybody.

That April, I raced up to Peoria for the birth. Jason's mother and I had never met but we instantly bonded. We were both first-time grandmothers, and it ended up we had something else in common: we both dearly loved Virginia.

As we waited for the birth, Sharon told me what a fine, upstanding young lady my daughter was. Virginia helped around the house when she wasn't working, had endless energy, and was a perfect partner for Jason. The two of them never fought, but they did laugh a lot. And in the decisions they made for the baby-to-be, such as what crib to buy and what would be the best toys and car seat to purchase, they researched and discussed and made careful, thoughtful choices. Together.

What a gift! I was able to see my daughter, through Sharon's eyes. She had turned into a woman I was proud of. Sharon and I hugged at the end of a long day; she was now "Grandma" and I was "Grammy." And I could breathe a little easier, because Virginia was back on track.

Today, Riley is almost five. Jason, Virginia and their daughter moved back to St. Louis over a year ago, much to my delight. "Grammy" gets to babysit sometimes and I cherish those evenings. My granddaughter is a spitfire, loves anything pink, is incredibly bright and remembers everything. (That last one will definitely bite her parents in the rear end later on.) As parents, they are patient and gentle and easygoing, although there are definitely expectations and consequences.

My brother-in-law once spoke of the difficulty of keeping sons and daughters out of trouble. He said the main goal of parenting was to keep them on the road, making sure they stayed "out of the ditches and between the lines."

Now, my daughter is on track for good. She is staying far from the ditches and within the lines.

~Sioux Roslawski

The Magic of Mothers & Daughters

Chapter 9

What Goes Around Comes Around

Of all the haunting moments of motherhood, few rank with hearing your own words come out of your daughter's mouth.

~Victoria Secunda

The Lessons We Teach

And mothers are their daughters' role model,
their biological and emotional road map,
the arbiter of all their relationships.
~Victoria Secunda

don't know which job is harder: being a good parent or being a good child. But something happened recently to show me that if you're good at being one of them, chances are you are good at the other. Jennifer was twelve and Carrie was nine when my parents came from Florida to live with us. Red-haired, sneaker-wearing Grandma Mona, the woman who sewed a hundred nametapes into all of their clothes each summer before camp; who, when we moved out of town, traveled 800 miles from New York to Georgia just for the weekend to celebrate their birthdays; who always smelled of Juicy Fruit and Ivory soap, had cancer.

The year she spent with us was difficult for everyone. Watching someone you love grow sicker is always painful, but when it goes on for months and it's happening right in your own house, it's especially hard. Home was always the most comfortable and safest place in the universe. No more. As a daughter, I did my best to treat my mother the way I imagined she would treat me if the situations were reversed. Nothing was ever more important to her than protecting, supporting and guiding me through life. I never doubted that she thought of me as her greatest accomplishment. Now I was in a position to prove I could give the same love back to her. Except that I had two daughters and a husband and a job and a house and if I put her first, I pretty much had to shove everyone else to the back burner.

Doctor's appointments and hospital stays conflicted with dance recitals and soccer games. Jen and Carrie said they understood when I didn't show up, but I still felt lousy. It seemed like every day I was making a choice about who was more important, and it was never my husband or children. What kind of lesson was I teaching my girls? I worried about missing almost a year of clapping in the bleachers and shopping at the mall. I started dreaming about the most ordinary of times... a typical weeknight dinner with the family, exchanging jokes and speaking in the kind of shorthand only those intimately connected could understand.

Then one day the doctor agreed to let my mother return to Florida for a few weeks between chemotherapy treatments. We were thrilled that she felt well enough to go and excited at the idea of being just us once again. Passover was coming up the following week and we got busy preparing for a traditional holiday celebration.

About 4:00, the day before the first Seder, the phone rang. The kitchen was a mess, with pots simmering, eggs boiling, stacks of the good dishes ready to be put on the table, and boxes of matzos waiting to be opened. It was my father calling from a hospital in Florida. My mother's blood count had fallen to a dangerously low level and she was admitted for emergency transfusions. It wasn't life threatening at this point but they couldn't promise how quickly she'd respond.

"Just tell her not to worry. I'll be there as soon as I can catch a flight," I heard my voice say automatically.

I hung up the phone. No one said a word.

"I'm so sorry," I began, suddenly remembering all the plans we had made for the school vacation coming up the next week. How we were going to catch up on eight months worth of cuddles and make Rice Krispy Treats and buy new sneakers. "But I have to go."

The next few hours passed in a blur. By 8:30 that night I was on a plane to Fort Lauderdale. As the plane climbed into the sky, I looked out the window and thought about how unfair life can be.

All I wanted was to be with my family. I couldn't bear disappointing them one more time.

My eyes filled and I searched my pocketbook for a tissue. Instead I pulled out a piece of Jennifer's stationery, carefully folded in half. "DO NOT OPEN UNTIL YOU'RE IN THE AIR!" Carrie's oversized, green Magic Marker bubble writing warned. My heart beat faster as I unfolded the note.

> *Please try not to worry about us; we'll be fine. We are both*
> *so proud of the kind of daughter you are. And we just wanted*
> *you to know we think that it's inherited.*

> *Love, Jennifer and Carrie*

I closed my eyes and took a deep breath. Sometimes, when you're a mom, the lesson you think you're teaching is not the one being learned. And sometimes that's a very good thing.

~Marcia Byalick

Refrigerator Magnets

Never apologize for showing feeling.
When you do so, you apologize for the truth.
~Benjamin Disraeli

nudged the refrigerator door shut and a paper fluttered to the floor. Tossing dinner preparations onto the counter, I scooped it up. Then I recognized the yellowing-with-age story written by my daughter. Meal prep stalled as I read it before reaffixing the brittle sheet onto the chaotic collage that is our refrigerator door. This makeshift altar is the ultimate place of honor in our home.

I once longed for a sleek, stainless steel, uncluttered kitchen, like those pictured in the decorator magazines languishing on my coffee table. Those refrigerator doors sparkled, sans crayon drawings or handwritten stories secured with magnets bearing emergency phone numbers or insurance ads. I coveted the perfect door.

Initially, the papers plastered the trendy avocado green I'd painted the door. I'd purchased the refrigerator secondhand, and it shuddered and groaned loudly, sometimes shaking the magnets and treasured stories off in protest. Eventually, the scribblings covered the hideous green. I never imagined Old Avocado would outlast my love of the decorating theme. But it trembled on, and we noted family triumphs each time we scrounged for a snack or prepared a meal.

Through the years, my daughter and I shared the corner kitchen table as our workspace, always in the shadow of the refrigerator door. Sometimes we had typical mother/daughter disagreements and clashed. I thought her skirt was too short; she thought her curfew was too rigid. At times, we labored to maintain our relationship. But no matter how loud or harsh the words between us had been, we met in an unspoken truce back at the kitchen table.

She struggled with homework; I struggled to write. Her writing began with scrawls of short sentences. Mine began with funny stories about family life. Hers eventually progressed to "My Summer Vacation" and "Why I Hate Boys." Mine progressed to press releases for her school team competitions and prom chaperone satires. Hers moved on to "Dear Diary" and "I Love Boys."

Sometimes, submitting to publications, I collected rejection slips. Consequently, I often felt like I wasn't accomplishing much. I judged that if I didn't have sales, I didn't have value. So one by one, my daughter's school stories accumulated. When the door brimmed over, too many pages fluttering with each opening and closing swish, I reluctantly filed them away, next to a folder with my own stories, and posted her new ones.

One day I looked up to see my daughter writing college application essays. All too soon, she was far from home, off to her own life. At last I could have my sterile refrigerator door.

My empty nest left me alone at the table with more time to write. I thought of taking down the writing trophies. But I pecked away and frequently looked up at the memories as Old Avocado labored in the background. The refrigerator door clutter softened the solitude.

The extra writing time and effort paid off; I occasionally sold a story or a column. Excitedly, I shared copies with my daughter, now living in another state. And before I visited her in her first tiny apartment, I ordered a new refrigerator, partially financed with my writing proceeds. After joyful greetings, she gripped my hand tightly for the "grand tour" and steered me to her kitchen. I cried when I saw the copies of my published stories posted on her refrigerator door.

Shortly after I returned home, the shiny ultra-modern refrigerator of my dreams arrived. Before the delivery person carted off Old

Avocado, I carefully transferred and taped the paper accumulation to the new door. And then I added a copy of my own latest published story.

~Hope Sunderland

86

Chicken Soup for the Soul

Cheer Leader

Cookies are made of butter and love.
~Norwegian Proverb

As I stepped off the school bus and looked up at the house, I suspected she knew. She was peering around the curtain through the kitchen window as I made my way up the driveway. My five siblings raced past me, but I slowly sauntered along, kicking the gravel as I approached the back door. The buttery smell of freshly baked cookies filled the air as I opened the door and slipped off my shoes. As my brothers madly reached for cookies, my sister slapped their hands away.

Mom was oblivious to the chaos as she dried her hands on her apron and looked at me, examining my eyes. Donning her oven mitt, she pulled out a cookie sheet with a fresh batch of chocolate chip cookies, all the while keeping one eye on my ravenous brothers and one on me going through my backpack. I threw down my backpack, and headed straight to my room with my head down. I shut my door, only to hear a light knock.

"Vicki, can I come in?" her quiet voice asked as I watched the doorknob turn. She untied her flour-stained apron, and held her arms out to me. "I called the office at school to find out. I know you didn't make it."

"You what?" I couldn't believe that she would be so nosy as to call the office to find out who made the cheerleading squad. But when I felt her arms embrace me, I immediately felt her empathy and started crying, while rehashing all the horrible details. Through my sobs, I somehow relayed the entire scene.

"Mom, they posted the girls who made the squad on a big white poster board taped right on the wall of the main office! I could see from down the hall that my name wasn't on it!

"Megan and Sara's names were on it! Can you believe they made the team but not me? They can't do aerials or back handsprings!"

She just listened and nodded, as I relayed the painful details of how my friends' names were on the list, but not mine. I cried profusely, retelling her all the earth-shattering minutiae and she just sat and listened, stroking my hair.

"Mom, I even forgot an entire verse of the Eskymos' Fight Song! Can you believe that?"

She looked away at that one, and I realized she was fighting giggles as she covered her mouth. "How can you laugh at that, Mom? It's not funny!"

"I'm sorry, Vick. It just reminds me of my own sophomore year when I tried out for the flag corps and I kept dropping my flag in tryouts!" Her blue eyes twinkled, as she looked straight into mine, then tipped her head back in laughter.

I couldn't help but giggle through my tear-filled eyes. "Did you make the team?" I asked, half-laughing and half-crying.

"Of course not. I was shaking so much that I was surprised I could flip the flag even once!"

We laughed together, and she wiped my eyes, holding my chin in her rough hands. "Vicki, I know you're devastated now, and I was disappointed too, but pretty soon, you'll find something else you love to do, and you'll look back and laugh at this."

I had to admit, I no longer felt like throwing up.

"Oh don't start," I laughed, hitting her playfully on the arm. "I'm getting sick of everyone telling me it'll be okay, and that I can always try out for basketball."

Still holding my chin in her hands, she said, "Vicki, we're all just trying to encourage you." Of course, she was right. I hugged her, and as I looked over her shoulder, I realized my two little brothers had cracked open the door, and were peeking through, watching us. She didn't budge though, and kept wiping my eyes until I smiled up at her.

Ever since I can remember, my mom always seemed to say just the right words, and has always given each of us the attention we needed. Even though she had five other people's problems to attend to, Mom made me feel like my problem was her only concern. Each one of us at different times was her only concern.

After wiping my tears and listening to my tale of woe, she said something that I'll never forget. Though I was devastated at the time, my mom knew exactly how to soothe my pain. From that day on, she ended our many talks with two simple sentences: "Vicki, keep your chin up. That way, you can always see what's coming next."

And she was right—through all the disappointments of high school, she somehow made me feel that the crisis at hand would pass and there would soon be something new to look forward to. Just one month after consoling me, she was the first to congratulate me with another plate of cookies when I made the gymnastics team.

I'll never forget that day, because my mom gave me the most simple, yet most important gift a mother can give her daughter. She didn't get me the Guess jeans, or the new stereo I had been begging for. She taught me compassion. She taught me that a mother puts her children's needs ahead of her own. And I have used her gift in helping my own two children through their most troubling times. Whenever I hug and encourage my kids with their grandmother's words, it always helps to dry their tears.

My mom raised my five siblings and me to "keep our chins up" and always look to the next challenge—and in true mom style, she never asked for anything in return—well, maybe just a little bite of a chocolate chip cookie.

~Victoria LaFave

Reprinted by permission of
Carolyn Hiler ©2011

Some Things Never Change

You can learn many things from children.
How much patience you have, for instance.
~Franklin P. Jones

I was touched. And a little apprehensive, too. Two daughters, totally adult, independent women, women with children of their own, had a proposition: it was fall, the time when there is some primal instinct women feel that translates into "I need to shop for something new to wear."

I've had that primal pull for years at almost the precise moment when the hot flash of summer is definitely behind us, and when I don't want to look at anything pastel again for thirty more seconds.

So I understood when Amy and Nancy, who happen to live in the same town less than a mile from one another, suggested that we meet midway between the eighty miles that separate them from me and shop together.

It felt both familiar—we spent a lot of time shopping together back in the days when we all lived under the same roof—and weird. It had been not just months, but years, since we greeted fall with a shopping trip together.

Through rose-colored glasses, I seemed to remember happy romps on those back-to-school odysseys. I thought I recalled how eagerly these daughters sought my advice, and even took it.

Ah, memory and its tricks…

But of course I said yes, and then we hammered out a date that worked for the three of us. That actually took longer than any shopping trip would. And their oldest sister, who has recently launched a new career complete with great challenges and great satisfactions, declined with thanks.

"It'll be so much fun!" said Nancy, the family optimist.

How tricky memory is. How fortunate that I'd accepted this invitation with temporary amnesia about the darker side of shopping with daughters, the side that has nothing to do with laughter and joy.

So it came to pass that on a recent Saturday, after surviving logistical nightmares that would stop a military general in his tracks, Nancy, Amy and I met at their favorite fashion discount store in central New Jersey. There was no way we'd shop anything but discount. That was a given.

I recorded, with that automatic maternal sensor, that both daughters looked well and seemed happy and fit. And the mission, after all, was simple: Nancy needed a coat. A warm, practical winter coat. Amy needed a glamorous dress, possibly velvet, for an upcoming event.

Tell me, then, how we ended up in the shoe department, with Nancy trying on hideous brown oxford-type shoes that I seemed to remember dimly on my own grandmother's feet? Evidently, those very shoes were high on the hit parade in Nancy's circle, which is actually quite fashion-savvy. Who knew?

Tell me, also, how we moved from the shoe department, where Nancy actually plunked down good money for the clunkies, to an area of the store where jeans of all styles, cuts and lengths were flashily displayed, leading impetuous Amy to try on what seemed like all of them.

"Love is patient," I reminded myself. And initially, I hung in there. Through the shoes, through the jeans, and later the shirts that might go with them, I smiled through gritted teeth at my daughters' choices.

They didn't actually want to hear my reactions, which were decidedly negative about almost everything they loved.

There were rambles through racks and racks of blazers that had nothing to do with winter coats or velvet dresses. I remained stoic. The picture of motherly endurance.

Not once did I mention focus. Not once did I remind my daughters that we had set a time limit on this afternoon delight, and that I, for one, was already starving and exhausted.

Then Amy asked for my honest opinion of the dress she had tried on, the one with the zigzag hemline and the droopy shoulders in a ghastly greenish color. So I told her. And suddenly, it was eighth grade again, and Amy and I were having our periodic fitting room fight, full of sound and fury, signifying nothing.

My skirmish with Nancy involved the forty-five minutes it took this terminally indecisive daughter to select not a sensible coat, but a decidedly funky T-shirt that seemed better suited to a teeny-bopper than a women coasting into her forties. Nancy, a psychologist, decided that the core issue was really not the shirt or her indecision, but about control. Mine.

Ah, mother/daughter shopping bliss! And oh, the wonderful relief of finally bidding two daughters goodbye as they juggled shopping bags full of treasures, at least as they define them, and I headed for home, ready to collapse into an exhausted heap.

Nancy never did get the winter coat. Amy never did find the velvet dress.

And I wished them both luck in the search... from a safe maternal distance half a state away.

Fall—and shopping—remain encoded in my DNA. But the rose-colored glasses have come off.

And I now understand that when it comes to shopping with my adult daughters, the best approach is... not to.

~Sally Schwartz Friedman

Just a Good Mother

Being a full-time mother is one of the highest salaried jobs in my field,
since the payment is pure love.
~Mildred B. Vermont

truly believe that my calling was to just be a good mother," my mother said, pouring us cups of coffee and then putting away the creamer. My mother says this contentedly. And often. Not as often, of course, as she doles out such motherly advice as, "Always make sure you have tissue in your purse. You never know when you'll find yourself inside a bathroom stall with an empty roll of toilet paper." But my mother makes reference to her passion for motherhood often enough to let me know she means it. She knows it in her bones: her purpose in life was to be my mother.

Still, I sometimes can't help but get the impression that perhaps she tells me this in order to convince me that, although her innate longing to nurture, raise, and guide me didn't render stock options, a 401K or a car allowance, it was still indeed a real job that she took tremendous pride in.

While my mother and I share many commonalities, we also possess the kinds of differences that are a reflection of the two distinct paths we have traveled. She married my father, her first serious boyfriend, a year before she graduated college, had me at the tender age of twenty-four, and deferred her career after making the no-brainer decision to stay home with me until I was old enough to enter elementary school. I, on the other hand, dove head first into the cold, rocky waters of a highly competitive career field—on-air television reporting—which precipitated a move to another state mere months after earning my Bachelor of Arts degree from her alma mater, spent my twenties footloose and fancy-free, and finally settled down and married at thirty.

Suffice it to say, my grueling career serves as a constant reminder of how different we are. When my mother was my age, she was helping me with my times tables at night and always made sure that a well-balanced meal graced the table. "A true dinner has a meat, a starch, and a vegetable," she would always say. Me? I spend my evenings cooped up in my office, hypnotized by the steady drone of fluorescent lighting while trying to make a deadline. And dinner—if I have one—is carryout from the local Coney Island where they know me by name.

I love having a career, and most days I love my insanely chaotic life. But something that happened to all of my girlfriends—something I have yet to experience—has opened my eyes to the fact that there is more to life than this.

That "something" is motherhood.

I'm not saying that I hear a ticking clock, or that I yearn to feel the subtle vibration from the pitter-patter of little feet just yet. But I do know that a well-written press release—no matter what kind of paper it's printed on—will never have that new baby smell or make me feel as proud as raising me has made my mother.

In experiencing motherhood through my friends, watching them as they watch their tiny miracles blossom, the joy is palpable. It is also unrivaled. Like me, my friends were intensely driven and focused on their career in their twenties, but the moment they became mothers, the grind they had worked so hard to establish became second fiddle to ensuring the rightful development of their offspring.

Where have I seen this before? I thought. It was like déjà vu—I had been here, but I couldn't quite put my finger on it. Then I realized that all I had to do was look around, and there it was. It was in the photo of me at age three, dressed as a mouse for Halloween, in a costume my mother, an impassioned seamstress, had created; it was in the photo of me on stage at my third grade talent show, a photo that was captured through the lens of my mother's camera as she stood front and center; it was also in the photo of me at a summer picnic with freshly braided hair, wildly thick hair that my mother carefully combed each night while I sat dutifully between her legs and watched the Nickelodeon channel.

Of course, my mother's unconditional love was supplemented by an acutely watchful eye during that hormonally challenged period otherwise known as adolescence, a time during which my mother surely thought: who are you and what have you done with my daughter? My mother snooped incessantly through my drawers, boldly reading my diary to determine whether I was running with the right crowd—and with good reason. I would spin a web of lies at the drop of a hat.

Thankfully, the hawk morphed back into a mother when the deceitful smart aleck had fully grown into womanhood. My mother had not only remained my mother, but had also gained a new title: best friend. In the twelve months leading up to my wedding day, she secretly penned a letter that she gave me upon my return from my honeymoon. In it is some of her most poignant advice yet:

Always be true to yourself; never do anything if it doesn't feel right to you. Make sure you are getting what you need. I don't mean that in a selfish, self-centered way, but in a way that serves your purpose, because if you are not happy and fulfilled, then you certainly cannot contribute to the happiness of Scott. It is up to you to be happy.

I realized then that "just a good mother" didn't seem to do her job title justice.

But enough of waxing poetic. I would be remiss if I didn't admit there are times when my mother's smothering I-know-best unsolicited advice causes my eyes to roll back in my head. But then, like clockwork, she'll release a nugget of wisdom that causes me to ponder whether I really know as much as I think I do. Yes, my innate stubbornness and independence make it hard for me to utter the phrase, "Okay, you were right," but don't think for one solitary second that

I'm not filing away her counsel for that anticipated rainy day when I will surely draw upon it.

"Just wait until you have kids," my mother always says. "And I hope you have a girl so you know exactly how it feels."

I used to reply by staring at her smugly in silence.

But now I always tell her, "I hope so, too. I would love nothing more than to just be a good mother."

~Courtney Conover

I'm a Barbie Girl

So, like a forgotten fire, a childhood can always flare up again within us.
~Gaston Bachelard

On my daughter's sixth birthday, she stepped into the magical world of Barbie. Her first doll was a Malibu Barbie. All her guests gave her Barbie presents. Her lucky doll had her own car, several fashionable outfits, and of course, a swimming pool. From that moment on there was no going back.

Each Christmas or birthday she received at least one Barbie doll. Her grandmothers would give her beautifully coiffed versions with stunning designer dresses. They fervently hoped that she would leave them in the boxes, their beauty preserved. My daughter was unable to resist playing with each one. Eventually she boasted a box full of Barbies, who unclothed, were almost indistinguishable, at least to me.

These dolls shared a townhouse full of miniature furniture, and coolest of all, an elevator. There is something about tiny, perfectly replicated items that is mesmerizing. Barbies swam in their own pool and drove their own pink sports car. They were living the good life.

Occasionally, I would pull out my Barbie. I had only one. I had played carefully with her as a child and I had taken meticulous care of her over the years. She was housed in a black patent case, a mini closet with hangers filled with clothes and small drawers full of shoes and accessories. Some of the clothes had been hand sewn by me as a child. One was even crocheted.

Taking out my Barbie was something of an event. Everything had to be carefully handled. Her tiny bracelets and sunglasses were a wonder. The amazing details of her clothes, from the top stitching on her jeans to the tailored lines of her cocktail dress, were marveled over.

My daughter loved these times and I knew she wanted my doll, but I remembered her box of clones, loved but indistinguishable. I knew the time would come when I would entrust my doll to her, but not yet.

After a time, my daughter also put her dolls on the top shelf of her closet. She might take them out on a rainy day and dress them up in their pretty dresses, but for the most part she had other pursuits. She was busy with school and friends. She was growing up.

Years at a time went by without her taking out her dolls. Like mine, they were pushed to the back of a shelf, forgotten. Eventually they were stored in the basement. Room was needed in the closet for my daughter's own clothes and accessories. I don't know if Barbie had been her influence, but she was enamored of lovely clothes, shoes, handbags, and jewelry. This passion increased as each year passed.

Watching TV together, one evening, we heard people who were speaking out against Barbie dolls. They said that little girls were growing up with impossible ideals of body image because of their dolls. My daughter and I were shocked.

"Have you ever thought of Barbie as anything but a pretty toy?" she asked me.

"Not really," I said.

We listened, appalled. You see we did not look anything like a Barbie doll. We both had very dark hair and we were certainly not fashion-model-thin nor did we ever aspire to be. If anything, we were more influenced by her fashions and the possibility that we could be anything… just like Barbie.

"Can you believe that they want to get rid of Barbie?" My daughter was stunned, as was I. "That's just wrong."

I thought about how our Barbies had been a bond between us, a common thread that ran through our lives. It had been a way for us to communicate, a way for her grandmothers to share in her life. We actually felt sad that little girls might grow up without the pleasure of having played with Barbie dolls.

My daughter is a woman now. She has recently begun to collect Barbies again. She is more selective and careful. They are still beautiful and still very affordable. She has them lined up, posed on their stands, on a shelf in her bedroom. In the middle of her collection stands my old Barbie in her black and white striped swimsuit and white sunglasses with the blue lenses. The new dolls are pretty but my original is still the coolest.

My daughter and I are, once again, talking Barbie. It remains one of those special threads between us. Sometimes, when visiting her grandmothers, you will hear them ask, "Do you still have the Barbies I gave you?" I have no doubt that one day, if she has a daughter of her own, or maybe a granddaughter, that thread will remain and her Barbies will be passed down to thrill another generation.

~Debbie Acklin

A Mother
Who Read to Me

Books are the bees which carry the quickening pollen
from one to another mind.
~James Russell Lowell

Mother slipped into my bedroom on the night of my sixth birthday, hands behind her back. "I have one more present for you," she said. "One I wanted to save until now."

Another present? But I'd already gotten roller skates and a paint set and a shiny yellow rain slicker. Not to mention chocolate cake with chocolate icing.

"Close your eyes and hold out your hands." I did. And in them she placed a brand-new hardcover book. A picture of a little girl with her arms wrapped around a pig graced the cover. "It's *Charlotte's Web* by E.B. White," Mother said. "The perfect story for a six-year-old."

I opened the book to page one. But since I was only in first grade, and since school had only just started, I didn't know most of the words.

"It might be too hard for you to read by yourself right now," Mother said. "But I thought I'd read a chapter to you every night if you want me to." I nodded. And so she began the timeless story of Fern and Wilbur and the spider that loved them with the magical first sentence I'll never forget: "Where's Papa going with that ax?"

Mother wasn't exactly true to her word. She didn't read me a chapter of *Charlotte's Web* every night. Sometimes she read three or four. In less than a week, we reached the final pages, sobbing together as she read the part where Charlotte dies. We sighed wistfully as the dear spider's children sailed away from Zuckerman's farm on their silk balloons and the book ended with the magical sentences I'll never forget: "It is not often that someone comes along who is a true friend and a good writer. Charlotte was both."

That's when I fell in love with reading.

More books followed. *The Bobbsey Twins*, Laura Ingalls Wilder's *Little House on the Prairie* series and *The Chronicles of Narnia* by C.S. Lewis. As time passed and my reading skills improved, Mother and I took turns reading chapters aloud, snuggled together—as we had been from the beginning—in the sagging oversized armchair in the corner of my bedroom.

Those golden times didn't last, of course. By the time I was old enough for *Nancy Drew* and *The Black Stallion* and Judy Blume books, I was a proficient reader, teetering on the brink of adolescence. My snuggle-up-and-read time with Mother came to an end.

But our shared love of books didn't.

When I read *To Kill a Mockingbird*, *Catcher in the Rye* and *The Grapes of Wrath* in high school, Mother did, too, so that we could talk about them. My letters and phone calls home from college began, "Let me tell you what I'm reading."

So it was no surprise when, just hours after the birth of my first child, Mother slipped into my hospital room with her hands behind her back. "I have a present for Meg," she said. "Close your eyes and hold out your hands."

I did. And in them she placed a well-worn hardcover book with a picture of a little girl, her arms wrapped around a pig, gracing the cover.

I didn't read it to Meg right away, of course. In fact, I waited until bedtime on her sixth birthday, after we had finished the chocolate cake with chocolate icing. She snuggled up next to me in the sagging oversized armchair that now sat in the corner of her bedroom as I opened *Charlotte's Web* to page one.

And then I read the magical first sentence aloud to her: "Where's Papa going with that ax?"

~Jennie Ivey

Monster in the House

Adolescence is a period of rapid changes. Between the ages of 12 and 17, for example, a parent ages as much as 20 years.
~Author Unknown

'm not going to school and you can't make me!" My fifteen-year-old daughter pounded her fists on the kitchen table. Plates rattled and a pitcher of orange juice careened to the floor. She bolted from the table and slammed her bedroom door, causing the pictures hanging in the hall to vibrate on their hooks.

"Reneé, come back here. Now!" Our daily morning battle had begun.

As soon as my husband left for work, Reneé turned from a mild-mannered teenager into a raging monster. The Hulk had nothing on her.

"She hates me," I complained to Harry that night. "Nothing I do is right. She said she wouldn't be caught dead in the clothes I picked out for her. She used to love going shopping with me. Now she just wants to be dropped off at the mall. Doesn't she realize that horrible things can happen to young girls alone?"

I had a horrible thought. "Do you think she could be on drugs?"

"She seems fine to me." He looked up from the newspaper. "I'm sure she's not on drugs. Stop worrying so much."

"That's because she's fine around you." Daddy's little girl only had to smile up at him and all was forgiven. He just didn't or couldn't see the emotional roller coaster Reneé was on. She was still his five-year-old golden princess, not an angry teenager leaving havoc in her wake.

"When you're not home, it's a different world."

"Sounds like the two of you have a problem." He turned back to his paper. "She's just growing up; things will work themselves out."

He didn't understand. The house was filled with conflict. I would say yes and she would automatically say no. Most family rules were broken and conversations were either shouting matches or ended in sullen silence.

After taking away her phone privileges for the second time in a month, I tried to reason with her. "Reneé, you know your curfew is 10:00. Not 10:30."

"You don't understand," she retorted.

"Help me understand," I said.

According to her, a list of the things I didn't understand would go from here to the moon.

I reached out to her. "What's happening? What is the problem? Are you on drugs?" My greatest fear was that my darling daughter was ruining her life and I had to stop her.

"Me?" she screamed. "You're the one with a problem."

The next day I called her pediatrician, Dr. Jim, and scheduled an appointment. He had treated her for colds and aches and sprains from soccer games. He had guided her through her childhood illnesses. She trusted him and so did I.

"Reneé must be on drugs. She's turned into a smart mouth, rule-breaking monster. She hates me," I sobbed.

"It can't be that bad," Dr. Jim calmly replied. "Reneé is a great kid. Bring her in and we'll find out what's going on."

Our appointment was the next morning. Reneé was angry and brooding. She wanted to be any place but at the doctor's office. When we arrived the nurse placed us in separate exam rooms.

I was apprehensive about what he would find out. The last thing I expected was for him to come into the small room with a smile on his face.

"What did she say? Did you do a blood test? Is she on drugs? Why is she acting this way? Why does she hate me?" I cried out.

Dr. Jim patted me on the shoulder. "Calm down. She's not on drugs."

"Then what's wrong?" I demanded.

"According to Reneé, there is a monster in your house," he grinned, "and it's you."

"Me!"

"She's concerned you're going crazy with all these rules and demands and it must be menopause or something. She wants me to check you out."

"Me!" I jumped up from the chair.

"Don't worry, you're fine." He said.

"But, Reneé…"

"Reneé has teenage-itis," Dr. Jim interrupted. "Happens to all thirteen-year-olds. She'll outgrow it."

"But."

He took out his medical pad and started to write. "Here." He handed me the scrap of paper. "When things get bad, read this."

I looked down at the words and cried.

"They only lash out at the one who loves them the most. The one who won't reject them regardless of how they act."

Dr. Jim was right. Reneé is now my best friend. One of my happiest days as a mother was when she thanked me for all the rules she once considered stupid and interfering.

Reneé went off to college and married a fine young man. She told me of friends who didn't turn out as well—they had been allowed to roam the mall without curfews, had dropped out of school, or went the drug route and messed up their lives.

I am no longer the meanest mom in the world. We shop and have lunch together. She calls often for advice.

It seems though that she has a monster in her house. My granddaughter, Lexi, just turned thirteen.

Monsters come and go, but mothers and daughters stay together forever.

~Jeri McBryde

Reprinted by permission of
Carolyn Hiler ©2011

92

My Three Mirrors

People like us, who believe in physics, know that the distinction between past, present, and future is only a stubbornly persistent illusion.
~Albert Einstein

Raising three beautiful daughters was such a blessing... sometimes! Oh, the "agony and the ecstasy" of life with four females in the same household.

When the girls were small I had so much fun dressing them alike, although they hated it. It was a pleasure showing them off to my friends, except those would inevitably be their moody days. And of course teenage girls are always so loving to their mother... when they want to be!

Now they are all grown up and I have watched three distinct personalities emerge, each reminiscent of myself, but in a completely different way. They were fed the same food, taught the same values, raised by the same guidelines. How are they all so different?

My oldest daughter was always a serious child. She caught on fast to anything presented to her and analyzed every topic. Anything that came at her too fast stressed her as she tried to digest it all. *Sesame Street* and the flashing letters were not for her! She worried about everyone and everything... and still does to this day.

My second daughter was also very bright. Although not quite as serious as her older sister, she was very methodical in most everything she did. She thought things through and strategized her plan of attack. She still does to this day.

Then there's my youngest. Smart, but happy-go-lucky, ready to have fun at the drop of a hat and not a worrier. She only seems to get upset when we worry about her!

They all have children of their own and I have now realized the apple doesn't fall far from the tree!

The oldest has two daughters. I see so much of their mother in them. When they reached the difficult teenage years, I tried to remind my daughter of her younger days. She saw no resemblance... did she have amnesia? Her girls are fun for me but I see so much of her serious ways in them. They are both smart, hard workers, and tackle anything sent their way. They love to question the system, challenge the rules... just enough to make life interesting!

My second daughter has a son. He is so much like her. In fact, he is exactly like her! Smart, methodical, and logical. He makes a plan and works his plan... just like his mother!

My youngest has two boys. The older one is smart, serious, but ready to have fun at any given moment. Her younger son is all fun.

I was eighteen years old when my first child was born. A baby having a baby! I worried about that first baby all the time. Was I doing the right thing, was she eating enough, was she warm enough, was she... was she... was she...?

No wonder she is so serious!

Four years later I had my second daughter. I was more relaxed. I worked part-time and tried to juggle family, job and social life. Methodical and logical in all my plans for life. Do I see myself in her? You bet I do.

Then there's my youngest. Three years later... it was all a breeze. I could do anything! Life was a piece of cake... I had it made! What fun everything was... no wonder she doesn't worry.

There is so much of us in our children. I can see myself at various stages of my life in every member of my family. They are my mirrors and I'm very proud of each and every one of them.

~Kristine Byron

The Magic of Mothers & Daughters

Chapter 10

Dreams Fulfilled

A daughter is the happy memories of the past,
the joyful moments of the present,
and the hope and promise of the future.

~Author Unknown

93

The Rest Is Unwritten

Turn your face to the sun and the shadows fall behind you.
~Maori Proverb

I can't believe I am doing this again. I am crying hysterically, hidden behind the closed bathroom door at work.

I seem to have it together everywhere else, but every time I come into work a dark, hellacious shadow invades my view. I don't belong here, yet I can't seem to find a way out. I have to face it—I hate my job!

I am in a role that does not play to any of my strengths. Every day I keep hoping my boss will recognize my good ideas and promote me, but I feel invisible here. Less than a year ago, I was making four times as much money, I was in a leadership role, and I was doing work that I loved. Then I was laid off. Now I am stuck in a dead-end job that I can't find any passion for. I look into the bathroom mirror and splash water on my face. I say to myself, "Get it together girl, you are living through the largest economic depression since the 1930s; be happy you even have a job."

I pull myself together long enough to finish my shift. As I exit my workplace, I gaze across the shopping center and see a beautiful version of what I'll likely look like in thirty years. To my amazement, my mother is approaching me. Before I can even ask what she's doing here, she explains: "I had a feeling you needed a friend today. So I cleared my schedule and came to say hi! Are you off work now?" I reach out for one of her world famous hugs, and say, "Mom, you are so amazing; your timing couldn't be better. Lets go get dinner."

For the past few months, my job situation has gone from okay to horrible. My mother has patiently listened as I've shared how things keep getting worse. As we sit down for dinner I go over the details of my day, but exclude the tale of my bathroom breakdown. Before I can finish the story, my mother reaches across the booth, grabs my hands and says, "What would it take… how much money would you need, to get peace of mind and quit? I'm convinced that you are blocking your true self by staying in this toxic environment."

As the words come out of her mouth, a weight miraculously lifts off my shoulders. I answer, "I have enough money in savings to hold me over until I find a job!" At this moment, I realize I have been trapping myself. No one is keeping me in this painful job except for me. My mother just reminded me that in life we always have choices. I can choose to be happy. One small comment from my mother opened the space in my mind to have a transformational shift. I realize that up until now, I have been making excuses, finding reasons to justify dealing with my unhappiness instead of seeking to change my circumstances. I just couldn't see the way out through the fear that was consuming me. My mother helped peel the blinders back.

I take my mother's advice and put in my two-week notice at work. My manager tells me that when I walked into work that day, I exuded a calm presence that she hadn't seen in me before. I don't want to tell her that the reason for my changed mood was that I finally felt free and alive again. When I tell her "I quit!" I don't just mean quitting this job. Internally, I understand that I'm also quitting my routine of excuses and justification. From now on, I resolve that I will always choose love over fear. Of course, I don't say any of this to my manager. Instead I simply smile and say, "Thank you for this opportunity, but I've realized that it is my time to leave."

As I push through the last two weeks in this job, I try to leave the fear behind. I try to trust in my safety net, but the reality is that I do not have another job lined up and I begin to worry. I feel that I'm taking a giant leap of faith. What if I don't get a job for months? The anxiety creeps back in. Precisely at that moment I get a text message from my mom. It reads, "Trust your heart; you are doing the right thing. Today is the first day of the rest of your life; the rest is still unwritten." I smile at my mother's words, and realize she is right; everything is in divine order. It seems like my mother's timing is yet again perfect. Literally five minutes after my mother's message I receive a phone call from my future employers. They want me to start full-time as soon as possible... making twice my current income!

I am immediately filled with gratitude. My mother was the guiding light who helped me get back on track. Mothers have a way of knowing and guiding when we go astray. I needed a wake-up call. My mother swooped in at the moment I most needed her to shower me with her wisdom and love.

~Shannon Kaiser

94

A True Daughter

It's such a grand thing to be a mother of a mother—
that's why the world calls her grandmother.
~Author Unknown

have known her since she was seventeen. That is more than half of her life. I did not give birth to her but my son fell in love with her and asked her to marry him. She became my daughter and I became her mother. It was a real treat to have another female around after all those years with a husband and three sons!

I have watched her grow up and evolve from a teenager into an amazing adult. She is very self-confident and smart, and at the same time, she is loving, compassionate, and fun. She brings sunshine and warmth into any room she enters.

We have fun together. We often will say the same thing at the same time. She claims we have the same brain and that we think alike. I remember when I was out shopping for earrings to give her for her birthday. When the saleswoman learned I was buying a gift for my daughter-in-law she gave me that "oh, poor you" look. She told me I should look at all of the earrings in the case and then pick the earrings I liked the very least because those would be the ones my daughter-in-law would like the best. I told her that, in this case, her plan wouldn't work. I picked the ones I liked the best and Crescent loved them too. I knew she would!

After my son and Crescent had been married for a number of years, we got the exciting news that she was pregnant. It was wonderful for me to see Crescent slowly change from a career woman into a mom. Her pregnancy was textbook perfect and she just glowed. At each ultrasound appointment we saw what our baby looked like and how he was developing. And make no mistake about it... this was OUR baby! Crescent has always stressed that this baby belongs to me, too, and she has always made me feel a special part of his life since the time he was conceived. I have always been included and I thank her for that.

It has been an amazing experience to watch Crescent transform from daughter to mother. I was so proud of the way she handled those first few months: from the sleepless nights to the frustrations of having a colicky baby to the joy of his first smile and to the laughter at his cute antics. That teenager I met years ago has become a mature, selfless, compassionate mother. I couldn't be any more proud of her if I had given birth to her myself.

Crescent had a very successful career. Before our baby was born she wasn't sure that she wanted to be a stay-at-home mom and we talked about it a lot. After he was born she told me that she just couldn't bear the thought of being away from him for even a little while: to miss his first smile, his first laugh, his first steps. I had been a stay-at-home mom and I told her that being a mom is the hardest job in the whole world. There are no days off, no promotions, no paid vacations. But motherhood is also the very best and most rewarding job in the whole world.

Our baby is almost a year old now. He's over his colic and is a joy to be around. Crescent's hard work and patience has started to pay off. He is developing his own personality and I can see some of her sweet traits in him already. Every day Crescent continues to grow as a mom. She tells me that I have been a role model for her. And for that I am so proud and blessed. How lucky our baby is to have such an amazing mom. And how lucky I am to have such a wonderful daughter.

~Barbara LoMonaco

95

A True Success

I've got a theory that if you give 100 percent all of the time,
somehow things will work out in the end.
~Larry Bird

"Dallas! Time to come in for dinner!" my mom called.

"Okay, give me a sec—just one more shot!" I took a deep breath, gazing up at the basketball hoop in our driveway. I shuffled my feet to the perfect position: right foot two inches behind the free-throw line, left foot a couple more inches back. I dribbled once, twice. Took another breath. Feeling the basketball's firm, familiar weight in my hands, I lifted it up to the shooting position, bent my knees, and released.

The ball soared towards the hoop in a straight, graceful arc, swishing cleanly through the net. Score! Twenty-four out of twenty-five free throws in a row. Almost perfect, but not quite. To me, it wasn't good enough.

After dinner, I went back outside and shot free throw after free throw until it became too dark to make out the hoop against the night sky.

The next morning, my mom drove me to the big free-throw shooting contest for which I'd spent countless hours practicing. I was nervous and quiet during the two-hour drive. If I won this contest, I would move on to the statewide competition.

It was the time of year when my mom was busiest at work. She was manager of her division and I knew she could use her time off to rest. But here she was, taking an entire Saturday to cheerfully drive down with me and cheer me on. More than anything, I wanted to make her proud.

We arrived at the high school gym where the competition was being held. The sound of bouncing basketballs echoed off the walls as kids warmed up before the big event. The stands were crowded with people. I pictured myself out there alone on the basketball court, shooting free throws in front of everyone, and my nervousness escalated.

"Don't be nervous, sweetheart!" my mom said, as if sensing my anxiety. "You'll do great! You've been practicing for weeks!" She helped me get checked in at the registration table, and then it was time for me to venture onto the basketball court and start warming up. Mom gave me a hug and headed for the stands.

There were four other girls competing in my age division. The competition was structured so we each shot five free throws at a time, for a total of twenty-five free throws. The girl with the best score at the end would move on to the statewide competition.

When it was my first turn, I walked out to the free-throw line, searching for my mom's face in the crowd. She caught my eye and gave a little wave and smiled at me. I felt my nerves calm a bit and reminded myself of all the free throws I had practiced shooting in my driveway at home.

Swish, swish, swish, swish, swish; I made all five free throws my first turn.

My confidence increased as the competition went on. Soon there were only two of us in the lead, neck and neck. We both went ten-for-ten, then fifteen-for-fifteen, then twenty-for-twenty.

The other girl took her final turn. Swish, swish, swish, swish, swish. A perfect twenty-five for twenty-five. In order to stay in the competition, I would have to make all five of my final free throws to force us into a tiebreaker.

I took a deep breath as I strode to the line. My mom gave me a thumbs-up from the stands.

Swish. Swish. Swish. Swish.

One more shot. I just needed to make this final shot to stay in the competition.

I shuffled my feet to the perfect position: right foot two inches behind the line, left foot a couple more inches back. I dribbled once, twice. Took a deep breath. I lifted the basketball up to the shooting position, bent my knees, and released.

The ball spun around the rim, as if in slow motion. It felt as if the entire gym were holding its breath. I watched the basketball roll around the rim of the hoop… rolling, rolling, rolling… out.

I had missed one shot. My final score was only twenty-four out of twenty-five.

After all that hard work, after all those hours of practice, after the long drive down on a Saturday morning, I had lost the competition. I felt like a failure. Like I'd let my mom down.

Fighting back tears, I congratulated the ecstatic winner. Then I shuffled toward the stands, toward my waiting mom. I looked down at my feet. Around me, the bouncing of many basketballs seemed to echo sadly on the gym floor.

Mom greeted me with a huge smile as she enveloped me in a hug. "Dallas, you were fantastic out there!" she said.

"But I lost," I sniffled. "I missed that last free throw."

"That's okay," my mom said, lifting up my face to meet her eyes. "Some things are out of our control. Sometimes the ball just doesn't roll in." She reminded me of the famous basketball coach John Wooden's definition of success: "Success is peace of mind, which is a direct result of self-satisfaction in knowing you did your best to become the best you are capable of becoming."

"Did you try your best?" she asked.

"Yes," I said.

"Did you put in the effort and practice as much as you could?"

"Yes."

"Then you're a true success," my mom concluded. "I could not be any prouder of you!"

I never thought that losing a free-throw contest would boost my self-esteem, but it did. Through my mom's genuine pride and encouragement, I was able to find pride and confidence in myself, no matter the circumstance. She helped me separate "success" from "perfection." I often think back to Coach Wooden's definition of success, and I strive to be the best person I am capable of being. And even today, when "the ball rolls out," so to speak, a hug from my mom always makes things better.

~Dallas Woodburn

Girl Scout

And Girl Scouting is not just knowing... but doing... not just doing, but being.
~Juliette G. Low

I can remember walking at least twenty blocks to those Brownie Girl Scout meetings every week. It was probably closer to five or six blocks, but I was only seven or eight years old, so it seemed farther.

I went faithfully every week... even though I was the only girl there who didn't have a vest or pretty uniform to wear. Even though I was the only girl there whose parents didn't drop her off, pick her up, or get involved in the troop in any way. Even though I never got to attend any of the outings, camps, or even sell cookies. Even though I didn't know my troop number or what that even was.

All I knew was that once a week I went to a place where everyone was nice to me. And even though I didn't know all their names, I knew that once a week I had lots of friends, at least for one night, because they said they were at the end of every meeting in our friendship circle. Someone always held my hand in the circle, and no one cared that I didn't have on a pretty uniform... they didn't care if my clothes weren't nice... if my hair was brushed... or that my parents never even paid my dues for that matter. What were dues anyway? I didn't know.

I don't remember the crafts we made or the projects we worked on. I don't remember family nights or my troop leader's name. I can only remember the feeling of belonging. I can only remember that for one night a week I wasn't the poor girl with tattered clothes. I wasn't the loner daydreaming in class while everyone laughed because I didn't hear the teacher call my name. I wasn't the girl with tangled hair that no one combed. I wasn't at home listening to the screaming or the sound of his fist when it collided with her skin.

I was safe, and I was with people who didn't mind me being there, even though I never registered or never contributed to the troop in any way. I wasn't in the way, and I was welcome just as I was. I was someone. I was significant enough to be someone's friend and that made all the difference to me... at least once a week.

So today, at twenty-seven, I am a proud, registered Girl Scout in troop 198. I still don't wear a vest or pretty uniform. But my pretty little girl gets the skirt, shirt, vest, hat, and even the hoodie. She (with my help) sold just over 500 boxes of cookies this year. She earned enough "cookie dough" to pay her way to camp this summer. I told her that her cookie dough points could be used to buy anything she wanted in the Girl Scout shop or to go camping. Without hesitation, she decided she wanted to go camping. And while I was telling her the options on which camps she could go to, she decided, without hesitation, that she'd be going to the "Mommy and me" camp this year with her mommy.

My little girl loves being a Girl Scout. She may take for granted the pretty uniform she wears and even the fact that she's a registered scout whose Mommy makes sure it's done right. But I know that she's learning the things that matter most. She's learning what accepting others for who they are is all about. She's learning that beauty is what's inside someone's heart and not in their size, shape, status, clothes, or color of their skin. She's learning to love through acts of service to her community and those around here. She's learning that hard work pays off. She's learning about integrity and building good character. She will grow up and forget all those crafts and projects even though they are the building blocks that make the picture whole. But she will never forget the good character that was instilled in her. And she will always remember it when it's time to apply those tools to her life and helping others. I know because I was a Girl Scout too.

~Tara Henson-Cameron

What I Gained When I Lost My Daughter

*Never be bullied into silence. Never allow yourself to be made a victim.
Accept no one's definition of your life; define yourself.*
~Harvey Fierstein

My little girl was a tomboy. Oftentimes strangers would refer to her as my son. "Pierce her ears," my sisters advised.

I grew her hair out, too, but it didn't change anything. Rachael didn't seem bothered by the comments and, in fact, sometimes seemed to enjoy hearing someone call her a boy.

We lived in Hawaii when Rachael was in third and fourth grades. On May 1st, the kids participated in the Lei Day celebration with music and hula dancing. The girls wore moo-moos and the boys, aloha shirts. I have a photo from that day—she looked pained. That was the last time I made her wear a dress.

In hindsight, a friend said: "It might have been a good idea to just let her stay home that day."

When she was fifteen we were living in San Diego. Rachael was excited about attending her first high school dance. When her date, Shawn, arrived, I took pictures of the two of them. As they got ready to leave, I kissed my daughter goodbye.

I'd already said everything that was on my mind—not the usual things parents tell their kids, such as don't drink and drive. Instead, I told her to be cautious and aware, to watch her back, reminding her that some people are intolerant and ignorant.

I wanted the easiest possible life for my daughter. I didn't want to see her get hurt, harmed, threatened, antagonized, or taunted. Often that's what people resort to when they meet up with someone different from themselves.

I said a prayer, then called my sister. "Rachael just left for the dance. I did the normal mom things, taking pictures and all, but it was hard."

My sister listened patiently as I cried.

"Shawn looked beautiful in a gorgeous dress, her hair styled, her make-up perfect. Shawn's parents may have to deal with emotions similar to mine, but at least they got to see their daughter looking like a woman," I sniffled. "Rachael had her hair slicked back and was wearing a tux."

At nineteen, Rachael changed her name to Caoinlean Caleb, saying she wanted to choose her own name, something that had meaning for her.

Less than a year later, I received an e-mail from my daughter. It was a short note but by the time I finished it, I was reading through a blur of tears.

> Hi Mom,
>
> I need to tell you something and I thought it would be best to e-mail you so that you could process it before we talk. I know you've always said that you want your children to be happy, and there is one thing in particular that I need right now in order to be happy. You know I've always been a tomboy, but it is more than that. I was born into the wrong body, and I need to fix that now. I hope you can understand that. If you have questions about it, you can ask me. Love you.

Agony is the word that comes closest to describing how I felt at that moment. The next few days were consumed with tears and heartache. I researched in an attempt to understand. I read that thirty percent of the transgender population commits suicide. At least my kid had the courage and strength to do what she felt was necessary to be true to herself—which could be keeping her alive. Or… should I say him?

It took a few days before I responded to the e-mail from "my little girl."

> Dear Rachael,
> I'm struggling right now and feeling a lot of pain. It's a grieving process—a loss. I do have many questions and in trying to understand I went online to do some research. I will wait with my questions until we talk. You know I love you no matter what. I hope you can understand how painful and difficult this is for a mother. We are not our bodies; we are our souls.
> Love, Mom
> P.S. I don't need any more ideas for articles or books (just trying to keep a sense of humor here).

We lived in different states and sometimes didn't see each other for several months, so I didn't realize she was already living as a guy—part of the process in order to obtain male hormones.

A few months after the e-mail, s/he started taking male hormones and went to San Francisco to have chest surgery—removal of her large D-cup breasts. A large scar was left from surgery. Hair was growing on his chest. He had new nipples. He shaved his face instead of his legs.

In the interest of keeping things humorous, he gave me a greeting card for new parents: "Congratulations! It's a boy." It was a sweet card. He recognized that I had a lot to deal with, too, in this decision he'd made. "Thanks for all of your support. I'm really proud of how you've been handling everything," he wrote.

It was a rough transition trying to remember he versus she, to see my former daughter now as a guy with a beard, sitting at the breakfast table without a shirt on. It was difficult explaining things to my other child, who was seven at the time. His nickname for Rachael was "Sissy."

Sometimes I was in the middle of telling a story from years ago when he was a she and wondered: Do I refer to my son or my daughter? He was a she back then. An article on trans-etiquette cleared up that question—always refer to the person in the gender they are now. Also early on, I'd talk to someone and couldn't remember if they thought I had a daughter or a son. These things aren't covered in Parenting 101.

Questions would pop in my head and even if my new son thought they were weird, he was kind enough to reply.

"Is your sex drive now like that of an eighteen-year-old guy versus a twenty-year-old woman?"

"Yes."

"Did you take a sudden interest in sports after starting hormones?"

"No."

My younger son asked if Caleb is better at playing catch now.

Although heartbroken, I knew I had only one choice—acceptance. There were times when "hey, girl" slipped out of my mouth. It was a conscious effort to say he and him—but now it's become second nature.

I was clueless as to what my child was going through in high school. There was not a lot of information available at the time—even back in 2000 you didn't see transgender on informational programs.

On occasion, I've pondered the question of whether I raised a daughter or a son. I guess it doesn't really matter. My child is a courageous, kind person who I'm proud to have as my kid, regardless of gender. The main thing is his happiness. My transgender child is the same person, with the same soul. I loved the daughter I lost and now I love the son I gained.

~Jo Eager

Reading with Rosie

We shouldn't teach great books; we should teach a love of reading.
~B.F. Skinner

I had my daughter, Rosie, hooked on books at an early age. I read to her every night. When Rosie was about eight we changed our routine. We took turns selecting our books and we also alternated reading out loud.

There was no discernible pattern in the books selected. I recall that we began with Robert Louis Stevenson's *Treasure Island*, enjoying the company of those rough sailors and stumbling over the eighteenth-century seamen's dialect. "Mummy, what is a 'pleasant sittyated grogshop'?" But we loved the book, and learned a lot about pirates and buried treasure.

We laughed and commiserated as we read through the chick lit series of the day, empathizing with the characters in Ann Brashares's *The Sisterhood of the Traveling Pants* and shrieking with laughter at the adventures of the eponymous heroine in Louise Rennison's *Confessions of Georgia Nicolson*.

Bram Stoker's *Dracula* took us weeks to read. But it was well worth it for the picture he painted of contemporary Victorian society. Nothing in Stephanie Meyer's *Twilight* series could compare to the suspense we felt anticipating the Count's next move, even though we were thousands of miles away and safely tucked in bed in our village in southwest Nova Scotia.

In due course Rose grew up and left for McGill University in

Montreal. It was a good fit. She had been educated in French and was enthusiastic about speaking the language; she rose to the challenges posed by the new B.A. and Sc. degree. She explored the cafés and boutiques of that cosmopolitan city, acquiring a taste for clothes from BCBG and French Connection, eventually developing an elegant style she could call her own.

Her first visit home to the Maritimes from university was at Christmas. In addition to a snappy, navy, velvet jacket from BEDO, there was another decoratively wrapped gift from her that was very thoughtful, very personal and very touching. Inside the box were six cassettes—an audio book. It was Sophie Kinsella's *The Shopaholic Takes Manhattan*, read by Rose, her narrative interrupted occasionally by a giggle or a cough, her voice evoking the enjoyment we shared in reading together in her younger years.

As I write this, Rosalind is a third-year medical student at Dalhousie University doing a surgical clerkship at the QE II Health Sciences Centre. Although we have less time these days to read together we continue to recommend reading material to each other. Our personal interests, hers for medicine, and mine for history, often overlap. We are currently loving *The Crimson Portrait* by Jody Shields, an exquisitely written novel about the development of plastic surgery during World War I. Our first written collaboration, a photo essay on an aspect of Canadian medical history, will be published this year in the Humanities section of the *Canadian Medical Association Journal*.

~Susan H. Young

Following in Our Footsteps

There is an itch in runners.
~Arnold Hano

I t was the day before the Bolder Boulder (an acclaimed 10K race boasting 53,000 runners) when I decided to take an easy run on the beautiful trails by my home. At fifty-three, I'm trying to accept that slowing down is just part of life and perhaps this year my goal on race day could be just enjoying myself. As I rounded the corner and started up one of the many familiar hills, a pretty young woman was jogging toward me. It was one of the nicest meetings I have had on the trail in over thirty years.

"Hi Mom," she said breathlessly, removing her ear buds.

We have three children, all of whom have watched my husband and me go running most mornings of their lives. It was so predictable that when my daughter was six years old, I commented, "You know honey, not every Mommy and Daddy go running every morning."

"Really Mommy, like who?" In other words, my children thought running was just part of being a parent.

My daughter is my youngest and soon to turn seventeen, following behind her two older brothers who are now twenty and twenty-three. That means, like most parents, we've had many years of trying to teach a healthy lifestyle to our children. Tennis lessons, ski lessons, skating and swim lessons, early years of soccer, basketball and golf camps filled their lives. But at some point, when it comes to sports, you have to let go and just hope they choose some activity that they enjoy with the added benefit of keeping themselves physically, emotionally, and spiritually healthy.

I always thought how happy I'd be if my children started running. But my daughter never seemed to like it too much when I'd come in sweaty and tired from a run. "You smell stinky, Mom!" My sons each ran the Bolder Boulder once, but after that their running shoes were left to gather dust in the back of their closets. Nevertheless, I kept running and racing while my children did not. In retrospect, the fact that my husband and I love running so much likely encouraged my children to avoid it all together.

But meeting my daughter on the trail that morning was a beautiful example of what parenting is all about. It really is so much more about what we do versus what we say. Of course, as a psychologist I always advise my clients that good parenting is all about modeling. But when it comes to my own parenting, my insecurities often get the better of me, making it hard to trust in the obvious. This morning, as my daughter passed me running in the other direction, finding her stride and separating in one brief moment, it felt like such a gift. We now have five pairs of running shoes on our front porch, since my sons have also recently found their way to the trails. So no matter how fast I run this Memorial Day, I've already felt the joy of winning and am reminded that doing what you love will bring home a medal for the whole family.

~Priscilla Dann-Courtney

A Sign of Love

The best teachers teach from the heart, not from the book.
~Author Unknown

I saw this sign in a classroom: "If you can read this, thank a teacher." It was a simple statement, yet it evoked such gratitude, such happy memories from childhood, I couldn't help but smile.

My mom was my teacher growing up. Since I was home schooled from kindergarten until fifth grade, it was she who taught me how to read. The sign brought back memories of her holding up *Hooked on Phonics* cards and rejoicing with me when I got the right answer. It made me remember trying to copy her perfectly formed letters as she patiently waited by my side. Her helpful presence was always there as I graduated from the short *Bob Books* to longer books at the library.

It was she who first introduced me to *Nancy Drew*, and because of her I still have a bookshelf full of all fifty-six of them. Snuggled against her on our couch as she read, I listened as she transported me to mysterious times and places. It was magical to be so enveloped in a world not my own. Her steady voice guided me through books I didn't have the ability to read yet, and I marveled at the treasure she held between her hands—this treasure she'd chosen to share with me. Sometimes while reading she'd even don a Scottish accent, just for me.

Each day she would decide upon a certain number of chapters we'd be reading. But as she finished that last sentence on the predetermined page, I'd prepare my plea: "Please, Mom! Just one more. I have to know what happens!"

She'd protest at first, but always acquiesced in the end. With one more chapter stirring my imagination, I always left content, dreaming of what would happen next and looking forward to the next episode.

Throughout the years, I never lost my love for reading. The magic and excitement never changed for me. What did change was my need to have my mom read to me. I could begin and finish a book when I wanted and I didn't need her to sit down with me to help me through it. Soon our precious reading time evaporated all together. Instead, I locked myself away in my room to read.

I became an independent teenager who still loved to read, but who had forgotten where she had first acquired that love. I grew to love writing, too, and found it was almost impossible to express myself in any other way. What had once enthralled me as a listener, I could now create! It was a whole new kind of magic, but with a forgotten source.

Until the day I saw the sign. Suddenly, it all rushed back to me. The memories of looking over her shoulder as she read, catching words I hadn't known before like gold flecks in a stream. Flying on as wonderful a magic carpet as Aladdin's, watching people and scenery flow below. The sound of her sipping from the cup of coffee she always brought, and her playful voice telling me to make a "duck butt" for a capital G. I smiled, realizing I had someone to thank.

I couldn't wait to rush home and tell her. As soon as I got back, I updated her about all the happenings from the day as she glided about the kitchen preparing dinner. Then I remembered.

"Oh! Mom. Thank you for teaching me how to read."

For the first time she stopped, casserole in her mitted hands. With a quizzical brow she asked, "What? Where did that come from?"

"Thank you for teaching me how to read. I read a sign in Mr. Jabbour's classroom today that said, 'If you can read this, thank a teacher.' Well, you're the one who taught me. So thank you."

A look of touched surprise came into her eyes. "Oh. Well, you're welcome, honey."

We shared a fond smile, each of us remembering a certain green couch where it all began. The memories only we could share. It was only a part of my childhood, but how special it was. But even more special was my mom, my teacher.

Because of her, I have found a passion and a career. Because of her, I have been encouraged, guided, and taught. Because of her, I am inspired to pass on to my own children one day the gift she gave to me.

~Elizabeth Veldboom

First Wonder

First wonder goes deepest;
wonder after that fits in the impression made by the first.
~Yann Martel

My daughter, age three, woke up one morning to find the world outside her window covered in white. Her eyes widened with awe. "Mommy, did you do that?"

I blew it when I replied too quickly, unaware that I needed to build a cache of admiration to serve me in years to come. "Nature did it."

Her eyes dimmed one notch, but not her astonishment. She ran to the kitchen sliding door and stood there, her nose and pajama-covered belly squeezed against the glass. She examined the leaves bearing the weight of fresh snow, the blades of grass peeking out along the patio line. "Did Daddy do it?"

An icicle pierced inside me with the pang of my lost omnipotence. "It's called 'snow' and it falls from the sky in winter when it's very cold outside." I paused, hoping she'd protest that I was joking, that I had been the one to make this magic happen. When she didn't, I added, "After breakfast we'll put on your new boots and new jacket and new hat and new gloves and we'll go play in the new white snow."

In the months and years that followed, I waited for that moment to come back, when I would say that "yes, I had done it"—whatever the wonder was. I yearned to experience again that first awe through her eyes. But while there were moments of wonder—the first time

I put her on horseback, the bead necklace I strung for her, the story I made up about the three kittens—none matched that short-lived absolute belief in my power to paint the world in white.

In fact, merely three years later, at age six, my daughter, anchored in life as a first grader, dismissed my correcting her usage of a word with, "You didn't go to first grade in America."

Within a few years, as far as my daughter was concerned, I gradually lost my faculties. I became an embarrassment for my eleven-year-old daughter and her friends when, as a driver of the carpool, I had the temerity to try to make conversation. Soon, I knew a lot less than other mothers: they allowed their children to watch TV instead of insisting on doing homework; their meals padded the bottom of the nutrition pyramid while I insisted on some balance.

Although I seemed to be taking stupid pills along with my morning vitamins, on some occasions this teenage daughter resigned herself to my presence and subjected me to long ranting about girls' cliques and backstabbing, intrigues in which I ached to intervene but held back. Soon, though, my not being "cool" about knowing that socks must be oversized and gather loosely around the ankles was replaced by a permanent not being "with it."

It was a surprise in our household when I was called upon for advice about college selection. Gradually, my trickle of drops of wisdom seemed to spurt again as I was asked to meet one boyfriend, then another, until I approved the one deserving of my daughter's wonder.

Suddenly, I went through a metamorphosis and became really smart all the time. I was recruited for trips to the bridal store, to the caterer, and to the florist. I was handed piles of magazines to pore over wedding details that were now the subject of my daughter's new series of awe.

She chose me to walk her down the aisle, and the feminist me was not one to argue.

As I stared at the magnificent creature that was my child in a wedding gown, I was the one filled with awe. Her dress, the aisle, the flower arrangements, the pillars, the chuppah, all shimmered in white tulle, silk and organza. And it occurred to me that finally I had graced the world around us with white.

In my ears came the long-lost words of the three-year-old: "Mommy, did you do that?"

"Yes, I did it, baby," I now said aloud, and kissed my daughter's cheek.

~Talia Carner

The Magic of Mothers & Daughters

Meet Our Contributors
Meet Our Authors
Thank You
About Chicken Soup for the Soul

Meet Our Contributors

Debbie Acklin has been a freelance writer for five years. She is always looking for a good subject for a story. Fortunately life is full of them if you keep your eyes and ears open! E-mail her at d_acklin@hotmail.com.

Jackie Allison writes, paints, and keeps a day job. She takes writing classes at the local community college. Jackie enjoys family, the outdoors, and golfing. She is currently editing a novella and a stage play, and has started work on her next novel. E-mail her at sunjack87@hotmail.com.

Michele Arduengo holds a PhD in biochemistry and cell biology and is a science writer and editor for a biotech company in Madison, WI. Columns from her Grits and Purls blog are syndicated in the *Milton Courier* hometown newspaper. She enjoys knitting and cross-country skiing. Contact her via e-mail at gritsandpurls@gmail.com.

Carol Band is an award-winning humor writer whose work appears in publications nationwide. In her spare time, she raises champion dust bunnies and kills houseplants. To read more, visit her website at www.carolband.com or her blog at www.carolband.wordpress.com.

Ann Barnett grew up in a factory town in Pennsylvania. Moving to New York she raised two daughters, taught school, and lived on the Hudson River in an old wooden boat. Now retired and living in Manhattan, she surrounds herself with good books, sharp pencils, and an up-to-date passport.

Steve Barr is one of the creators of the 1-2-3 Draw app for iPads. He's also the author and illustrator of the *1-2-3 Draw Cartoons* series of art instruction books. You can see more of his work at www.stevebarr. drawbooks.com.

Ann Blakely recently retired and is enjoying a life of doing all that is interesting and fun. She has always written short stories, just for fun, and to share her thoughts. She enjoys travel, gardening, volunteer work, reading, taking continuing education courses and spending time with her grandchildren. E-mail her at annl.blakely@hotmail. com.

Cynthia Lynn Blatchford is an aspiring writer with hopes that she can help others heal through the written word based on her own life experiences. E-mail her at cindy_700@hotmail.com.

Lil Blosfield is the Chief Financial Officer for Child and Adolescent Behavioral Health in Canton, OH. She has had several stories published in the *Chicken Soup for the Soul* series. She loves writing and especially loves sharing her stories with family and friends. E-mail her at LBlosfield40@msn.com.

Pam Bostwick's many articles appear in Christian magazines, newspapers and anthologies. Although she is visually and hearing impaired, she enjoys her new condo and its peaceful, sunny surroundings. She mentors others, and adores her seven children and thirteen grandchildren. Pam happily remarried on 7/7/07. E-mail her at pamlove7@comcast.net.

Dianne Bourgeois is the author of *Pugs* (Animal Planet Pet Care Library). She is the former editor of *Pug Phoenix* and the author of the humor column "Pug Tales" which appeared in *Pug Talk* magazine. Dianne's favorite hobby is dollhouse miniatures. She lives with a feisty little Papillon named Lily.

Leigh Ann Bryant, a survivor of battered women's syndrome, is now remarried with three sons. Her passions include writing and speaking to educate others about domestic violence, as well as travel and being with family. She loves the Lord, and is involved in high school and prison ministries. Learn more at www.leighannbryant.com.

Marcia Byalick is a young adult novelist, a columnist for several Long Island publications, a frequent contributor to *The New York Times* and *Newsday*, and a teacher of memoir writing. She's passionate about helping adults and children write down the stories of their lives before the stories evaporate and are lost forever.

Kristine Byron worked as a trainer for Tupperware and in later years as an interior designer. She loves to cook and entertain. Kristine also loves to travel with her husband and spend quality time with her five grandchildren.

Author **Talia Carner's** heart-wrenching suspense novels, *Puppet Child* and *China Doll*, were hailed for exposing society's ills. Her latest novel, *Jerusalem Maiden*, depicts a woman's struggle for freedom and passion against her society's religious dictates. Carner's short stories and essays have appeared in anthologies and literary publications. Learn more at www.TaliaCarner.com.

Mary Beth Case is in her first year at the College of William & Mary. She plans to major in biology or neuroscience but will always keep a journal handy for when the writing mood strikes!

Christy Chafe is a freelance author living in Hudson, OH, with her husband and three children. She holds a degree in Creative Writing (Miami University) and a Master's degree in English (Xavier University). Christy enjoys reading, writing, hiking and skiing. Visit her blog, Notes From the Journey, at http://blog.hudsonucc.org.

Amber Chandler is a middle school English teacher in Hamburg,

NY. She is inspired by her children Zoey and Oliver, but especially by her husband Matt. She'd like to thank her mother-in-law Chris, who is the stay-at-home Nana, allowing Amber to pursue her dreams.

J.D. Chaney is a retired teacher, published novelist and freelance writer. He lives in the Bay Area with his wife and 17-year-old daughter. His hobbies include traveling, running, reading and watching his beloved San Francisco Giants.

Jan Cline is a freelance writer, speaker and writers' conference director from Spokane Valley, WA. She leads a writing group in her area and enjoys golf, traveling and grandchildren. Jan has had many articles and short stories published. Learn more about her at www.jancline.net.

Courtney Conover is a writer and yogini who just took on her most challenging role yet: Mother. She and her husband Scott welcomed their first child, a son, in 2011. This is Courtney's eighth contribution to the *Chicken Soup for the Soul* series. Read her musings on motherhood at courtneyconover.blogspot.com.

Danika Cooley is a writer with a passion for God's word and small people. Her work appears in children's periodicals. Danika's blog, Thinking Kids, can be found at www.thinkingkids.wordpress.com. **Amber Vanderzanden** is twenty-three years old and plans to become a dental hygienist. Amber loves being outside and writing.

Priscilla Dann-Courtney is a freelance writer and clinical psychologist living in Boulder, CO, with her husband and three children. Her book, *Room to Grow*, is a collection of personal essays previously published in national newspapers and magazines. Her passions include family, friends, yoga, running, skiing and baking.

Angel Dionne is a fourth-year student at the University of Maine at Fort Kent. She is currently studying English Literature and hopes to obtain her PhD. Her greatest aspiration is to become a published author. In her spare time she enjoys reading, writing, and traveling. E-mail her at paper_lantern4@hotmail.com.

Tricia Downing is a professional speaker and athlete. In 2000 she was hit by a car while riding her bicycle and was paralyzed. Tricia credits the examples her mother set regarding faith, resilience and resolve for getting her through the difficult experience. Learn more at www.trishdowning.com or e-mail her at ladyterp_td@hotmail.com.

Drema Sizemore Drudge is an MFA student at Spalding University. The mother of two grown children, Drema teaches at the Learn More Center. She and her husband Barry (and fish, Chicklet) live in North Manchester, IN. Drema is currently writing a novel.

Jo Eager is a freelance writer and broadcast journalist in San Diego, CA. She has written for radio, television, newspaper, and magazines. Jo spent many years as a radio DJ. Currently, she reports news and traffic for television from a news helicopter. She moonlights as a Zumba fitness instructor.

Malinda Dunlap Fillingim keeps the two quarters her daughter Hope gave her many years ago as a reminder of what is really important in life. E-mail her at fillingam@ec.rr.com.

Kim Cooper Findling's essays have appeared in *Horizon Air*, *Oregon Quarterly*, *Hip Mama* and *High Desert Journal*. She authored *Day Trips from Portland, Oregon: Getaway Ideas for the Local Traveler* and *Chance of Sun: An Oregon Memoir*. Kim lives in Bend, OR, with her husband and two daughters. See www.kimcooperfindling.com.

Judith Morton Fraser, actress, writer, counselor specializes in creative processes and teaches: The Symbols of the Medicine Wheel and Focusing. Daughter Tiffany is a yoga instructor, son Neal a master chef, and husband Ian a musical director. Her young adult book, *Grandmas Never Die*, is on Amazon.

The mother of three adult daughters, **Sally Friedman** regards them as her most important work. Now mothers themselves, they have provided much of the material for the essays she has been writing for four decades. A graduate of the University of Pennsylvania, she resides in Moorestown, NJ. E-mail her at pinegander@aol.com.

Chantel Friesen resides in Alberta, Canada, with her husband and children. She loves music, the creative arts and time spent with family. Her life's adventures have given her much to write about. E-mail her at chari.friesen@ymail.com.

Nancy Lowell George is a freelance writer in Richardson, TX. She is the mother of one daughter and two sons.

Alyson Gerber is a writer living in New York City. Her work has been published in *The Jewish Daily Forward*, *Heeb Magazine*, AOL, The Frisky, YourTango, *New York Press* and *The Huffington Post*, among many others. She is currently earning her MFA degree in Writing for Children at The New School.

Rachel Gilmore, M.Ed. , has been a writer all her life but has been working as a freelancer since 1998. Rachel currently provides feature stories for AOL's Patch in her hometown of Frankfort, IL, including two weekly columns. For more information, visit http://blog.thegilmoregirl.com.

Carmen Goldthwaite earned a bachelor's and a master's from Texas Christian University and followed a journalistic career path. Later she joined her mother in an early edition of the coffee house craze before returning to TCU to teach journalism and write stories of Texas women in a column titled "Texas Dames."

Patricia Gordon is a retired elementary school teacher, mother and grandmother. She holds teaching degrees from Illinois State University and Western Michigan University. She now teaches music education at Grand Valley State University and loves to write about her family. She also writes fiction as Patricia Kiyono.

Cindy Gore lives in Richmond, VA, where she is on staff at her church as Education Pastor. Cindy spends her time discipling ladies and writing. She enjoys swimming and spending time with her dog Bosco.

Tessa Graham works for the BC provincial government and writes in her spare time. She has been published in *Island Parent*, *Today's Parent* and *Pacific Yachting*. Shortly after her daughter's diagnosis, she and her husband began to plan for the family's future. In 2009/10, they took a sabbatical and moved to southwest France (http://talesfromouryearinfrance.blogspot.com).

Nina Guilbeau, a Royal Palm Literary Award winner, has written a women's fiction novel, *Too Many Sisters*, and an e-book, *Birth Order and Parenting*. Her work was also published in the short story anthology *From Our Family to Yours*. She loves to read thrillers, but her current writing interest is romance!

Stacey Gustafson received her B.A. from Washington University in St. Louis. She writes humorous short stories based on her suburban family and everyday life. Most readers relate to her experiences and enjoy the laughable perspective. She lives in Pleasanton, CA, with her husband and two children. E-mail her at gustafson1@comcast.net.

Therese Guy owns and operates a Taekwondo studio in Nebraska. She writes humorous stories about growing up in the Midwest. She comes from a family of storytellers. E-mail her at therese-tkd@juno.com.

Carol Harrison, B.Ed is a Distinguished Toastmaster, motivational speaker and author of the book *Amee's Story*. She also has stories in four other *Chicken Soup for the Soul* books. She enjoys spending time with family and friends, reading and scrapbooking. E-mail her at carol@carolscorner.ca or visit her website www.carolscorner.ca.

"Almost" a native of Denver, **Nancy Hegan** is a thirty-nine-year resident, a daughter, mother and grandmother. She is retired and has years of experience to write about. Nancy loves writing essays and short stories. She has no desire to write a novel, but that remains to be seen.

Tara Henson-Cameron is an avid inspirational writer, and her various writings have been published in college literary magazines. She is a member of the Air National Guard and mother to six. She enjoys writing, photography, and being a mom. She plans to publish inspirational books for women and young adults.

Carolyn Hiler is an artist and writer living in the mountains outside Los Angeles. When not drawing, painting, or hiking with her two adorable mutts, she works in private practice as a psychotherapist and art therapist in Claremont, CA. Carolyn posts cartoons almost every day at www.azilliondollarscomics.com.

Linda J. Hinds has been teaching and writing for many years. She is now retired, but still substitute teaches and continues to write. Linda enjoys traveling, movies, walking, and being with her family and friends. She plans to enjoy life to its fullest.

Deanna Ingalls holds a bachelor's degree in accounting but finds her true passion teaching kindergarten at her church. Her writing includes children's fiction and inspirational essays on motherhood. She lives in Alabama with her husband and their three teenagers. E-mail her at teachingauthor@gmail.com.

Jennie Ivey lives in Tennessee. She is a newspaper columnist and the author of numerous works of fiction and nonfiction, including stories in several *Chicken Soup for the Soul* anthologies. Visit her website at www.jennieivey.com.

Mary Ulrich Jackson is a graduate of The University of Texas. She lives in Austin with her husband Bob and their two adopted daughters from China: Amy Lening and Bonnie Noel.

Shauna Hambrick Jones holds a master's degree in Counseling from West Virginia University and served at-risk teens for fifteen years. She is working on her Master's of Fine Arts degree in creative writing from West Virginia Wesleyan College. Her passions include her husband, her son, reading, writing, and lounging oceanside.

Shannon Kaiser is an inspirational travel writer, author, adventure junkie and art director. Shannon is founder of playwiththeworld.com, an adventure site dedicated to helping others love life fully. Connect with her there.

Amanda Kendle is an Australian travel lover who has lived in Japan, Slovakia and Germany. She has traveled to some forty countries, with trips to Russia, Finland and Tunisia being highlights. In between trips she teaches others about blogging and social media. Follow her travel writing at www.notaballerina.com.

Mimi Greenwood Knight is a mama of four living in South Louisiana with her husband David and way too many pets. She's blessed to have over 500 essays and articles in magazines, anthologies and on websites including in over twenty *Chicken Soup for the Soul* books. She enjoys gardening, baking, birding and Bible study.

Victoria Koch is a home school teacher with her local school district. She often works with teen mothers. Her daughter is grown and now drives her own car! Victoria is a writer of personal essays and has a blog at victoriasvisiblevoice.blogspot.com.

Amanda Koehler graduated from La Salle University in 2007. She is a freelance writer and full-time editor in Philadelphia. Amanda enjoys books, movies, TV and being with her family and friends. She's glad to share this memory of her mother, who died from brain cancer in 2009. E-mail her at amanda.e.koehler@gmail.com.

Terri Lacher is a freelance writer who calls herself a Cali-Zona-Texan, finally settling in her East Texas home with her husband Bob and Golden Lab Samson. Her offbeat humor is sprinkled throughout her inspirational short stories, poetry and bi-monthly newspaper columns. E-mail her at btlacher@sbcglobal.net.

Victoria LaFave is a writer and marketing coordinator for nine Catholic schools in Michigan's Upper Peninsula. She has been published in several *Chicken Soup for the Soul* books, along with *My Teacher Is My Hero*. Her stories have also appeared in *Parents*, *FamilyFun* and *Woman's Day* magazines. E-mail her at vrlafave@sbcglobal.net.

Cathi LaMarche is the author of the novel *While the Daffodils Danced* and has contributed to numerous anthologies. She currently teaches eighth grade English and is working on her second novel. She resides in St. Louis with her husband, two children, and three dogs.

Mary Elizabeth Laufer has a degree in English Education from SUNY Albany. As a Navy wife and mother of two, she moved around the country for twenty years, working in schools and libraries. Her stories have been published in magazines, newspapers and anthologies. She lives in St. Cloud, FL.

Tiana Lawson is a native New Yorker, who received her Bachelor of Arts degree in Mass Communications with a concentration in Print Journalism. She is now considering graduate school and hopes to pursue a career as a magazine freelance journalist. E-mail her at TLawson17@aol.com.

Kathy Levine has written copy for the publishing, advertising and retail worlds for thirty years. Her essays have appeared in *The New York Times* and *Newsday* and she volunteers for Literacy Nassau. The mother of two daughters, she just became a grandmother for the first time. E-mail her at katlev@optonline.net.

Janeen Lewis is a freelance writer with a degree in Journalism from Eastern Kentucky University. She lives in central Kentucky with her husband and two children and enjoys long phone conversations with her very forgiving mother. Janeen no longer borrows her mom's car without permission.

Barbara LoMonaco has worked for Chicken Soup for the Soul as an editor and webmaster since 1998. She has co-authored two *Chicken Soup for the Soul* book titles and has had stories published in various other titles. Barbara is a graduate of the University of Southern California and has a teaching credential.

Crescent LoMonaco is a retired hairdresser and salon owner. She combined her knowledge of salon experience and love of writing to write the "Ask a Stylist" column for the *Santa Barbara Independent*. Crescent currently lives with her husband and son in Summerland, CA. E-mail her at crescentlo@aol.com.

Jeri McBryde is retired and lives in a small southern town outside of Memphis, TN. She spends her days reading and writing. She loves crocheting and chocolate. Her family is the center of her life.

Inspirational author **Anita Mellott** holds post-graduate degrees in Communications and Journalism. She worked as an editor with Habitat for Humanity International, and headed the Department of Journalism at Mount Carmel College, Bangalore, India. When she's not homeschooling, she blogs at From the Mango Tree: www.anitamellott.com, and may be contacted there.

Stephanie Wolff Mirmina is an elementary school reading specialist who is currently enjoying being a stay-at-home mom. She lives with her husband and two boys in Arlington, VA. Her previous work can be seen in *Chicken Soup for the New Mom's Soul* and *Chicken Soup for the Soul: Stay-at-Home Moms* (formerly titled *Chicken Soup for the Soul: Power Moms*).

Alice Muschany is close to retiring after working forty years for an electronics company. She's looking forward to the freedom to pursue her hobbies that include hiking, biking, writing and photography. Her eight grandchildren make wonderful subjects. E-mail her at aliceandroland@gmail.com.

Caitlin Q. Bailey O'Neill has previously been published in two other *Chicken Soup for the Soul* books. When not reminiscing on a fairytale childhood, she enjoys photography, theater, gardening, and spending time with her husband Chris and her family. Caitlin can be reached via e-mail at PerfectlyPunctuated@yahoo.com.

Joan Oen is a teacher who loves to write. She lives with her family in Minnesota. She has a Bachelor of Arts degree in Communication/Literature Education and a Master of Arts degree in Human Development. Joan is pursuing publication of her young adult novella, *We Watched Moonbeams*. E-mail her at joan.oen@comcast.net.

Kelly Reidenbaugh received her Bachelor of Arts of English degree from Old Dominion University in 2011. She currently writes proposals for a government contractor in the Washington, D.C. area. Her mother's strength and courage is her greatest writing inspiration.

Natalie June Reilly, author and college student, is the daughter of a beautiful woman named Hope. Save some unsolicited feedback, she's been her beacon of hope all of her life, her best friend, grand-mother to her two boys and the one person Natalie looks to for guidance — still.

Dan Reynolds' work is seen by millions of people via greeting cards for American Greetings, Papyrus, NobleWorks, and other companies. He is the most frequent cartoon contributor to *Reader's Digest*, and also regularly appears in *Esquire*, *Christianity Today*, *The Saturday Evening Post*, *Catholic Digest*, and many other titles.

Bobbi Dawn Rightmyer is a freelance writer published in *Kentucky Monthly*, *New Southerner*, *The Journal of Kentucky Studies*, *Speaking Out! Vol. II*. She has four chapbooks: *Out of My Comfort Zone*, *Care and Feeding of Nightmares*, and *Bobbi's Mercer Memories Vol. I and II*. Her first book, *Harrodsburg*, was released August 2011.

Jacqueline Rivkin lives in New York City with her teenage daughter, Natasha, also a writer. Jacqueline has a master's degree from the Columbia University Graduate School of Journalism and has contributed to publications including *Newsday*, *Self* and *Jet*. This is her third essay in the *Chicken Soup for the Soul* series.

Mother, grandmother, writer and speaker, **Karen Robbins** and her husband are also travel addicts. She writes of their adventures at her blog, Writer's Wanderings, http://karenrobbins.blogspot.com. She has also coauthored *A Scrapbook of Christmas Firsts* and published her first e-book, *Murder Among The Orchids*.

Kathryn Roberts lives and writes in Portland, ME. She received her BFA degree in Creative Writing and English Literature from Goddard College. Her work has appeared in various publications including *NAP Literary Magazine*, *Girls' Life* magazine, and the *Sun Journal*.

Sallie A. Rodman is an award-winning author whose work has appeared in numerous *Chicken Soup for the Soul* anthologies. She has a

Certificate in Professional Writing from Cal State Long Beach. Sallie is working on a book entitled *Panic Demons, My Life with Panic Disorder and Agoraphobia*. E-mail her at sa.rodman@verizon.net.

Patricia M. Rompca resides in Indiana. She owns a landscaping business with her husband, Len. Patty enjoys sewing, reading and most especially, spending time with her four children and their families. E-mail her at pattyrompca@hotmail.com.

Sioux Roslawski, a third grade teacher in St. Louis, as well as a teacher consultant with the Gateway Writing Project, dotes on her brilliant and beautiful granddaughter Riley, enjoys her daughter and her son, and rescues Golden Retrievers for Love a Golden Rescue. Please contact her at http://siouxspage.blogspot.com.

Carol S. Rothchild has a master's degree in writing from Johns Hopkins University and directs editorial for (the incredible!) *Joy of Mom*. A freelance writer/editor, she's contributed to education, media, web, marketing, advertising, anthologies, and magazines—complete with celebrity interviews and backyard fashion shoots. E-mail her at carsusnh1@comcast.net.

Kathryn Rothschadl received her BA from the University of Wisconsin-Whitewater. She is a freelance writer and self-published *Connected*, her first work of fiction, in 2010. She lives in Waukesha, WI with her husband and two children. E-mail her at kathrynlytle@wi.rr.com or visit her website at www.kathrynlytle.com.

Marcia Rudoff is a newspaper columnist, memoir writing instructor and freelance writer in Bainbridge Island, WA. She is the author of *We Have Stories—A Handbook for Writing Your Memoirs* and a frequent contributor to *Chicken Soup for the Soul* books.

Sue Sanders' essays have appeared in national and local magazines and newspapers, including *Salon*, *Parents*, *Babble*, and *The Oregonian*.

Her stories have been included in the anthologies *Ask Me About My Divorce* and *Women Reinvented*. She lives in Portland, OR, with her daughter, husband, dog and three chickens.

Natalie Scott received her Bachelor of Arts degree in English with a concentration in Journalism from the University of Delaware in 2005. She is a writer for Easter Seals. She is married to Nicholas Scott and they have a daughter named Eleanora Lynn who has preceded her to heaven.

Michelle Sedas is author of *Welcome The Rain*, *Live Inspired* and coauthor of *The Power of 10%*. She is co-founder of Running Moms Rock and host of the Inspired Living Café. Michelle graduated from Texas A&M University and lives in Texas with her husband and children. Visit Michelle at www.michellesedas.com.

Carol Sharpe began writing very early in life and continues to enjoy it. She has been published in fourteen books and newspapers. Carol lives in British Columbia.

Penny Smith, a seminary graduate, has taught in conferences and retreats at home and abroad. Her writings cover a variety of genres, appearing in numerous Christian periodicals. She authored *Gateways To Growth and Maturity Through the Life of Esther*. E-mail Penny at psmithgtg@verizon.net or www.pennyesmith.blogspot.com.

Davalynn Spencer is a writer, speaker, and adjunct professor of writing at Pueblo Community College in Colorado. She enjoys playing the piano and guitar, and has published a book of devotions for women. E-mail her at davalynnspencer@hotmail.com.

Sharon M. Stanford is the fiction editor for *Aquarius Press* in Detroit, MI. She has been published in *Chicken Soup to Inspire a Woman's Soul*, as well as winning *Ebony* magazine's short story contest in 2000. She also does writing workshops and manuscript critiques. Sharon can be contacted via e-mail at sstanford87@yahoo.com.

Lynn Sunday graduated, with honors, from Syracuse University in 1973, with degrees in Fine Art and Education. She is an artist turned writer, and lives with her husband and dog in Northern California. Her personal essays have appeared in many publications, including the *Chicken Soup for the Soul* series. E-mail her at Sunday11@aol.com.

Hope Sunderland is a retired registered nurse who hung up her enema bucket and bedpan to start writing. She enjoys politics, reading, biking, and swimming. She writes what she hopes is humor from her home in South Texas on the Gulf Coast. E-mail her at hopecc2000@yahoo.com.

Annmarie B. Tait resides in Conshohocken, PA, with her husband Joe Beck. In addition to writing stories Annmarie also enjoys cooking, crocheting, and singing Irish folk music. Annmarie has stories published in several *Chicken Soup for the Soul* volumes and many other anthologies. E-mail Annmarie at irishbloom@aol.com.

Lisa Tiffin is a freelance writer from upstate New York, where she lives with her husband and twin sons. She has a weekly column in the Rochester *Democrat and Chronicle* and has had a variety of essays, magazine articles and short fiction published. Learn more about her at www.lisatiffin.com.

Elizabeth Veldboom is a freelance writer and a student in Jerry B. Jenkins Christian Writers Guild. She lives in a small town in Colorado, and would like to thank the Lord for making her dreams come true. Visit her blog anytime at www.thefearlist.wordpress.com.

Samantha Ducloux Waltz is an award-winning freelance writer in Portland, OR. Her personal stories appear in the *Chicken Soup for the*

Soul series, numerous other anthologies, *The Christian Science Monitor* and *Redbook*. She has also written fiction and nonfiction under the name Samellyn Wood. Learn more at www.pathsofthought.com.

Laura Wisniewski is a registered nurse, stress management coach, writer, speaker, and storyteller. Laura uses lessons from her recovery from compassion fatigue to educate and encourage people who overdo helping others. Her website is www.HealingtheHelper.com.

Dallas Woodburn is a twenty-four-year-old author of two collections of short stories and editor of *Dancing With The Pen: an anthology of today's best youth writing*. Learn more about her nonprofit youth literacy foundation Write On! at www.writeonbooks.org. Connect with Dallas via www.dallaswoodburn.com and dallaswoodburn.blogspot.com.

Susan Young lives in Nova Scotia and works for Western Counties Regional Library. She studied Art History at Concordia University (Montreal) and at Penn State. She has published numerous art-related articles but this is her first contribution in the genre of inspirational nonfiction. E-mail her at susanyoung@auracom.com.

Meet Our Authors

Jack Canfield is the co-creator of the *Chicken Soup for the Soul* series, which *Time* magazine has called "the publishing phenomenon of the decade." Jack is also the co-author of many other bestselling books.

Jack is the CEO of the Canfield Training Group in Santa Barbara, California, and founder of the Foundation for Self-Esteem in Culver City, California. He has conducted intensive personal and professional development seminars on the principles of success for more than a million people in twenty-three countries, has spoken to hundreds of thousands of people at more than 1,000 corporations, universities, professional conferences and conventions, and has been seen by millions more on national television shows.

Jack has received many awards and honors, including three honorary doctorates and a Guinness World Records Certificate for having seven books from the *Chicken Soup for the Soul* series appearing on the New York Times bestseller list on May 24, 1998.

You can reach Jack at www.jackcanfield.com.

Mark Victor Hansen is the co-founder of Chicken Soup for the Soul, along with Jack Canfield. He is a sought-after keynote speaker, bestselling author, and marketing maven. Mark's powerful messages of possibility, opportunity, and action have created powerful change in thousands of organizations and millions of individuals worldwide.

Mark is a prolific writer with many bestselling books in addition to the *Chicken Soup for the Soul* series. Mark has had a profound influence in the field of human potential through his library of audios, videos, and articles in the areas of big thinking, sales achievement, wealth building, publishing success, and personal and professional development. He is also the founder of the MEGA Seminar Series.

Mark has received numerous awards that honor his entrepreneurial spirit, philanthropic heart, and business acumen. He is a lifetime member of the Horatio Alger Association of Distinguished Americans.

You can reach Mark at www.markvictorhansen.com.

Amy Newmark is Chicken Soup for the Soul's publisher and editor-in-chief, after a thirty-year career as a writer, speaker, financial analyst, and business executive in the worlds of finance and telecommunications. Amy is a *magna cum laude* graduate of Harvard College, where she majored in Portuguese, minored in French, and traveled extensively. She and her husband have four grown children.

After a long career writing books on telecommunications, voluminous financial reports, business plans, and corporate press releases, Chicken Soup for the Soul is a breath of fresh air for Amy. She has fallen in love with Chicken Soup for the Soul and its life-changing books, and really enjoys putting these books together for Chicken Soup's wonderful readers. She has co-authored more than three dozen *Chicken Soup for the Soul* books and has edited another three dozen.

You can reach Amy through the webmaster@chickensoupforthesoul.com.

Thank You

We owe huge thanks to all of our contributors. We know that you poured your hearts and souls into the thousands of stories that you shared with us, and ultimately with each other. As we read and edited these stories, we were truly inspired, and we shared many of our own stories about mother/daughter relationships.

We could only publish a small percentage of the stories that were submitted, but we read every single one and even the ones that do not appear in the book had an influence on us and on the final manuscript. We owe special thanks to our editors Barbara LoMonaco and D'ette Corona, who in addition to their other duties as webmaster and assistant publisher, respectively, took on the task of reading every submission to this book and narrowing the list down to the finalists, shaping the chapters, and finding the wonderful quotations that add richness to each story. Our editors Madeline Clapps and Kristiana Glavin performed their normal masterful jobs of proofreading the manuscript and coordinating our production process for this book.

We also owe a special thanks to our creative director and book producer, Brian Taylor at Pneuma Books, for his brilliant vision for our covers and interiors.

~Amy Newmark

Improving Your Life
Every Day

Real people sharing real stories—for eighteen years. Now, Chicken Soup for the Soul has gone beyond the bookstore to become a world leader in life improvement. Through books, movies, DVDs, online resources and other partnerships, we bring hope, courage, inspiration and love to hundreds of millions of people around the world. Chicken Soup for the Soul's writers and readers belong to a one-of-a-kind global community, sharing advice, support, guidance, comfort, and knowledge.

Chicken Soup for the Soul stories have been translated into more than forty languages and can be found in more than one hundred countries. Every day, millions of people experience a Chicken Soup for the Soul story in a book, magazine, newspaper or online. As we share our life experiences through these stories, we offer hope, comfort and inspiration to one another. The stories travel from person to person, and from country to country, helping to improve lives everywhere.

Chicken Soup for the Soul

www.chickensoup.com